NORTHERN ATOLLS

UNDERSTAND

SURVIVAL GUIDE

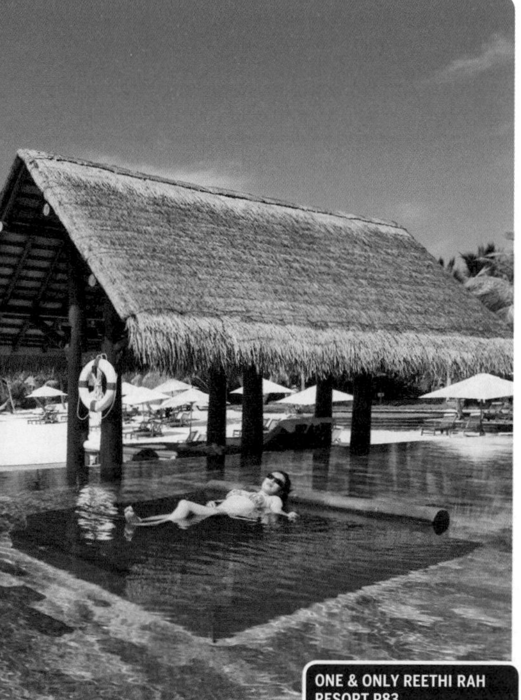

ONE & ONLY REETHI RAH RESORT P83

SPECIAL FEATURES

Welcome to Maldives

Unrivalled luxury, stunning white-sand beaches and an amazing underwater world make Maldives an obvious choice for a true holiday of a lifetime.

Resorts for Everyone

Every resort in Maldives is its own private island, and with over 100 to choose from the only problem is selecting where you want to stay. At the top end, the world's most exclusive hotel brands compete with each other to attain ever-greater heights of luxury, from personal butlers and private lap pools to in-room massages and pillow menus. It's not surprising that honeymooners and those seeking a glamorous tropical getaway have long had the country at the very top of their wish lists. But there's also plenty of choice beyond the five- and six-star resorts.

Unbelievable Beaches

Maldives is home to perhaps the best beaches in the world; they're on almost every one of the country's nearly 1200 islands and are so consistently perfect that it's hard not to become blasé about them. While some beaches may boast softer granules than others, the basic fact remains: you won't find consistently whiter-than-white powder sand and luminous cyan-blue water like this anywhere else on earth. This fact alone is enough to bring well over a million people a year to this tiny, remote and otherwise little-known Indian Ocean paradise.

Underwater World

With some of the best diving and snorkelling in the world, the clear waters of Maldives are a magnet for anyone with an interest in marine life. The richness and variety is astonishing; dazzling coral walls, magnificent caves and schools of brightly coloured tropical fish await you when you get down to the reef. In deeper waters lurk manta rays, turtles, sharks and even the world's largest fish, the whale shark. The best bit? The water is so warm many people don't even wear a wetsuit.

Independent Travel

Maldives has undergone seismic change in the past 10 years, since inhabited islands have been opened to tourism and locals permitted to build their own guesthouses. Travellers no longer have to stay in resorts and remain separate from the local population, something that kept backpackers away for decades. Island hopping by public ferry, speedboat and domestic flights has opened up this incredible country to visitors on almost all budgets. A number of islands in Male and Ari atolls are now big centres for a booming guesthouse industry, with dozens of options on each.

Why I Love Maldives

By Tom Masters, Writer

I first came to Maldives with no idea how different it was to the rest of the world, how fragile or challenging life seems here at the mercy of the sea, with so few resources locally available. I instantly formed a bond of respect and friendship with the people who make these inhospitable coral islands home. It's such a contradiction that this is also where to find some of the world's most luxurious hotel properties, and this is a paradox – among many – that I continue to enjoy every time I return to this astonishingly beautiful country.

For more about our writers, see p192

Above: Six Senses Laamu resort (p124)

Maldives

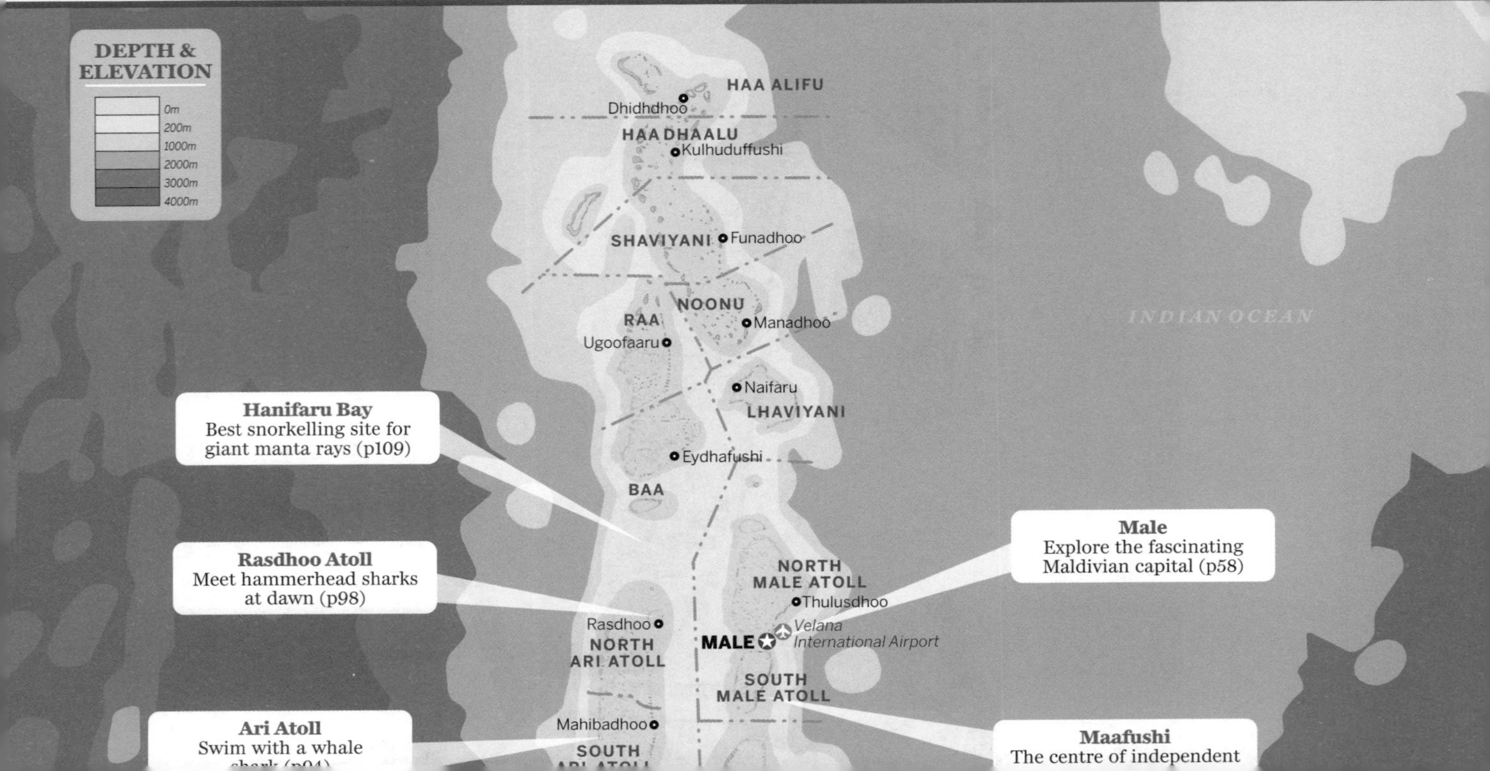

0 100 km
0 50 miles

DEPTH & ELEVATION

0m
200m
1000m
2000m
3000m
4000m

HAA ALIFU
Dhidhdhoo
HAA DHAALU
Kulhuduffushi
SHAVIYANI
Funadhoo
NOONU
RAA
Manadhoo
Ugoofaaru
Naifaru
LHAVIYANI
Eydhafushi
BAA
NORTH MALE ATOLL
Thulusdhoo
Velana International Airport
MALE
SOUTH MALE ATOLL
Rasdhoo
NORTH ARI ATOLL
Mahibadhoo
SOUTH
INDIAN OCEAN

Hanifaru Bay
Best snorkelling site for giant manta rays (p109)

Rasdhoo Atoll
Meet hammerhead sharks at dawn (p98)

Ari Atoll
Swim with a whale

Male
Explore the fascinating Maldivian capital (p58)

Maafushi
The centre of independent

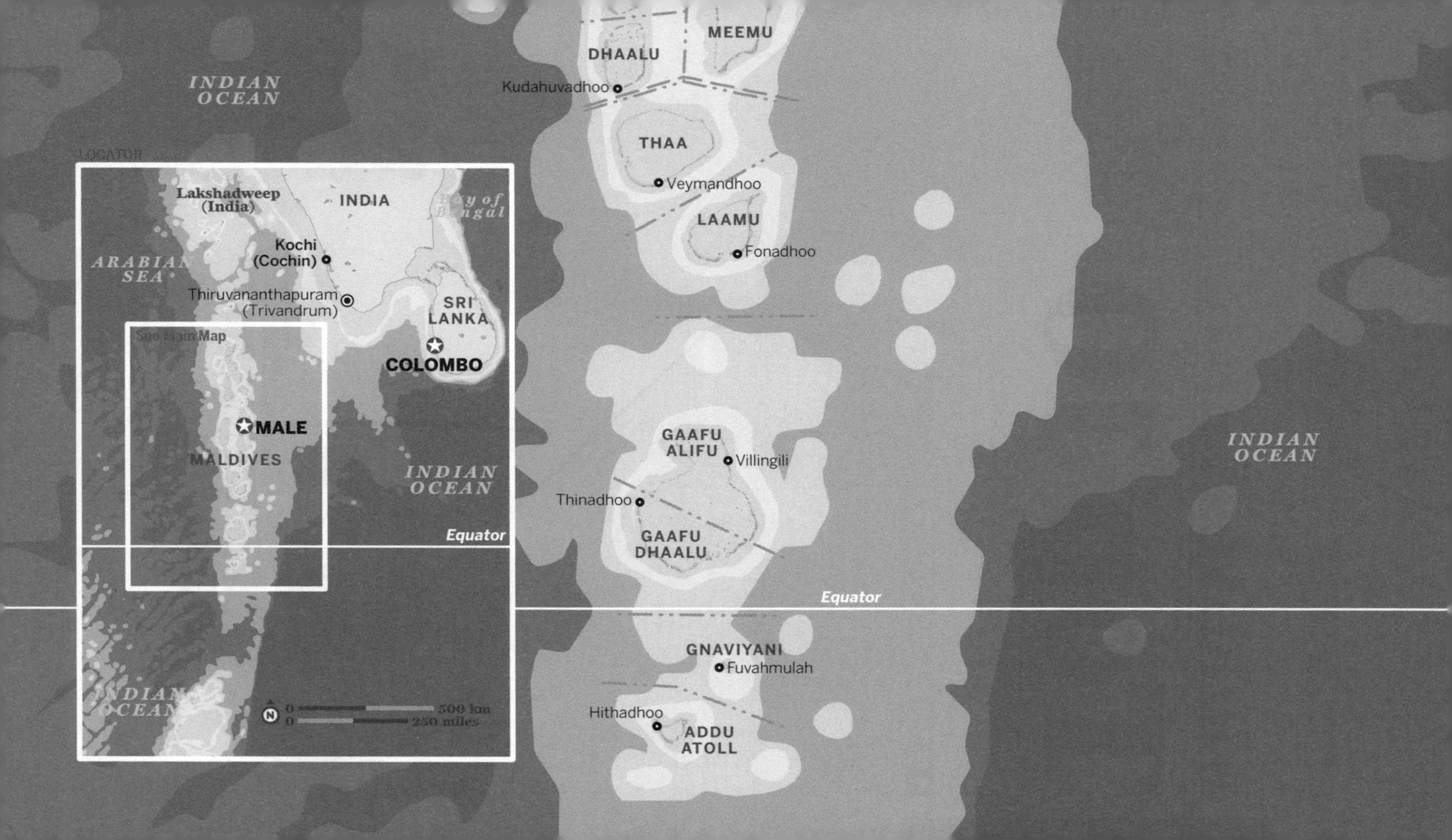

INDIAN OCEAN
LOCATOR
Lakshadweep (India)
INDIA
Bay of Bengal
ARABIAN SEA
Kochi (Cochin)
Thiruvananthapuram (Trivandrum)
SRI LANKA
COLOMBO
See Main Map
MALE
MALDIVES
INDIAN OCEAN
Equator
INDIAN OCEAN
0 500 km
0 250 miles
DHAALU
MEEMU
Kudahuvadhoo
THAA
Veymandhoo
LAAMU
Fonadhoo
GAAFU ALIFU
Villingili
Thinadhoo
GAAFU DHAALU
Equator
GNAVIYANI
Fuvahmulah
Hithadhoo
ADDU ATOLL
INDIAN OCEAN

Maldives' Top 10

1

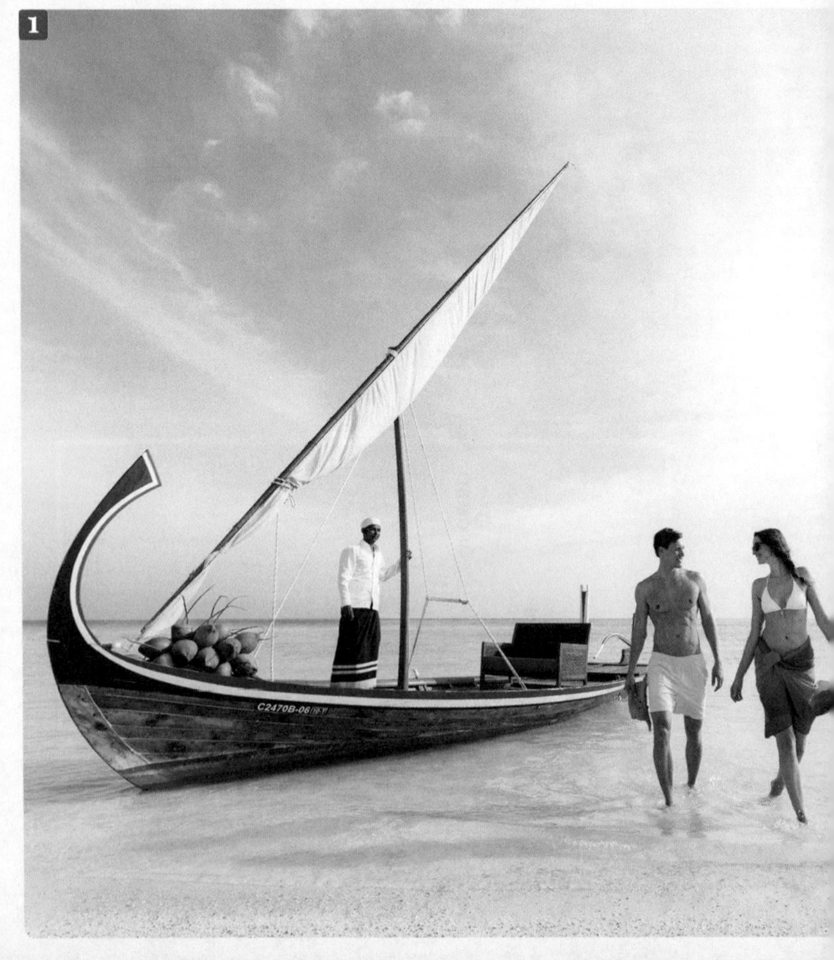

Becoming a (Luxurious) Castaway

1 Nearly every resort (p19) offers some variation on this theme: you and your partner or family are given a picnic basket (in the most luxurious resorts it may be a full meal set up for you by staff) and dropped off on an uninhabited, pristine island by dhoni. The crew then jump back on the boat and leave you to your own devices on a white-powder beach surrounded by a turquoise lagoon. Explore the island, dine on great food, sunbathe and swim – this is the modern castaway experience.

Hanifaru Bay

2 Maldives' most famous snorkelling site (p109) is this plankton-rich bay in the Baa Atoll Unesco Biosphere Reserve, where you can often see dozens of giant manta rays gliding acrobatically through the water as they filter their food. It's an incredible experience when they appear in great numbers and the water is clear. Hanifaru is also regularly visited by those fellow plankton eaters, the whale sharks. Resorts and inhabited islands nearby arrange trips to Hanifaru Bay daily.

CAROLINE VON TUEMPLING/GETTY IMAGES ©

2

DIVEDOG/SHUTTERSTOCK ©

Learning to Dive

3 You simply *have* to get beneath the water's surface in Maldives; the corals, tropical fish, sharks, turtles and rays all make up an unforgettably alien world, which is best experienced by diving (p30). All resorts and many guesthouses have diving facilities, and you won't regret deciding to learn here. Maldives boasts excellent safety standards, modern equipment, passionate and experienced dive staff and – best of all – the water is so warm many people don't even bother diving in a wetsuit.

Staying in an Island Guesthouse

4 The guesthouse (p50) phenomenon in Maldives has only been around for a few years, yet it has already become a truly unique way to experience the 'real' Maldives on an inhabited island: interact with locals, eat traditional food and experience something totally different to life in a resort. The best guesthouses are those on remote atolls, far from the modernity of Male, where friendly local families will literally treat you like one of their own, take you to desert islands, and let you fish, dive and snorkel.

hilling on Maafushi

5 Maafushi (p92) is the first inhabited island in Maldives to become a big aveller centre, with some 30 guesthouses d hotels now operating. It's probably e best place for a cheap beach holiday Maldives, with lots of competition and w prices for accommodation, diving, orkelling and other excursions. There's so a good bikini beach, which means visi-rs can swim without offending the local pulation. What's more, at just a couple of urs away from the international airport, s also very easy to reach.

Diving with the Hammers

6 Hammerhead sharks, definitely one of the weirdest-looking creatures in the sea, can be observed in abundance in Maldivian waters – if you know where to look for them. There are few more thrilling experiences than a dawn dive, descending free fall into the deep blue to 30m and coming upon a huge school of hungry hammerhead sharks waiting to be fed. The best place to do this is at the world-famous Hammerhead Point (p98) (aka Rasdhoo Madivaru) in Rasdhoo Atoll.

Swimming with a Whale Shark

7 The largest fish in the world, the whale shark (p101) is prevalent in Maldivian waters, especially in the south of Ari Atoll and during a full moon when the currents between the atolls are at their strongest. Swimming with one of these gentle giants is an incredible experience – they average almost 10m in length – and it's also totally safe: despite their immense size, whale sharks feed only on plankton.

Taking a Seaplane

8 There are few destinations where the mode of transport by which you arrive could be called a highlight, but that's because there are few places in the world where you need seaplanes (p177) to reach your hotel. These zippy Twin Otters function like taxis in a country with no roads, and taking off from the water is an unforgettable experience, as is observing the spectacular coral atolls, blue lagoons and tiny desert islands from above.

7

ANDREA IZZOTTI/SHUTTERSTOCK ©

JOHN BORTHWICK/GETTY IMAGES ©

ʌale: Maldives' ʌicrometropolis

9 The Maldivian capital (p58) is definitely the best place to get to know ·cals and see what makes them tick. The ·rightly painted houses, crowded markets ·nd convivial teashops where you can chat ·regulars and share plates of delicious ·hort eats' are just some of the highlights ·this unusual capital city – and they per·ctly complement the resort experience. ·on't miss the National Museum, the best ·verview of Maldives history anywhere ·the country, or the Old Friday Mosque, ·omplete with its carved coral tombstones.

Watching a Bodu Beru Performance

10 Whether you're staying at a resort or on an inhabited island, the cultural highlight of almost any trip to Maldives is seeing a dance and drum performance (p164) known as *bodu beru,* which means 'big drum' in Dhivehi. These traditional all-male performances are a thrilling and genuine experience, even if they can feel rather contrived in your resort's restaurant. The drum ceremony starts off slowly and builds gradually to an incredible climax, during which some dancers enter a trance-like state.

Need to Know

For more information, see Survival Guide (p167)

Currency

Maldivian rufiyaa (Rf)

Language

Dhivehi; English is widely spoken.

Visas

Nobody coming to Maldives requires a visa for a stay of 30 days or less.

Money

Credit cards can be used in resorts and most guesthouses. ATMs can be found in Male and the bigger inhabited islands.

Mobile Phones

Local SIM cards can be bought in Male or other inhabited islands, but not at resorts. Most phones will automatically roam in Maldives.

Time

Maldives Standard Time (GMT/UTC plus five hours)

When to Go

Tropical climate, wet/dry seasons

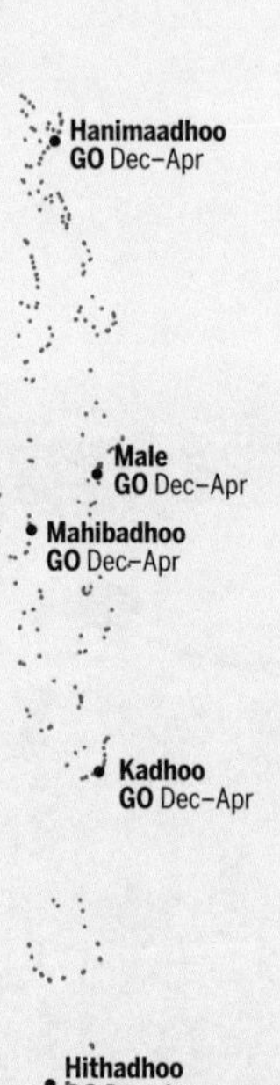

High Season (Dec–Feb)

- Maldives enjoys its best weather.
- Expect little rain, low humidity and blue skies.
- Christmas and New Year involve huge price hikes and often minimum stays of five days or more.

Shoulder (Mar–Apr)

- Great weather continues until the end of April, when temperatures are at their hottest.
- The surf season begins in March and continues until October.
- Prices jump during Easter.

Low Season (May–Nov)

- Storms and rain more likely, but weather warm and resorts at their cheapest.
- Prices rise in August for European summer holidays.
- Marine life is more varied on the western side of atolls at this time.

Useful Websites

Lonely Planet (www.lonelyplanet.com/Maldives) Destination information, hotel bookings, traveller forum and more.

Visit Maldives (www.visitmaldives.com) Official tourism site.

Maldives Independent (www.maldivesindependent.com) Balanced English-language online newspaper.

Atoll Transfer Ferry and speedboat timetables, routes and tickets.

Two Thousand Isles (www.twothousandisles.com) An excellent blog about life in Maldives.

Guesthouses (www.guesthouses.mv) Comprehensive listing of guesthouses in Maldives.

Important Numbers

Country code	☎960
International access code	☎00
Ambulance	☎102
Fire	☎118
Police	☎119

Exchange Rates

Australia	A$1	Rf12.15
Canada	C$1	Rf12.44
Euro zone	€1	Rf19.08
Japan	¥100	Rf14.12
New Zealand	NZ$1	Rf11.25
Switzerland	CHF1	Rf16.44
UK	UK£1	Rf21.37
US	US$1	Rf15.42

For current exchange rates, see www.xe.com

Daily Costs

Budget: Less than US$400

- Budget resorts cost US$150–350 per night.
- Guesthouses are cheaper at around US$60–100 per night.
- Reach guesthouses cheaply by taking public ferries for US$5–10.

Midrange: US$400–850

- Midrange resorts start from US$350 per night.
- Full board or all-inclusive options can save money.
- Speedboats to resorts cost around US$200–300.

Top end: More than US$850

- Top-end rooms start at US$750.
- Seaplane transfers generally cost anything from US$400 return.
- Expect a meal in a top-end resort to cost a minimum US$150 per person.

Opening Hours

The Maldivian working week runs from Sunday to Thursday; Friday and Saturday are the weekend. Friday sees many businesses closed. Most shops close for between 15 and 30 minutes at prayer time, which can be unusual to Western shoppers. Typical business hours outside resorts are as follows:

Banks 8am–1.30pm Sunday to Thursday

Businesses 8am–6pm Sunday to Thursday

Government offices 7.30am–2pm Sunday to Thursday

Restaurants noon–10pm Saturday to Thursday, 4–11pm Friday

Arriving in Maldives

Velana International Airport (p176) Resorts in South and North Male Atoll transfer guests from the airport by speedboat (10 to 70 minutes). Chartered seaplane transfers from the airport operate daily until around 5pm (seaplanes cannot fly after dark) to resorts outside South and North Male Atoll. Late arrivals need to overnight in Male and take a seaplane the next day. The Male ferry leaves 24 hours a day to the capital (Rf10, five minutes, every 10 minutes). Buses to the island of Hulhumale leave from outside the airport terminal every half-hour (Rf20).

Getting Around

Transport in Maldives is either fast and rather expensive, or reasonably priced and very slow.

Air Internal flights connect Male to 12 regional airstrips at least daily. Chartered seaplanes collect arrivals at **Velana International Airport** (p176) and fly them direct to their resorts.

Boat Most transport in Maldives is by boat, for obvious reasons. Resorts collect guests from Male or regional airstrips by speedboat, a fast and comfortable way to travel. Independent travellers will need to use the slow but cheap public ferry system or newly introduced (and pricier!) private speedboat transfers to inhabited islands.

Car Most islands are totally car-free, with the exception of Male and a few other larger inhabited islands.

For much more on **getting around**, see p177

What's New

Domestic Airports

Brand new airstrips have opened in Dhaalu (p105) and Raa Atolls (p108), and another new runway is being built in Noonu Atoll (p107). It will open in 2019, and will make getting around by air easier than ever.

China-Maldives Friendship Bridge

This US$250 million infrastructure project – a massive gift from China and a significant new development for the capital – will connect Male to the airport islands of Hulhule and Hulhumale. (p60)

Speedboats

A growing trend is the private speedboat services linking Male and Velana International Airport to inhabited islands in nearby atolls, slashing travel times for independent travellers and making the atolls more accessible than ever.

St Regis Vommuli

Urban sophisticates will love the stunning architecture, gorgeously understated public areas and city-hotel sensibility of the new St Regis resort, brand new to Dhaalu Atoll. (p122)

Soneva Jani

Perhaps the most eagerly anticipated new resort opening in Maldives, Soneva Jani is a luxury resort on steroids: massive water villas with retractable roofs, private pools and their own water slide await the lucky few who can afford them. (p107)

Ritrella Cruise Hotel

The largest live-aboard in Maldives, the Ritrella takes diving and surfing trips to a new level of comfort and modernity on this fabulous yacht. (p36)

Alcohol boats

More and more boats with bar licences now dock off inhabited islands where alcohol is illegal. Travellers wanting a few beers can then take a free transfer to the boat, drink and pay the bill before heading back to the island.

Sirru Fen Fushi

The first resort in pristine Shaviyani Atoll, Sirru Fen Fushi opened its doors in 2018 and is an absolutely stunning luxury island that marks an exciting start to tourism here. (p105)

Rasrani Bageecha

The brand new Rasrani Bageecha – until recently the shady and quiet Sultan's Park in the centre of Male – is now an entertainment area, complete with bright lights, fountains and rides. A garish addition to the city for sure, but one that kids will enjoy. (p63)

OZEN by Atmosphere at Maadhoo

This brand new luxury all-inclusive is the first new resort to open in South Male Atoll in over a decade. It's a gorgeous place and currently offers the best high-end all-inclusive in the country. (p91)

For more recommendations and reviews, see **lonelyplanet.com/Maldives**

If You Like...

Luxury

Cheval Blanc Randheli (p108) The Louis Vuitton resort that has everyone talking, as well as the highest room rates in the country.

One & Only Reethi Rah (p83) An old-time classic, this superlative place is the playground of millionaires and royalty.

Four Seasons Landaa Giraavaru (p112) Less bling and more class, the Four Seasons has the feel of a giant social club.

Velaa Private Island (p108) The personal creation of one individual, VPI effortlessly competes with the best international hotel chains.

Six Senses Laamu (p124) With its wooden structures, sustainable ethos and comic sans font, this is barefoot luxury at its relaxed best.

Romance

Cocoa Island by COMO (p90) Simple luxury with little fuss, this gorgeous island is perfect for high-end romance.

Anantara Kihavah Villas (p112) With sumptuous rooms and one of the best beaches in the country, this place is heaven for couples.

Gili Lankanfushi (p82) There are few things more romantic than spending the day in your giant overwater villa here.

Soneva Fushi (p113) With stunning beaches, beautiful private villas and thick jungle vegetation, this is a totally romantic destination.

Cool Design

St Regis Vommuli (p122) Extraordinary public areas, a floating reception and memorable manta ray–inspired water villas.

Amilla Fushi (p111) Some of the most stylish villas in the country in this slice of Palm Beach on an Indian Ocean island.

W Maldives (p95) This modern and chic place redefines the Maldives resort into something contemporary.

One & Only Reethi Rah (p83) Perhaps the best rooms in the country: all the villas here look like Balinese palaces.

Diving & Snorkelling

Adaaran Select Meedhupparu (p109) The remote location in Raa Atoll means that divers have 30 dive sites essentially to themselves.

Cinnamon Hakuraa Huraa (p118) A remote location means pristine dive sites where you're highly unlikely to be bothered by other divers.

Ellaidhoo Maldives by Cinnamon (p95) Attracts divers with over 100 sites within easy reach, as well as the finest house reef in the country.

Reveries Diving Village (p124) One of the most diving-focused guesthouses in the country, this is a great mixture of diving resort and boutique hotel.

Equator Village (p131) Some of the cheapest and best diving in Maldives is available at this former British naval base.

Good Food

Gili Lankanfushi (p82) It's hard not to be blown away by the culinary brilliance at one of the three restaurants here.

Four Seasons Resort Maldives at Kuda Huraa (p84) Its signature Indian restaurant Baraabaru is simply superb, but don't miss pizza at Reef Club.

COMO Maalifushi (p124) This luxury resort has some mind-blowingly good food.

Six Senses Laamu (p124) Superb Japanese, Vietnamese and Mediterranean cuisine, and probably the best breakfast buffet in the country.

Family Holidays

Conrad Maldives Rangali Island (p101) This megaresort on two islands has everything imaginable to keep kids entertained.

Four Seasons Landaa Giraavaru (p112) This high-end option is always popular with families for its great kids club and numerous activities.

Kurumba Maldives (p79) Set up more like a grand country club, here you'll find a great kids club and boundless entertainment options.

Shangri-La Villingili Resort & Spa (p131) While the parents relax, the kids can enjoy the kids club and teenagers the Cool Zone.

Kuredu Island Resort & Spa (p115) One of the best midrange resorts for families, Kuredu has a great range of activities, a kids club and lots of excursions.

Surfing

Cinnamon Island Dhonveli (p81) The most surf-focused resort in the country, Dhonveli has access to perfect left Pasta Point.

Coke's Beach (p85) A popular guesthouse on the island of Thulusdhoo, with access to two great breaks.

Canopus Retreats Thulusdhoo (p85) An excellent guesthouse with plenty of surfing choices nearby.

Six Senses Laamu (p124) This top-end resort is also the best place to access Ying Yang, one of the biggest breaks in Maldives.

Reveries Diving Village (p124) As well as being a great base for divers, this guesthouse is excellently located to access six surf spots in Laamu Atoll.

Top: Velaa Private Island resort (p108)

Bottom: Water villas at Gili Lankanfushi resort (p82)

Plan Your Trip

Choosing a Resort

Don't worry about the judicious use of Photoshop in brochures – almost every resort in Maldives will get you a superb beach, amazing weather and turquoise waters overlooked by majestic palms. Indeed, so uniform is the perfection, it's often hard to take memorable photographs here – they all just look like they've been lifted from a holiday brochure.The standard of facilities and accommodation in Maldivian resorts varies enormously, from budget and extremely average accommodation to the best of everything – if you can afford to pay through the nose for it. Your choice of resort or guesthouse is absolutely key to getting the holiday you want, though, so take plenty of time and weigh up as many options as possible before settling for the place or places you decide to book. There are plenty of factors you need to take into consideration when selecting a resort.

Top Resorts

Best Rooms

Jumeirah Vittaveli (p90) Huge and sumptuously furnished villas with enormous outdoor bathrooms, surrounded by lap pools and enjoying direct beach access.

Best Pool

Anantara Kihavah Villas (p112) Long enough for swimming lengths and fun for kids too.

Best Beach

Kanuhura (p115) The endless white-sand beach is unbeatable, and the resort owns a private desert island for you to boat over to for a picnic lunch.

Best Restaurant

Six Senses Laamu (p124) You're spoiled for choice here, but our favourite Six Senses restaurant is Leaf, where sublime Vietnamese cuisine is served at lunch and Mediterranean fare for dinner.

Atmosphere

Every resort cultivates a distinct atmosphere to appeal to its guests. Before choosing a resort decide on the type of holiday you want and the atmosphere most conducive to providing it. Honeymooners who find themselves surrounded by package-tour groups and screaming children may quickly come to regret their decision. Similarly, divers and surfers may find the social-life vacuum in a resort popular with honeymooners and couples a little claustrophobic after a week on a live-aboard.

Romance

Romance is big business in Maldives, where more than a few visitors are on their honeymoon, renewing their vows or just having an indulgent break. Almost anywhere is romantic. That said, the more budget the resort, the more families and groups you'll get, and the intimacy of the romantic experience can be diminished if it's peace, quiet and candlelit dinners you're after. Nonetheless, romance doesn't necessarily mean huge cost. It's hard to think of anywhere more lovely than little Makunudhoo Island, for example, where there's no TV or loud music, just gorgeously simple and traditional houses dotted along the beach, and vegetation thick with trees planted by past honeymooners.

However, the maxim of getting what you pay for is still true here – the loveliest, most romantic resorts are usually not the cheaper ones.

Be aware that you cannot at present get married in Maldives, although this may change in the near future. However, if you really want to, you can organise non-legally-binding services and effectively have your wedding here even if the legal formalities are completed elsewhere.

Nearly all midrange and top-end resorts can organise such ceremonies, so check websites for details and special packages. Honeymooners are often eligible for special deals and some added extras.

High Style

Few countries in the world have such a wealth of choice in the luxury market as Maldives. Most major luxury-hotel brands have or hope to have a presence here, and at times things can look like a never-ending glossy travel magazine, bringing ever higher levels of comfort and pampering.

And the pampering on offer here is almost legendary. You'll have your own *thakuru,* Man Friday or Guest Experience Manager (all various terms for personal butler), who will look after you during your stay. And you'll nearly always have a sumptuous villa stuffed full of beautifully designed furniture and fabrics, a vast, decadent bathroom (often open air) and a private open-air area (in a water villa this is usually a sun deck with a direct staircase into the sea).

Now most resorts in this category also include private plunge pools – some big enough to do lengths in, but all a wonderful way to cool off or wash off the salt after a dip in the sea.

Food in these resorts is almost universally top notch. There will be a large choice of cuisine, with European and Asian specialist chefs employed to come up with an amazing array of dishes day and night.

Social life will be quiet, and will usually revolve around one of the bars. Most of the market here are honeymooners, couples and families, but kids will certainly not run riot (most resorts impose a limit on the number of children), and even if they do, there will be enough space to get away from them. Although the general feel is romantic and stylish, activities will not be ignored – everything from diving to water sports and excursions will be well catered for.

Essentially, if you can afford this level of accommodation (and you're looking at a minimum of US$1000 per room per night, plus food), you are guaranteed an amazing time, whatever your interests.

Diving

All resorts have their own diving school and every resort has access to good diving. It's very hard to say that one resort has better diving than another, when in fact all the sites are shared, but there are a few resorts that have obvious advantages, such as remote OBLU by Atmosphere at Helengeli (p77), which offers access to some 40 dive sites, many of which are not used by any other resorts.

You'll find a similar situation in and around Ari Atoll, where the dive sites are excellent, including Kuramathi Island Resort (p181) and Ellaidhoo Maldives by Cinnamon (p95). Above all, divers should go for resorts that are focused on diving, as prices will be lower, and there will be more enthusiasm for the activity than elsewhere.

Back to Nature

Maldives has built much of its tourism industry on the desert-island ideal: the fantasy of simplicity, tranquillity, beach and sea. Of course, the fact that many places also provide a butler, a gourmet restaurant and a fleet of staff who cater to your every whim makes the whole experience somewhat more luxurious than being a real castaway.

These resorts tend to be well designed, use imported woods and natural fibres and have little or no air-conditioning outside the bedroom. The simplicity of such places (even at top-end resorts, which admittedly add supreme style and comfort to the mix), not to mention their peacefulness and relaxed feel, is what attracts people. These 'no shoes, no news' resorts are great for a romantic break, a honeymoon or total escape.

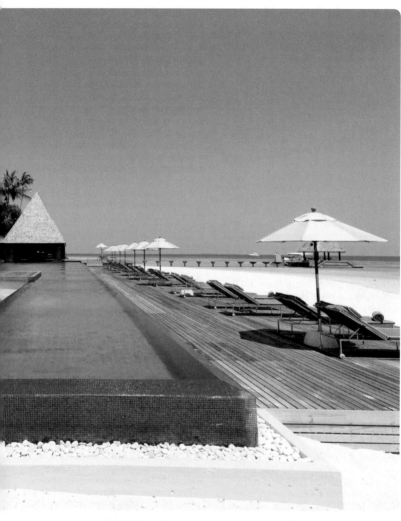

Top: Anantara Kihavah Villas resort (p112)

Bottom: Breakfast at a Maldivian resort

BLUEORANGE STUDIO/SHUTTERSTOCK ©

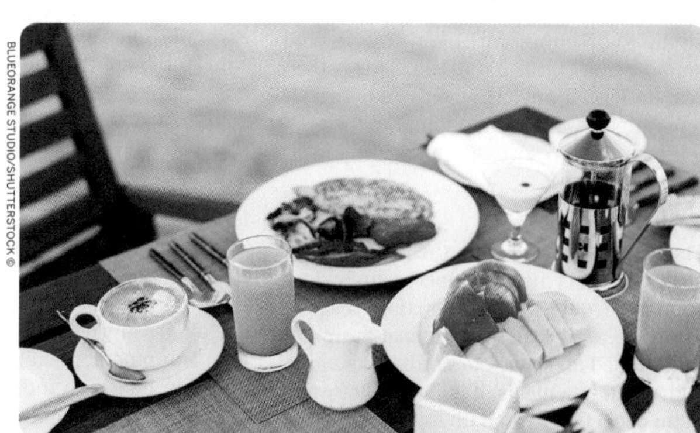

Ecotourism

Ecotourism can so often be a gimmick that it's important to know who's serious and who's just trying to attract a larger number of visitors.

Despite the lip service paid by many resorts, relatively few have genuine ecotourism credentials. Look for resorts that offer educational programs, sustainable development, environmentally friendly building practices, minimal use of air-conditioning and electricity in general, and a resort ethos that fosters environmental awareness and care (ie offering you not only Evian when you ask for water, but also water that has been desalinated on-site).

The resorts we recommend in this category are leading the way in the use of materials, their interaction with the local ecosystem and the activities they offer guests. Those that are serious about their commitment to ecotourism include Gili Lankanfushi (p82), Soneva Fushi (p113), Rihiveli by Castaway Hotels & Escapes (p89) and Six Senses Laamu (p124).

Guesthouses

Guesthouses are a relatively new initiative in a country where tourism and the local population were always kept scrupulously apart. There are now scores of these small hotels dotted around the country, and the experience offered here is one totally different to that found in resorts.

Forget the infinity pool and cocktails – you're on a dry local island here and swimming costumes aren't culturally acceptable save on the so-called 'bikini beaches' where foreigners can enjoy swimming in areas screened off from conservative locals – but you can still enjoy the beach on nearby uninhabited islands, do lots of diving, snorkelling, surfing, fishing, island hopping and cultural tourism. This is the best option for anyone who finds being separate from the local population in a self-contained resort an unappealing idea.

Safari Cruises

The massive expansion in the market for safari cruises has meant an increasingly sleek approach from the tour companies that run them. A typical, modern boat is air-conditioned and spacious, and serves varied and appetising meals. It will have hot water, a sun deck, fishing and diving gear, wi-fi, a full bar, a projector/TV for watching movies and cosy, comfortable cabins. Costs start at around US$120 per person per day, including the US$6 green tax and all meals, plus roughly US$80 per day for diving trips. There's usually a minimum daily (or weekly) charge for the whole boat, and the cost per person is lower if there are enough passengers to fill the boat. You'll be charged extra for drinks, which are priced comparably to most resorts.

The most basic boats are large dhonis with a small galley and communal dining area, two or three cramped cabins with two berths each, and a shared shower and toilet. The bigger, better boats have air-conditioning, more spacious accommodation, and a toilet and shower for each cabin.

Activities

Few people will want to spend an entire holiday sunbathing and swimming, so resorts are careful to provide a program of excursions and activities for guests. Bear in mind that this is the only way you'll be able to leave the island during your stay, public transport from resort islands being nonexistent and opportunities for sightseeing almost as scarce.

While all resorts have a diving centre, the uniformity ends there; you'll have to check to see if the resort you're planning to visit has a water-sports centre or its own spa, organises guided snorkelling, lays on marine biology lectures or morning yoga sessions or has a resident tennis coach.

For example, only Kuredu Island Resort (p115), Velaa Private Island (p108) and Shangri-La Villingili (p131) offer golf courses, while Soneva Fushi (p113) and Soneva Jani (p107) are the only resorts to offer an observatory.

Snorkelling & Diving

All resorts cater for divers and snorkellers, and most organise twice-daily diving excursions and sometimes snorkelling trips too, especially if there's not good snorkelling on the house reef. If you're keen on diving, it's always cheaper to bring your own equipment, including snorkel, mask and fins, plus buoyancy control device (BCD) and dive computer.

Most top-end resorts supply free snorkelling equipment to guests, but it normally attracts a charge at budget and midrange places. Dive schools are generally of an exceptionally high safety standard, as regulated by Maldivian laws. Most resorts have at least 10 sites nearby and you can visit them in rotation. If there's a particular dive site you want to visit, you should contact the dive school at the resort and check it'll be running a trip there during your stay.

Water Sports

In addition to diving schools, most resorts have a water-sports centre. These vary enormously. Some offer the most basic array of kayaks and windsurfing, while others run the gamut from water skiing to kite-boarding and wakeboarding. The best resorts for sailing and windsurfing have a wide lagoon that's not too shallow, and lots of equipment to choose from. Non-motorised water sports tend to be free in better resorts, while they're all charged in budget and midrange ones in general.

Good resorts for sailing and windsurfing include: Kanuhura (p115), Four Seasons Landaa Giraavaru (p112), Kuredu Island Resort & Spa (p115), Sheraton Maldives Full Moon Resort & Spa (p79), Shangri-La Villingili Resort & Spa (p131), Ayada Maldives (p127), Four Seasons Resort Maldives at Kuda Huraa (p84), Huvafen Fushi (p83), LUX* Maldives (p102), Sun Aqua Vilu Reef (p122), W Maldives (p95), Kurumba Maldives (p79) and Meeru Island Resort & Spa (p78).

Surfing

The best resorts for surfing are Cinnamon Island Dhonveli (p81) and Adaaran Select Hudhuranfushi (p82), which are both blessed with their own breaks and are very popular with surfers during the season.

The popularity of surfing is increasing in Maldives, with surfer arrivals going up massively in the past few years. However, it's really only these two resorts that are perfectly located near good breaks, although nearby resorts, such as Four Seasons Resort Maldives at Kuda Huraa (p84) and Paradise Island Resort & Spa (p80) can organise boat trips.

Meemu Atoll is also great for surfing and is largely unvisited by travellers, despite there being two nearby resorts making access fairly easy. Another fantastic option to avoid the crowds and explore a pristine region of the country is to join a 'surfari' – check with your resort or travel agent.

Spa Treatments

As a destination that has become synonymous with relaxation, Maldives offers a huge array of treatments in purpose-built spas. These include many different types of massage, beauty treatments, Ayurvedic (Indian herbal) medicine, acupuncture and even traditional Maldivian treatments.

All midrange and top-end resorts have a spa, and even most of the budget resorts now have them. The best are sometimes booked up in advance, so plan ahead. With staff often from Bali, Thailand, India and

RESORT TIPS

➡ It's always worth checking a resort website yourself and even contacting the resort for specific, up-to-date information, as things change regularly. Is there construction work happening on the island or nearby? Is the spa finished yet? Does it still offer kite-boarding? Also, be aware that many resort websites are not regularly updated. While there are exceptions, it's never a good idea to take the information there as fact – check when the page was last updated and also read up on the resort online.

➡ Check the dive-centre website. It might provide a discount if you block book your dives before your arrival. Email them for specific dive information and to check that they will definitely be visiting any site you want to dive at during your stay.

➡ If the trip is a honeymoon, or second honeymoon, or if you will be celebrating an anniversary or birthday, let your resort know – there's usually something laid on in such circumstances. Some resorts require a wedding certificate before they do anything, though.

RESORT BASICS

You'll be met at the airport by your resort representative, who will usually take your passport from you for the duration of your stay, something that is quite normal in Maldives, despite feeling rather odd.

Unless you're arriving in the late afternoon or evening, you'll soon be transferred to your resort – either by a waiting dhoni, speedboat, airplane or seaplane. You may have to wait for other passengers on the same transfer to get through customs, but it shouldn't be too long. Be aware that if you're heading to a resort, this is your last chance to buy things at a relatively normal price, such as toiletries or a local SIM card.

Travellers needing to take a seaplane connection who arrive after 3pm will have to spend a night at the airport hotel or at a hotel in Male or Hulhumale; seaplane transfers are not carried out after dark, so they generally do not leave Male after 4pm. Speedboat transfers can be done at any time of day or night, however.

On arrival at the resort you'll be given a drink, asked to fill out a registration form and taken to your room. Resort staff will bring your luggage separately. In no resort in Maldives are cash tips expected – you tip by paying the service charge included.

Room Types

Most resorts have several types of room, ranging from the cheapest garden villas to deluxe over-water suites. A garden villa will not have a beach frontage, while a water villa will be on stilts over the lagoon. More expensive rooms tend to have a bathtub as well as a shower, a minibar instead of an empty fridge, tea- and coffee-making facilities (and often an espresso machine), a sound system and maybe even a plunge pool, which are now de rigueur in newly built resorts.

Seasons & Supplements

High-season room rates are December to March for single/double occupancy. Rates also spike over Easter and in August. The cheapest time to visit Maldives is from April to July and from September to November.

Extra people can usually share a room, but there's normally a charge for the extra bed, which varies from resort to resort, as well as additional costs for meals. Bear in mind that there's also the obligatory US$6 per person per night green tax which is collected by the resort. This is only US$3 per person per night in guesthouses.

For children two years and younger, usually just the US$6 green tax is payable. From two to 12, the child supplement will be more, though usually less than a full adult rate.

Be aware that most resorts in Maldives quote their prices exclusive of taxes, which are significant. In general all resorts add on a 10% to 12% service charge as a tip for staff and a 12% general services tax (GST). Therefore bear these extras in mind when you're totalling up a trip's cost – the 'plus pluses', as they're known, essentially add around an extra 25% of all your resort costs, as they're added to food, drinks, activities and transfers too! We've included all taxes in our room prices.

Pricing Periods

Pricing patterns vary with the resort and the demands of its main market – some are incredibly detailed and complex, with a different rate every week. The basic pattern is that Christmas–New Year is the peak season, with very high prices, minimum-stay requirements and big surcharges for the often obligatory Christmas and New Year's Eve dinners. Early January to late March is high season. Chinese holidays such as Chinese New Year and the first week of October can also see price hikes. The weeks around Easter may attract higher rates (though less so than Christmas). From Easter to about mid-July is low season (and the wettest part of the year). July and August is another high season. Mid-September to early December is low season again.

Sri Lanka, you're in safe (if expensive) hands. Resorts well known for Ayurvedic therapy include Adaaran Select Meedhupparu (p109), Taj Exotica (p91), Vivanta by Taj Coral Reef (p77), Four Seasons Landaa Giraavaru (p112) and Olhuveli Beach & Spa (p89).

Day Trips

From a resort, day trips are one of the very few ways you'll be able to see something of the 'real' Maldives. Even if you are an independent traveller, this is still a good way to see otherwise inaccessible islands, and all guesthouses offer such excursions.

Almost all the resorts in North and South Male Atolls offer day trips to Male. There's enough to see and enough shopping to make this trip worthwhile, and it's a great way to get a feel for Maldivian culture, as terrifyingly polite resort staff are replaced by a friendly and down-to-earth city populace.

Another popular excursion is a trip to an inhabited island, which allows you to see a small island community, traditional housing, craftwork and lifestyle. The trips often feel rather contrived, but can still be immensely enjoyable depending on how friendly the locals are and how many people are around (with children often in school or studying in Male, and menfolk away for work, some islands feel like ghost towns). While it's often more enjoyable to explore an island on your own, the resort guides can be helpful in making contacts and telling you in detail about local life.

Fishing

Just about any resort will do sunset, sunrise or night-fishing trips, while many resorts can also arrange big-game fishing trips. These work out cheaper if there are several participants, as costs are high: from $450 for a half-day trip for up to four people. Large boats, fully equipped with radar technology, are used to catch dorado, tuna, marlin, barracuda and jackfish among others.

Food & Drink

What you eat in Maldives varies tremendously, but essentially boils down to your budget and your choice of resort. At the top end, you'll be cooked for by Michelin-starred chefs, while at the lower end the buffet – the standard dining option – is of extremely variable quality. The adage that you get what you pay for is especially relevant here.

Alcohol is also becoming more of a feature at resorts – many have spent years building up wine cellars.

One & Only Reethi Rah (p83) claims to have over 8000 bottles of wine in its cellar, while Huvafen Fushi (p83)'s wine cellar is a work of art itself, buried deep below the island and hired out for private dinners at great expense.

Meals

Typically, breakfast is a buffet wherever you stay in Maldives. At the bottom end, there will be a fairly limited selection of cereals, fruit, pastries and yoghurts. At the midrange and top end you'll have an enormous spread, usually including omelette stations, fresh fruit, good coffee, freshly baked pastries, curries, rice dishes, sushi, full English-style breakfast, meat platters and oodles of sweet cakes.

In budget resorts, lunch and dinner will usually be a buffet as well. This can quickly become repetitive, and while you'll never go hungry, you may find yourself craving some variety.

Some budget resorts have à la carte restaurants where you can dine to have a change of cuisine and scenery – if you're on an full-board deal, meals like this will normally be charged as extras. However, for the most part there's little or no choice at the budget end.

Dinner will usually have the biggest selection, and may be a 'theme night' specialising in regional cuisines such as Asian, Indian or Maldivian.

Almost all resorts serve locally caught fish and seafood, and these are an absolute highlight. Expect gorgeous fresh tuna, scallops, reef fish, crab and octopus in all but the most basic of resorts.

If you're in a midrange or top-end resort, you'll have a totally different experience. Almost all resorts in these categories have at least two restaurants, with a few exceptions for small islands where the restaurants are à la carte and have sufficiently long or changing menus to keep you satisfied for a week or more. The larger resorts will have multiple choices.

Another alternative to the usual buffet is a 'speciality meal'. This might be a barbecue or a curry night, served on the beach and open to anyone who pays an extra charge. Or it can be a much pricier private dinner for two in romantic surroundings – on an uninhabited island, on the beach, or on a sandbank a short ride from the resort island.

Most resorts will do special meals on request, and nearly all resorts offer in-room dining (room service) for those enjoying themselves too much to leave their villas.

Meal Plans

Many guests are on full-board packages that include accommodation and all meals. Others take a half-board package, which includes breakfast and dinner, and pay extra for lunch. Some resorts offer a bed-and-breakfast plan, and guests pay separately for lunch and dinner.

The advantage of not paying for all your meals in advance is that you permit yourself the freedom to vary where you eat (assuming your resort has more than one restaurant). However, at good resorts your full-board plan is usually transferable, meaning you can eat a certain amount at other restaurants, or at least get a big discount on the à la carte prices.

Room-only deals are also sometimes available, but they're rarely a great idea. Never underestimate the sheer expense of eating à la carte in Maldives at any level, although at the top end it's positively outrageous – think US$75 per head without alcohol for a decent lunch.

Self-catering is of course not possible, and there's nothing worse than being unable to eat properly due to financial constraints. Unless you're very comfortable financially and want to eat in a variety of different places, it's definitely a good idea to book full-board or at least half-board meal plans.

All-inclusive plans are some of the best value of all, although in general they're associated with the core package-tourist market and tend to be available only in budget resorts; though in recent years a number of luxury all-inclusive resorts have been opened. In budget and midrange resorts all-inclusive plans typically include all drinks (non-brand-name alcohol, soft drinks and water) and some activities and water sports/diving thrown in for good measure. Always investigate carefully exactly what's on offer meal-wise before you make a decision – the meal plan can make an expensive package worthwhile or a cheap one a rip-off.

At luxury all-inclusives, you'll get good wines and brand-name spirits for your (not inconsiderable) daily rate.

Entertainment

Maldives is not a premium destination for entertainment. What little of it there is can be naff and uninspiring, and the resorts that put on a nightly DJ or live band often find them poorly attended. Simply put, honeymooners, divers and families, the core demographic of Maldivian tourism, don't really come here for any kind of

EATING LOCAL IN RESORTS

It used to be rare to find Maldivian food in tourist resorts – but now many resorts do a Maldivian night once a week, which is very enjoyable if not totally authentic. The main dishes are fresh reef fish, baked tuna, fish curries, rice and *roshi* (unleavened bread). The regular dinner buffet might also feature Maldivian fish curry. Now almost ubiquitous is the serving of Maldivian breakfast favourite *mas huni* at breakfast: a healthy mixture of tuna, onion, coconut and chilli, eaten with *roshi*. This is a delicious way to start the day and many visitors get hooked. If there's nothing Maldivian on the menu, you could ask the kitchen staff to make a fish curry or a tray of 'short eats' – they may be making some for the staff anyway. Small resorts and top-end resorts are usually amenable to special requests. Otherwise, do a trip to Male or an island-hopping excursion to a fishing village and try out a local teashop. They're always a fascinating and tasty cultural experience.

entertainment, preferring quiet romance, daytime activities and early bedtimes.

That said, don't miss a performance of traditional Maldivian *bodu beru (*big drum) players, who perform regularly at resorts. Even better, if you're staying on an inhabited island, you might see the real thing performed by local youths after nightfall. This is definitely a cultural and entertainment highlight – the passion and excitement of the performance alone is remarkable – and shouldn't be missed.

A couple of clubs worth mentioning when it comes to evening entertainment are W Maldives (p95), Finolhu (p113), Niyama Private Islands (p122) and Huvafen Fushi (p83), all of which have clubs and frequently book international DJs to perform.

Beaches

Very few resorts in Maldives do not have an amazing beach. Some beaches suffer a great deal from erosion, but resorts work very hard to redress this with sandbags and seawalls in certain places.
These can of course be unsightly, but they are necessary to hold the islands' beaches in place. Obviously, the more expensive the resort, the more effort is made to ensure that sandbags are never visible. Every beach is cleaned each morning by teams of employees, and this is necessary, as even the fanciest of resorts gets dozens of plastic bottles and other flotsam washing up on them every day.

Here is a list of our favourite beaches in the country: Anantara Kihavah Villas (p112), Sun Siam Iru Fushi Maldives (p107), Kanuhura (p115), One & Only Reethi Rah (p83), Kuredu Island Resort & Spa (p115), Soneva Fushi (p113), Reethi Beach Resort (p109), Coco Palm Dhuni Kolhu (p110), Smartline Eriyadu (p81), Angsana Ihuru (p79), Bandos Island Resort (p80), Baros (p181), Banyan Tree Vabbinfaru (p85), Gili Lankanfushi (p82), Rihiveli by Castaway Hotels & Escapes (p89), Paradise Island Resort & Spa (p80), Hideaway Beach Resort & Spa (p177), W Maldives (p95), Veligandu Island Resort & Spa (p99), Sun Aqua Vilu Reef (p122), Huvafen Fushi (p83) and Conrad Maldives Rangali Island (p101).

This doesn't mean that resorts not on this list don't make the grade!

Children

If you're bringing children to Maldives, it's very important to get your choice of resort right, as only some resorts have kids clubs or babysitters available, and activities for older children can be limited at resorts more used to welcoming honeymooning couples. If you aren't looking for kids clubs and your offspring are happy to spend the day on the beach, then almost every resort will be suitable. Note that several resorts do not accept children and this has been mentioned in reviews.

In general, kids will love Maldives, although more than a week might be pushing it unless you're staying in a big family resort where there are plenty of other children for them to play with and lots of activities. Nowadays nearly all top-end resorts have kids clubs. These can be impressive places, with their own pools and a host of activities, which means parents can drop off kids (usually under 12) at any time, for free during the day. A few top-end resorts also have clubs for teenagers.

Luxuries

You've come to the right place if this is your main interest. Maldives' top-end resorts (and even some of its midrange options) offer an eye-watering range of treatments, pampering and general luxury.

Currently indispensable in the luxury industry is the personal *thakuru,* or butler, otherwise known as a Man or Woman Friday or villa host. The *thakuru* is assigned to you throughout your stay. They'll be your point of contact for all small things (restocking the minibar, reserving a table for dinner), but given that one *thakuru* will often be looking after up to 10 rooms at a time, the term 'personal' is pushing it a bit, especially when even in the best hotels in the country there are often language problems and some service issues.

The home of pampering at most resorts is the spa. Until recently they were considered optional for resorts, whereas now they are usually at the very centre of the luxury experience. Expect to pay from about US$100 for a simple massage at a budget or midrange place, to US$500 for a long session of pampering at a top-end resort.

RESORT RATINGS

We've ranked the resorts we cover in Maldives with scores out of three for the beaches, the child-friendliness, the quality of the diving nearby, the suitability for couples, the food on offer and how much we love the rooms. Three is the very highest standard in its field, while zero means that the resort has nothing worth mentioning on a subject; for example, if it doesn't accept kids, it gets a zero for child-friendliness.

	BEACHES	CHILD-FRIENDLY	DIVING	COUPLE SUITABILITY	FOOD	ROOMS
Adaaran Select Hudhuranfushi (p81)	3	2	3	2	2	2
Adaaran Select Meedhupparu (p109)	3	2	2	2	2	3
Amilla Fushi (p111)	3	3	3	3	3	3
Anantara Kihavah Villas (p112)	3	3	3	3	3	3
Angsana Ihuru (p79)	3	2	2	2	2	2
Asdu Sun Island (p75)	2	1	1	1	1	2
Ayada Maldives (p127)	3	3	3	1	3	3
Bandos Island Resort (p80)	2	3	1	2	2	1
Banyan Tree Vabbinfaru (p85)	3	1	2	3	2	2
Baros (p84)	3	0	2	3	3	3
Biyadhoo Island Resort (p87)	2	1	3	1	2	1
Cheval Blanc Randheli (p108)	3	2	3	3	3	3
Cinnamon Island Dhonveli (p81)	2	1	2	2	2	2
Cinnamon Hakuraa Huraa (p118)	3	2	3	2	2	2
Ellaidhoo Maldives by Cinnamon (p95)	1	1	3	2	2	2
Coco Palm Dhuni Kolhu (p110)	3	2	3	3	2	2
Cocoa Island by COMO (p90)	3	1	3	3	3	2
COMO Maalifushi (p124)	2	2	3	3	3	3
Conrad Maldives Rangali Island (p101)	3	3	3	3	2	2
Constance Halaveli Maldives (p97)	3	1	3	3	2	2
Embudu Village (p87)	1	1	3	2	1	1
Equator Village (p131)	1	2	3	1	1	1
Filitheyo Island Resort (p119)	3	1	3	2	2	2
Finolhu (p113)	3	1	3	2	2	2
Four Seasons Resort Maldives at Kuda Huraa (p84)	2	3	2	3	3	2
Four Seasons Landaa Giraavaru (p112)	3	3	3	3	3	3
Gili Lankanfushi (p82)	3	2	3	3	3	3
Huvafen Fushi (p83)	3	2	2	3	3	3
Hideaway Beach Resort & Spa (p104)	3	3	3	3	2	2
Jumeirah Vittaveli (p90)	2	3	3	3	3	3
Kandolhu Maldives (p97)	3	1	3	3	2	3
Kanuhura (p115)	3	3	3	3	3	2

	BEACHES	CHILD-FRIENDLY	DIVING	COUPLE SUITABILITY	FOOD	ROOMS
Kuramathi Island Resort (p98)	3	2	3	2	2	2
Kuredu Island Resort & Spa (p115)	2	3	3	2	2	2
Kurumba Maldives (p79)	2	3	2	2	3	2
LUX* Maldives (p101)	3	2	3	3	2	3
Makunudu Island (p80)	3	1	2	3	2	1
Meeru Island Resort & Spa (p78)	3	2	2	2	2	2
Mirihi (p100)	3	2	3	2	2	2
Naladhu Private Island (p91)	2	3	3	3	3	3
Niyama Private Islands (p122)	3	2	3	3	3	2
OBLU by Atmosphere at Helengeli (p77)	2	2	3	2	2	2
Olhuveli Beach & Spa (p89)	3	2	3	2	2	2
One & Only Reethi Rah (p83)	3	3	3	3	3	3
OZEN by Atmosphere at Maadhoo (p91)	2	2	3	3	3	3
Paradise Island Resort & Spa (p80)	3	3	2	2	1	1
Park Hyatt Maldives Hadahaa (p127)	3	2	3	3	2	3
Reethi Beach Resort (p109)	3	2	3	3	2	2
Rihiveli by Castaway Hotels & Escapes (p87)	3	2	3	2	2	3
Shangri-La Villingili Resort & Spa (p131)	3	3	3	3	2	3
Sheraton Maldives Full Moon Resort & Spa (p79)	2	2	2	3	2	3
Sirru Fen Fushi (p105)	3	2	3	3	3	3
Six Senses Laamu (p124)	2	2	3	3	3	3
Smartline Eriyadu (p81)	2	1	3	2	1	1
Soneva Fushi (p113)	3	3	3	3	3	3
Soneva Jani (p107)	1	3	2	3	3	3
St Regis Vommuli (p122)	3	2	3	3	2	3
Summer Island (p82)	2	2	3	2	2	2
Sun Aqua Vilu Reef (p122)	3	3	3	2	2	2
Sun Siam Iru Fushi Maldives (p107)	2	3	3	2	2	2
Taj Exotica (p90)	3	2	2	3	3	3
Velaa Private Island (p108)	3	2	3	3	2	3
Veligandu Island Resort & Spa (p99)	3	2	3	2	2	2
Vivanta by Taj Coral Reef (p77)	2	2	3	2	2	3
W Maldives (p95)	3	0	3	3	3	3

Diving at the British Loyalty Wreck (

Plan Your Trip

Diving, Snorkelling & Surfing

Unless you take some time to explore the magical world underneath the water in Maldives, you're seeing just one part of this wonderful country. Glance into the deep blue all around and you'll see why Maldives is a favourite destination for divers from around the world.

Top Diving Sites

British Loyalty Wreck

A torpedoed oil tanker (p131) in Addu Atoll that is now covered in soft corals.

Dhidhdhoo Beyru

The best place (p100) in Maldives to swim with whale sharks.

Fish Head

A spectacular thila dive (p95) with multiple layers, levels and extremely diverse marine life.

Hammerhead Point

A deep dawn dive (p98) that takes you to see dozens of hammerhead sharks in North Ari Atoll.

Helengeli Thila

One of North Male Atoll's best dive sites (p75), bursting with corals and pelagics.

Manta Point

Addu Atoll's best dive site (p131), with giant swooping rays who visit the cleaning station here.

Manta Reef

From December to April, this large cleaning station (p100) offers the chance to see mantas.

Diving in Maldives

Taking the plunge into the deep blue is one of the most exciting things imaginable and the rewards are massive, especially in Maldives, which is rightly known as a world-class scuba-diving destination. The enormous variety of fish life is amazing, and there's a good chance you'll see some of the biggest marine creatures – a close encounter with a giant manta or a whale shark is unforgettable. However, it's important to know that coral in Maldives will take years to recover from the severe bleaching that occured in 2016.

Where to Dive

There are hundreds of recognised and named dive sites, with dozens accessible from nearly every resort. In general there are four types of dive sites in Maldives.

Reefs Along the edges of the reef, where it slopes into the deep water, is the best part of the reef to dive on. There's lots of life, including small tropical fish, and bigger creatures often swim by.

Kandus These are channels between islands, reefs or atolls. The strong current makes them a breeding ground for plankton, which attracts whale sharks, and they're also a place where soft corals thrive.

Thilas & Giris Thilas are coral formations that rise from the atoll floor and reach to between 5m and 15m before the surface of the water, while a giri rises almost to the surface. Both brim with life.

Wrecks Maldives' treacherous shallows have made it a rich place to do wreck dives, even if most of those regularly visited are purposely sunk craft where coral has subsequently grown.

Learning to Dive

Diving is not difficult, but it requires some knowledge and care. It doesn't require great strength or fitness, although if you can do things with minimum expenditure of energy, your tank of air will last longer.

There's a range of courses, from an introductory dive in a pool or lagoon to an open-water course that gives an internationally recognised qualification. Beyond that, there are advanced and speciality courses, and courses that lead to divemaster and instructor qualifications. Courses in Maldives are not a bargain, but they're no more expensive than learning at home and this way you are assured of high standards, good equipment and extremely pleasant conditions. On the other hand, if you do a course at home, you'll have more time for actual diving when you get to Maldives.

The best option for learners is to do an open-water referral course in your home country (ie all the theory and basics in the pool), allowing you to complete the course in Maldives in just two days rather than the four or five needed for the full course. After all, you didn't fly halfway around the world to sit in a room watching a PADI DVD, did you? If you do this, ensure you have all your certification from the referral course with you; otherwise you'll have to start from scratch.

If you're at all serious about diving, you should do an open-water course. This requires nine dives, usually five in sheltered water and four in open water, as well as classroom training and completion of a multiple-choice test. The cost in Maldives is from US$600 to US$950. Sometimes the price is all-inclusive, but there are often a few extra charges. You can do the course in as little as five days, or take your time and spread it over a week or two. Don't try it on a one-week package – transfers and jet lag will take a day or so, and you shouldn't dive within 24 hours before flying. Besides, you'll want to do some recreational dives to try out your new skills.

The next stage is an advanced open-water course, which involves five dives (including one night dive) and costs from US$400 to US$700, depending on the dive school. Then there are the speciality courses in night diving, rescue diving, wreck diving, nitrox diving and so on.

Dive Schools & Operators

Every resort has a professional diving operation and can run courses for beginners, as well as dive trips and advanced technique courses that will challenge even the most experienced diver. The government requires that all dive operations maintain high standards, and all of them are affiliated with one or more of the international diving accreditation organisations.

> **DIVING SEASONS**
>
> **January to April** Generally considered the best months for diving, with fine weather and good visibility.
>
> **May and June** Can have unstable weather – storms and cloudy days are common until September.
>
> **October and November** Tend to have calmer, clearer weather, but visibility can be slightly reduced because of abundant plankton in the water. Some divers like this period because many large fish, such as whale sharks and mantas, come into the channels to feed on the plankton.
>
> **December** Can have rough, windy weather and rain.

Diving cou

Similarly, all guesthouses will have an arrangement with a dive centre on the same island, and in some cases, they'll have an in-house dive centre.

Certificates

When you complete an open-water course, you receive a certificate that is recognised by diving operators all over the world. Certificates in Maldives are generally issued by the Professional Association of Diving Instructors (PADI), the largest and the best-known organisation, but certificates from Confédération Mondiale des Activités Subaquatiques (CMAS; World Underwater Federation), Scuba Schools International (SSI) and a number of other organisations are also acceptable.

Diving Safaris

On a diving safari, a dozen or so divers cruise the atolls in a live-aboard boat fitted out for the purpose. You can stop at your pick of the dive sites, visit uninhabited islands and inhabited islands, find secluded anchorages and sleep in a compact cabin. If you've had enough diving, you can fish, snorkel or swim off the boat.

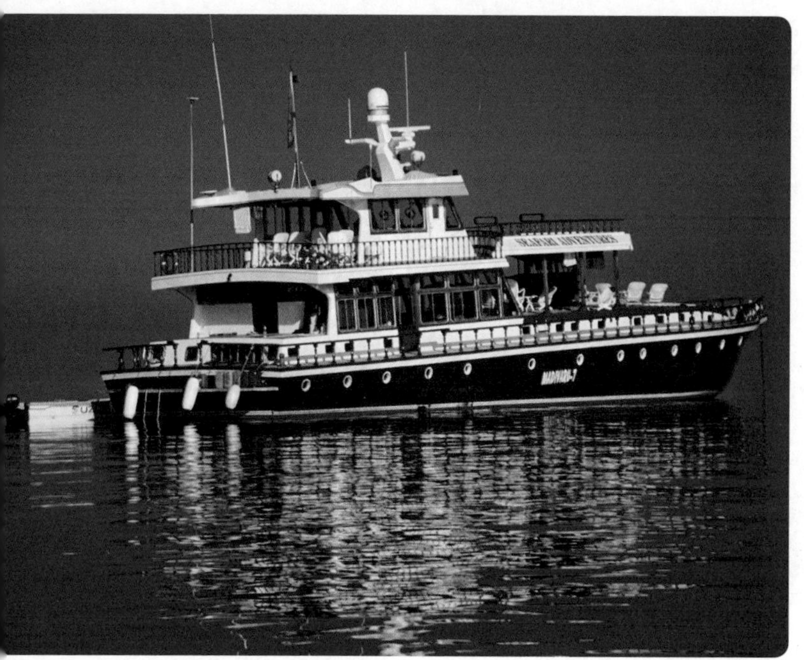

Diving safari boat

The massive expansion in the market for safari cruises has meant an increasingly sleek approach from the tour companies that run them. A typical, modern boat is air-conditioned and spacious, and serves varied and appetising meals. It should have hot water, a sun deck, fishing and diving gear, a mobile phone, a full bar, a TV room, wireless and cosy, comfortable cabins.

Costs start at around US$150 per person per day, including the US$8 per day per bed tax and all meals, plus roughly US$80 per day for diving trips. There's usually a minimum daily (or weekly) charge for the whole boat, and the cost per person is lower if there are enough passengers to fill the boat. You'll be charged extra for drinks, which are priced comparably to most resorts.

The most basic boats are large dhonis with a small galley and communal dining area, two or three cramped cabins with two berths each, and a shared shower and toilet. The bigger, better boats have air-conditioning, more spacious accommodation, and a toilet and shower for each cabin.

Choosing a Safari Boat

There are over 100 safari boats operating in Maldives, so you'll need to do some research. When you're considering a safari-boat trip, ask the operator about the following:

Boat size Generally speaking, bigger boats will be more comfortable, and therefore more expensive, than smaller boats. Most boats have about 12 berths or less. Few boats have more than 20 berths, and those that do may not be conducive to the camaraderie you get with a small group.

Cabin arrangements Can you get a two-berth cabin (if that's what you want)? How many cabins/people are sharing a bathroom?

Comforts Does the boat have air-con, hot water and desalinated water available 24 hours?

Companions Who else will be on the trip, what language do they speak, have they done a safari trip before? What are their interests: diving, sightseeing, fishing, surfing?

Food and drink Can you be catered for as a vegetarian or vegan? Is there a bar serving alcohol, and if so, how much is a beer and a bottle of wine etc?

ANDREY NEKRASOV/GETTY IMAGES ©

1. Tiger shark **2.** Laced moray eel **3.** Hawksbill turtle swimming with blueline snappers **4.** Whale shark

3

AQUAPIX/SHUTTERSTOCK ©

Big Creatures of the Deep

Marine life on the reef is fabulous, colourful and fascinating, but what divers and snorkellers really want to see are the big creatures of the deep. Indeed, an encounter with an enormous whale shark can be the experience of a lifetime.

Sharks

If you're lucky, you'll see a wide range of sharks in Maldives. Reef sharks are commonly seen everywhere, and tiger sharks frequent Gnaviyani and Ari Atoll, but one of the most impressive sights in the country is a school of hammerheads at Rasdhoo Madivaru – aka Hammerhead Point (p98) – in Rasdhoo Atoll.

Moray Eels

The moray eel and its slightly manic expression as it leans out of its protective hole are standard sights on almost any Maldivian reef, and some can be playful with divers. Be careful of its bite, though – once it closes its teeth, it never lets go.

Turtles

Turtles often swim around the reefs and can be curious around snorkellers and divers. Five different types of turtles swim in Maldivian waters. The most common are green and hawksbill turtles.

Rays

These creatures are a favourite with divers. Smaller stingrays and eagle rays often rest in the sand, while enormous manta rays can have a 'wingspan' of around 4m, and seeing one swoop over you is an extraordinary experience.

Whale Sharks

These gentle giants eat nothing but plankton and the odd small fish, but somehow have evolved to be the biggest fish in the world, measuring up to 12m in length. They can often be spotted cruising Dhidhdhoo Beyru (p100) on the edge of South Ari Atoll.

Recreation Does the boat have wi-fi, fishing tackle or a sun deck? Does the boat have sails or is it propelled by motor only?

Safari Boat Operators

Safari boats often change ownership, get refitted or acquire a new name. The skipper, cook and divemaster can change too, so it's hard to make firm recommendations. The following boats have a good reputation, but there are many others offering decent facilities and services. The boats listed here all have a bar on board, oxygen for emergencies and some diving equipment for rent. Universal's *Atoll Explorer* is like a mini-cruise ship with a swimming pool on deck, while the *Ritrella Cruise Hotel* is the biggest live-aboard in Maldives at 58m.

The official Maldives tourism website (www.visitmaldives.com) has reasonably up-to-date details on almost every safari and cruise boat.

Adventurer 2 (☎335 6734; www.maldivesdiving.com)

Atoll Explorer (☎999 9615)

Four Seasons Explorer (☎660 0888; www.fourseasons.com/maldivesfse)

Gulfaam (☎332 2019; www.voyagesmaldives.com)

Manta Cruise (☎976 1209; www.twentysixatolls.com)

Ritrella Cruise Hotel (☎334 0555; www.ritrella.com)

Sting Ray (☎331 4811; www.maldivesboatclub.com)

Sultan of Maldives (☎332 0330; www.sultansoftheseas.com)

Equipment

Dive schools in Maldives can rent out all diving gear, but most divers prefer to have at least some of their own equipment. It's best to have your own mask, snorkel and fins, which you can also use for snorkelling. The tank and weight belt are always included in the cost of a dive, so you don't need to bring them – sealed tanks are prohibited on aircraft anyway, and you'd be crazy to carry lead weights.

Wetsuit

The water may be warm (27°C to 30°C) but a wetsuit is often preferable for comfortable diving. A 3mm suit should be adequate, but 5mm is preferable if you want to go deep or dive more than once per day. Alternatively, it's totally possible to dive in a T-shirt if you don't feel the cold too much.

Regulators & BCDs

Many divers have their own regulator (the mouth piece you breathe through), with which they are familiar and therefore confident about using. BCDs (Buoyancy Control Devices) are the vests that can be controlled to inflate and deflate and thus increase or decrease your buoyancy, a vital tool for safe diving. Both pieces of equipment are usually included in full equipment packages, though serious divers will usually bring their own.

Dive Computer

These are now compulsory in Maldives. They're available for rent, for US$5 to US$10 per dive, or as part of a complete equipment package. Again, many serious divers have their own that they bring with them, as it saves money very quickly after the initial purchase.

Logbook & Other Accessories

You'll need this to indicate to divemasters your level of experience, and to record your latest dives, which are then authenticated by the divemaster and stamped by the school.

Other items you might need are an underwater torch (especially for cave and night dives), a waterproof camera, a compass, and a safety buoy or balloon, most of which are available for rental.

Some things you won't need are a spear gun, as spear-fishing is prohibited, and diving gloves, which are discouraged since you're not supposed to touch anything anyway.

Diving Costs

The cost of diving varies between resorts and guesthouses, and depends on whether you need to rent equipment. Diving with an operator on an inhabited island is nearly always cheaper due to the dive centre's lack of monopoly, so many budget-minded divers head directly for a guesthouse.

A single dive, with only tank and weights supplied, runs from US$60 to US$120, but is generally around US$70 (night dives cost more). If you need to rent

Right: Diving among red fan coral

a regulator and a BCD as well, a dive will cost from US$70 to US$150. Sometimes the full equipment price includes mask, snorkel, fins, dive computer and pressure gauge, but they can cost extra. A package of 10 dives will cost roughly from US$350 to US$700, or US$450 to US$800 with equipment rental. Other possibilities are five-, 12- and 15-dive packages, and packages that allow you as many dives as you want within a certain number of consecutive days.

The very best diving operators will bill you at the end of your stay, having worked out which tariff is most economical for you based on the diving you've done. In addition to the dive cost, there is a charge for using a boat, which can be as much as US$20 per dive.

There may also be a service charge of 10%, plus a general sales tax of 12% if diving is billed to your room, so the prices really do add up.

Ideally book your dives ahead of time, confirming the total price and shop around between resorts to find the best deals.

Protecting the Marine Environment

The waters of Maldives may seem pristine but, like everywhere, development and commercial activities have inevitably had adverse effects on the marine environment. The Maldivian government recognises that the underwater world is a major attraction, and has imposed many restrictions and controls on fishing, coral mining and tourism operations. Twenty-five protected marine areas have been established, and these are subject to special controls.

The following rules are generally accepted as necessary for conservation, and most of them apply equally to snorkellers and divers.

CORAL BLEACHING IN MALDIVES

Catastrophic coral bleaching events in 2016 killed between 60% and 90% of Maldives' famously beautiful corals in just a few weeks, and now sadly the diving in the country is a pale imitation of what it was prior to the event. As climate change marches onwards, it seems likely that more and more of these fragile creatures will be destroyed. Many reefs in Maldives look like graveyards today, with little life left on them but the grey remains of dead corals.

That said, despite coral's fragility, it also is growing back surprisingly quickly even in places totally devastated by the bleaching. Soft corals and sea fans were less affected than hard corals, and many of these are flourishing again just a few years later. Soft-coral gardens thrive still at some dive and snorkelling sites, especially around channels that are rich with water-borne nutrients.

The underlying hard-coral structure is still there of course – new coral grows on the skeletons of its predecessors, so it's important not to break the dead coral structures. Indeed, the healthiest living coral has many metres, perhaps kilometres, of dead coral underneath. New coral is growing on reefs all over Maldives, though the large and elaborately shaped formations will take many years to build. The first regrowth often occurs in crevices on old coral blocks, where it's protected from munching parrotfish. The massive Porites-type corals seem to come first, but they grow slowly – look for blobs of yellow, blue or purple that will eventually cover the whole block in a crust or a cushion or a brainlike dome. The branching corals *(Acropora)* appear as little purplish trees on a coral block, like a pale piece of broccoli. Growing a few centimetres per year (15cm in ideal conditions), they will eventually become big, extended staghorn corals or wide, flat-topped tables.

The recovery for coral is not uniform. Some parts of a reef can be doing very well, with 80% or 90% of the old surfaces covered with new and growing coral, while 100m along the same reef, new coral growth cover is less than 20%. Reef formation is a very complex natural process, but surprisingly the marine ecosystem as a whole seems to be undamaged by the coral bleaching. Fish life is as abundant and diverse as ever.

Snorkelling with a clownfish

➡ Do not use anchors on the reef, and take care not to ground boats on coral. Encourage dive operators and regulatory bodies to establish permanent moorings at popular dive sites.

➡ Avoid touching living marine organisms with your body or dragging equipment across the reef. Polyps can be damaged by even the gentlest contact.

➡ Never stand on corals, even if they look solid and robust. If you must hold on to prevent being swept away in a current, hold on to dead coral.

➡ Be conscious of your fins. Even without contact the surge from heavy fin strokes near the reef can damage delicate organisms. When treading water in shallow reef areas, take care not to kick up clouds of sand. Settling sand can easily smother the delicate organisms of the reef.

➡ Collecting lobster or shellfish is prohibited, as is spearfishing. Removing any coral or shells, living or dead, is against the law. All shipwreck sites are protected by law.

➡ Take home all your rubbish and any litter you may find as well. Plastics in particular are a serious threat to marine life. Turtles can mistake plastic for jellyfish and eat it. Don't throw cigarette butts overboard.

➡ Do not feed fish. You may disturb their normal eating habits, encourage aggressive behaviour or feed them food that is detrimental to their health.

➡ Practise and maintain proper buoyancy control. Major damage can be done by divers descending too fast and colliding with the reef.

➡ Take great care in underwater caves. Spend as little time within them as possible as your air bubbles may be caught within the roof and thereby leave previously submerged organisms high and dry. Taking turns to inspect the interior of a small cave will lessen the chances of damaging contact.

Snorkelling

Snorkelling is the first step into seeing a different world. Anyone who can swim can do it, it's cheap (and often free) to use the equipment and the rewards are immediately evident. The colours of the fish and coral are far better at shallow depths, because water absorbs light. This means a visual feast awaits any snorkeller on any decent reef.

Where to Snorkel

Usually an island is surrounded firstly by a sand-bottomed lagoon, and then by the reef flat *(faru)*, a belt of dead and living coral covered by shallow water. At the edge of the reef flat is a steep, coral-covered slope that drops away into deeper water.

These reef slopes are the best areas for snorkelling – around a resort island this is called the 'house reef'. The slope itself can have interesting features such as cliffs, terraces and caves, and there are clearly visible changes in the coral and marine flora as the water gets deeper. You can see both the smaller fish, which frequent the reef flats, and sometimes much larger animals that live in the deep water between the islands but come close to the reefs to feed. You can also take a boat from your resort to other snorkelling sites around the atoll.

The best resorts for snorkelling have an accessible house reef around at least part of the island, where deep water is not far offshore. There are usually channels you can swim through to the outer-reef slope. To avoid grazing yourself or damaging the coral, always use these channels rather than trying to find your own way across the reef flat.

Equipment

Every resort and guesthouse will have snorkelling equipment that you can rent, though it's often free at smarter places. It's definitely better to have your own equipment, though, as it's cheaper in the long run and sure to fit properly. You can buy good equipment at reasonable prices in Male, though you're better off buying your gear at home before you leave.

SNORKELLING SAFELY

Don't snorkel alone, and always let someone else know where and when you'll be snorkelling. Colourful equipment or clothing will make you more visible. Beware of strong currents or rough conditions – wind chop and large swells can make snorkelling uncomfortable or even dangerous. In open water, carry a safety balloon and whistle to alert boats to your presence.

Snorkelling over co

Surfing

Surfing has been slow to take off in Maldives, but in recent years, particularly since the development of independent tourism, there's been a strong growth in surfer numbers. There's some great surf throughout the country, although breaks are generally only surfable from March to November.

The period of the southwest monsoon (May to November) generates the best waves, but March and April are also good and have the best weather. June can have bad weather and storms, but it is also a time for big swells. The best breaks occur on the outer reefs on the southeast sides of the atolls, but only where a gap in the reef allows the waves to wrap around.

Where to Surf

The most accessible surf breaks are in the southeastern part of North Male Atoll. Half a dozen resorts and a few guesthouses are within a short boat ride, but check with them if you plan to surf, as only a few of them cater for surfers by providing regular boat service to the waves.

Catching a wave

Cinnamon Island Dhonveli (p81) is the resort that's best set up for surfers – the reliable waves of the 'house break', Pasta Point, are just out the back door, while Sultan's and Honky's are close by. A surfside bar provides a great view of the action. Surfing packages include unlimited boat trips to the other local breaks with surf guides who know the conditions well, leaving and returning on demand.

Adaaran Select Hudhuranfushi (p82), a few kilometres northeast of Dhonveli, is a bigger, more expensive resort with more facilities. It also has its own, exclusive surf break. A bar and a viewing terrace overlook the wave, which has hosted international surfing competitions.

Surfing Safaris

Most of the safari boats in Maldives claim to do surfing trips, but very few of them have specialised knowledge of surfing or any experience cruising to the outer atolls. Ideally, a surfing safari boat should have an experienced surf guide and a second, smaller boat to accompany it, for accessing breaks in shallower water and getting in close to the waves. A surfing safari ('surfari') boat should also be equipped with fishing and snorkelling gear, for when the surf isn't working or you need a rest.

An inner-atolls surfari will just cruise around North Male Atoll, visiting breaks that are also accessible from resorts in the area. If the swell is big and the surf guide is knowledgable, the boat may venture down to South Male Atoll to take advantage of the conditions. A one-week inner-atoll surf trip will start at around US$1000 per person. This might be cheaper than resort-based surfing, but it won't be as comfortable, and it won't give access to a handy and uncrowded house break.

An outer-atolls surfari is the only feasible way to surf the remote waves of Gaaf Dhaal or Meemu – an experienced outer-atoll guide is essential. If you're looking to surf in Meemu, the boat will probably pick you up in Male and then head south. If you're going surfing in Gaaf Dhaal, you'll normally take a Maldivian flight to the domestic airport on the island of Kaadedhoo, where the boat crew will meet you.

You need at least six people to make a safari boat affordable; the surfing specialists should be able to put together the necessary numbers. Don't book into a safari trip that is primarily for diving or cruising. Allow at least two weeks for the trip.

Surf Breaks

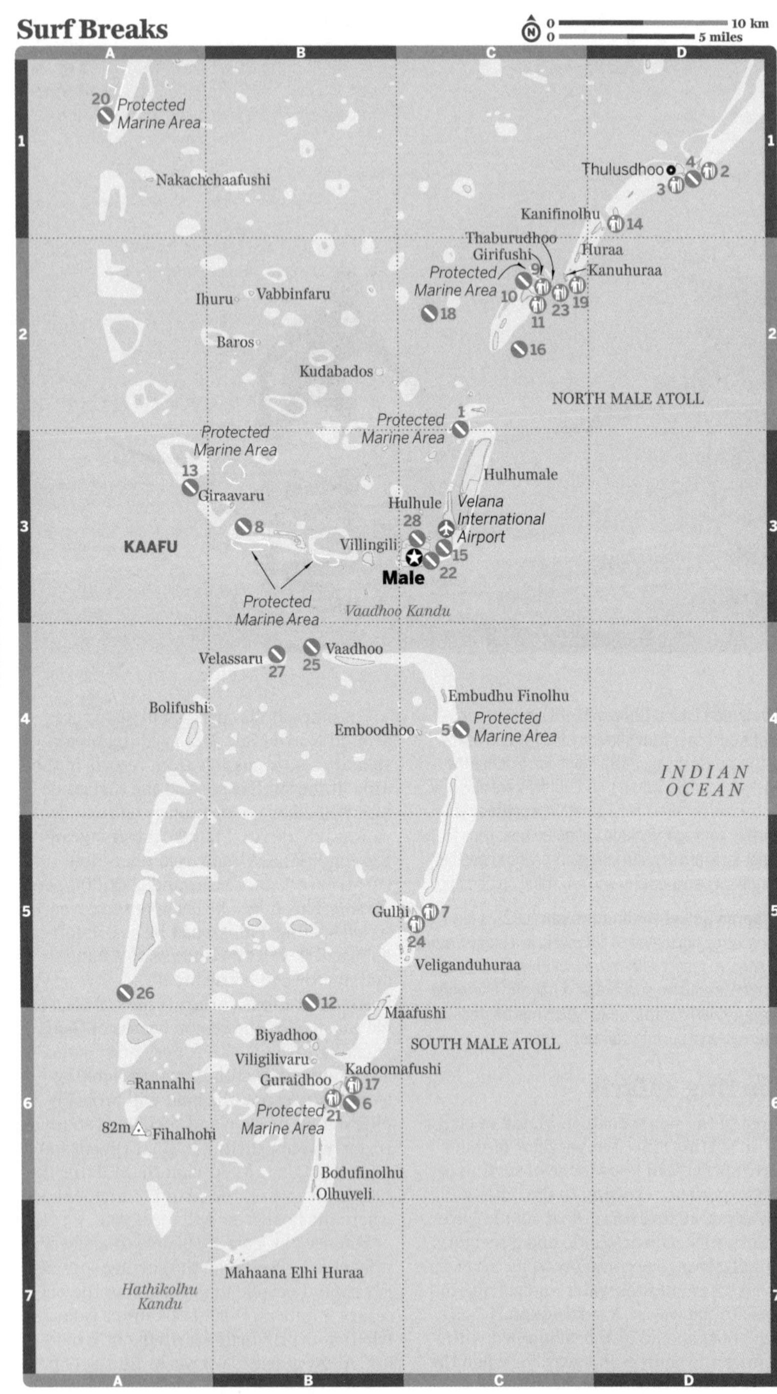
0 10 km
0 5 miles
20 Protected Marine Area
Nakachchaafushi
Thulusdhoo
4
2
3
Kanifinolhu
14
Thaburudhoo
Girifushi
Huraa
Kanuhuraa
Protected Marine Area
9
10
11
23
19
Ihuru
Vabbinfaru
18
Baros
16
Kudabados
NORTH MALE ATOLL
Protected Marine Area
1
Protected Marine Area
13
Giraavaru
Hulhumale
Hulhule
Velana International Airport
28
8
KAAFU
Villingili
15
22
Male
Protected Marine Area
Vaadhoo Kandu
Vaadhoo
Velassaru
27
25
Embudhu Finolhu
Bolifushi
Emboodhoo
5
Protected Marine Area
INDIAN OCEAN
Gulhi
7
24
Veliganduhuraa
26
12
Maafushi
Biyadhoo
SOUTH MALE ATOLL
Viligilivaru
Kadoomafushi
Guraidhoo
17
Rannalhi
6
21
Protected Marine Area
82m
Fihalhohi
Bodufinolhu
Olhuveli
Mahaana Elhi Huraa
Hathikolhu Kandu

Surf Breaks

Activities, Courses & Tours

1 Banana Reef......C2
2 Chickens......D1
3 Coke's......D1
4 Colosseum......D1
5 Embudhoo Express......C4
6 Guraidhoo Kandu......B6
7 Guru's......C5
8 Hans Hass Place......B3
9 Honky's......C2
10 HP Reef......C2
11 Jailbreaks......C2
12 Kuda Giri......B5
13 Lion's Head......A3
14 Lohi's......D1
15 Maldive Victory......C3
16 Manta Point......C2
17 Natives......B6
18 Okobe Thila......C2
19 Pasta Point......C2
20 Rasfari......A1
21 Rip Tides......B6
22 Sea Explorers Dive School......C3
23 Sultan's......C2
24 Twin Peaks......C5
25 Vaadhoo Caves......B4
26 Vaagali Caves......A5
27 Velassaru Caves......B4
28 Whale Submarine......C3

A 10-night surfari will cost from about US$2000 per person, including domestic airfares.

Surf Travel Operators

The following agents specialise in surf travel and book tours and safaris to Maldives.

Atoll Travel (☎+61 3 5682 1088; www.atolltravel.com; 4 Bridge St, Foster, Victoria, Australia)

Maldives Scuba Tours (www.scubascuba.com)

Surfatoll (Map p59; www.surfatoll.com; M Bolissafaru, 2nd Floor, Orchid Magu)

Surf Travel Company (☎in Australia +61 2 9222 8870; www.surftravel.com.au)

Turquoise Surf Travel (☎in France +33 1 85 34 45 37; www.turquoise-voyages.fr)

World Surfaris (☎in Australia +61 7 5444 4011; www.worldsurfaris.com)

Maldives Surf Breaks

North Male Atoll

This is where the best-known breaks are, and they can get a bit crowded, especially if there are several safari boats in the vicinity.

Chickens (p75) A left-hander that sections when small, but on a bigger swell and a higher tide it all comes together to make a long and satisfying wave. It's named for the old poultry farm onshore, not because of any reaction to the conditions here.

Coke's (p75) A heavy, hollow, shallow right-hander; when it's big, it's one of the best breaks in the area. This is a very thick wave breaking hard over a shallow reef, so it's definitely for experienced, gutsy surfers only. Named for the Coca-Cola factory nearby on the island of Thulusdhoo, it's also called Cola's.

Honky's (p75) During its season, this is the best wave in Maldives. It's a super-long, wally left-hander that wraps almost 90 degrees and can nearly double in size by the end section.

Jailbreaks (p75) A right-hander that works best with a big swell, when the three sections combine to make a single, long, perfect wave. There used to be a prison on the island, hence the name.

Lohi's (p75) A solid left-hander that usually breaks in two sections, but with a big enough swell and a high enough tide the sections link up.

Pasta Point (p75) A perfect left that works like clockwork on all tides. There's a long outside wall at the take-off point, jacking into a bowling section called the 'macaroni bowl'. On big days the break continues to another section called 'lock jaws', which grinds into very shallow water over the reef. It's easily reached from the shore at the Chaaya Island Dhonveli resort, whose guests have exclusive use of this break.

Sultan's (p75) This is a classic right-hand break, and the bigger the swell, the better it works. A steep outside peak leads to a super-fast wall and then an inside section that throws right out, and tubes on every wave.

South Male Atoll

The breaks in South Male Atoll are smaller than those in North Male Atoll and generally more fickle.

Guru's (p87) A nice little left off the island of Gulhi; it's good for manoeuvres and aerials when conditions are good.

Twin Peaks (p87) A small left-hander that can nevertheless get some big swell.

Rip Tides (p87) A long and fast right-hander.

Natives (p87) A small right-hander, rarely more than a metre.

REEFS IN BRIEF

An overview of some of the best and most popular reefs in the country:

Reef	Atoll	Reef Type
Banana Reef	North Male	reef & kandu
Devana Kandu	Vaavu	kandu & thila
Embudhoo Express	South Male	kandu
Fotteyo	Vaavu	kandu
Fushifaru Thila	Lhaviyani	kandu & thila
Kuda Giri	South Male	giri & wreck
Kuda Kandu	Addu	kandu
Kuredhoo Express	Lhaviyani	kandu
Maa Kandu	Addu	reef & kandu
Macro Spot	Dhaalu	giri
Manta Reef	Ari	reef & kandu
Milaidhoo Reef	Baa	kandu
Orimas Thila	Ari	thila
Panetone	Ari	kandu
Rakeedhoo Kandu	Vaavu	kandu
Hammerhead Point (Rasdhoo Madivaru)	Ari	outer-reef slope
Two Brothers	Faafu	giri
Vaadhoo Caves	South Male	kandu

Outer Atolls

Only a few areas have the right combination of reef topography, wind directions and orientation to swell. Laamu and Addu both have surfable waves on occasions, Laamu in particular has regular surf visitors staying at Reveries Diving Village (p124) and Six Senses Laamu (p124).

South of Male, Meemu Atoll has several excellent surf breaks on its eastern edge including Veyvah Point, Boahuraa Point and Mulee Point, which are gradually being explored by more adventurous surfers.

In the far south, Gaafu Dhaalu has a series of reliable breaks that are accessed by safari boats in season.

From west to east, the named breaks are Beacons, Castaways, Blue Bowls, Five Islands, Two Ways (also called Twin Peaks; left and right), Love Charms, Antiques and Tiger.

Plan Your Trip

Eat & Drink Like a Local

Your culinary experience in Maldives could be, depending on your resort, anything from haute cuisine ordered from a menu you've discussed with the chef in advance, to bangers and mash at the all-you-can-eat buffet in the communal dining room. What it's unlikely to be in either case is particularly Maldivian, given the disconnection of resorts from local life. However, anyone staying in Male or on an inhabited island should take advantage of this opportunity to try real Maldivian food.

Food Experiences

Essentially all that grows in Maldives are coconuts, yams, mangoes, papayas and pineapples; the only other locally occurring products are fish and seafood, which explains the historical simplicity of Maldivian cuisine. However, as trade with the Indian subcontinent, Africa, Arabia and the Far East has always brought other, more exciting influences, the result is far less bland than it could be.

The Indian influence is clear in local cuisine above all; Maldivian food is often hot and spicy. If you're going to eat local food, prepare your palate for spicy fish curry, fish soup, fish patties and variations thereof. A favourite Maldivian breakfast is *mas huni,* a healthy mixture of tuna, onion, coconut and chilli, eaten cold with *roshi* (unleavened bread, like an Indian chapati) and tea.

Your culinary experience in Maldives could be, depending on your resort, anything from haute cuisine ordered from a menu you've discussed with the chef in advance, to bangers and mash at the all-you-can-eat buffet in the communal dining room. What it's unlikely to be in either

Favourite Fish

Fish is the staple diet of Maldives, but some types of seafood are enjoyed with particular enthusiasm.

Tuna Maldives' favourite fish, the core ingredient of many *hedhikaa* (Maldivian finger snacks) and also eaten dried, stewed, grilled, and for breakfast!

Swordfish A resort favourite, often served fried or grilled, but islanders prefer skipjack, tunny, wahoo and other members of the tuna family.

Octopus Not often found in resorts, but loved on inhabited islands, and typically served in a curry sauce.

Lobster Common in Maldivian waters, but usually reserved for menus at the top resorts in the islands.

case is particularly Maldivian, given the disconnection of resorts from local life. However, anyone staying in Male or on an inhabited island should take advantage of this opportunity to try real Maldivian food.

Meals of a Lifetime

Gili Lankanfushi (p82) Sumptuous Japanese at By The Sea or just the incredible buffet at the main restaurant.

Four Seasons Resort Maldives at Kuda Huraa (p84) Have incredible Indian at Baraabaru or enjoy pizza cooked in a clay oven at Reef Club.

Huvafen Fushi (p83) Feeling Koi for Izakaya-style Japanese cooking or Forno for pizza.

Soneva Fushi (p113) Treehouse-style Fresh in the Garden is one of Maldives' most unforgettable restaurants.

Amilla Fushi (p111) Excellent food can be had in one of the many restaurants here.

Cheap Treats

For snacks and light meals, Maldivians like *hedhikaa*, a selection of finger foods. In homes the *hedhikaa* are placed on the table and everyone helps themselves. In teashops this is called 'short eats' – a choice of things like *fihunu mas* (fish pieces with chilli coating), *gulha* (fried dough balls filled with fish and spices), *keemia* (fried fish rolls in batter) and *kuli boakiba* (spicy fish cakes).

Look out for *kavaabu*, small deep-fried dough balls with tuna, mashed potato, pepper and lime – a very popular 'short eat' with local people.

Sweets include little bowls of *bondi bai* (rice pudding), tiny bananas and *zileybee* (coloured coils of sugared, fried batter). Generally, anything small and brown will be savoury and contain fish, and anything light or brightly coloured will be sweet.

Dare to Try

If you feel like trying something both exotic and dear to Maldivian people, go for *miruhulee boava* (octopus tentacles). This is not commonly found in resorts or in Male, but is often prepared in the atolls as a speciality should you be lucky enough to visit an inhabited island. The tentacles are stripped and cleaned, then braised in a sauce of curry leaves, cloves, garlic, chilli, onion, pepper and coconut oil – delicious.

The Maldivian equivalent of the after-dinner mint is the areca or betel nut, chewed after a meal or snack. The little oval nuts are sliced into thin sections, some cloves and lime paste are added, the whole lot is wrapped in an areca leaf, and the wad is chewed whole. It's definitely an acquired taste, and the kind of thing that few foreigners try more than once!

Local Specialities

'Maldive fish', is a big export of Maldives, a tuna product that is cured on the islands and often sold abroad, where it is widely used as a supporting ingredient in Sri Lankan cooking. It is also used as the principal ingredient of several Maldivian dishes such as *mas huni*.

A main meal will include rice or *roshi* or both, plus soups, curries, vegetables, pickles and spicy sauces. In a teashop, a substantial meal with rice and *roshi* is called 'long eats'.

The most typical dish is *garudia*, a soup made from dried and smoked fish, often eaten with rice, lime and chilli. The soup is poured over rice, mixed up by hand and eaten with the fingers.

Another common meal is *mas riha*, a fish curry eaten with rice or *roshi* – the *roshi* is torn into strips, mixed on the plate with the curry and condiments, and eaten with the fingers.

A cup of tea accompanies the meal, and is usually drunk black and sweet, sometimes with frothy powdered milk.

Bis hulavuu is a popular snack – a pastry made from eggs, sugar and ghee and served cold. You may well be invited to try some if you visit an inhabited island.

How to Eat & Drink

When to Eat

Many Maldivian resorts have multiple restaurants, but even if your resort only has one, you'll be able to find something to eat whenever hunger strikes. Buffets are the norm for breakfast, lunch and dinner, and some à la carte restaurants are only open for dinner, but the cafe by the poolside can normally provide snacks at any time of day.

At guesthouses on inhabited islands, meals are normally provided at breakfast, lunch and dinner, but the timing can be adjusted to meet guests' needs. Local restaurants and teashops on inhabited islands usually open from early morning until late at night, but some upmarket restaurants in Male only open for lunch and dinner.

Where to Eat

Maldives has some absolutely superb eating options at its better resorts. Budget resorts and restaurants on inhabited islands tend to be rather less exciting, but quality does exist.

Restaurants Every Maldivian resort has at least one restaurant, and better ones have as many as six or more.

Guesthouses Nearly all guesthouses have restaurants and serve meals to their guests. They generally welcome nonguests as well.

Cafes & Teashops These simple local eateries serve up cheap and delicious *hedhikaa* ('short eats' or snacks) and are the best place to try local dishes and interact with Maldivians.

Eating at Resorts

In budget resorts you won't usually have any choice about where to eat, as most cheaper resorts have just one restaurant. Midrange places typically have two or more to afford some variety, and top-end resorts often boast three or more. Buffets (nearly always for breakfast, sometimes for lunch and dinner too) allow for lots of different cuisines and plenty of choice. À la carte dining is more popular for lunch and dinner, and is nearly always the case in finer establishments.

Eating on Inhabited Islands

In Male, where there's a much broader choice, the most obvious place for authentic Maldivian 'short eats' is in a teashop. In recent years traditional teashops (confusingly sometimes also called 'hotels') have modernised so that they look less forbidding and are now more pleasant places at which to eat, with air-con and an attempt at interior decoration.

Larger towns elsewhere will also have teashops and these are a great way to sample real Maldivian food.

If you're staying on a smaller inhabited island though, guesthouses will be where you eat for the most part, as so few islands have sufficient restaurants for you to eat comfortably elsewhere. Even in places where independent travel is now well established, such as Maafushi, eating options, while common, are rarely particularly good, and all-you-can-eat buffets are the norm.

Eating with Kids

In resorts menus sometimes have kids' sections, giving youngsters a choice of slightly less sophisticated foods, ranging from spaghetti to fish fingers and chicken nuggets.

Even if there's nothing dedicated to the kids' tastes, resort buffets are usually diverse enough to cater to even the fussiest eaters.

However, it's always best to check what resorts offer before booking a holiday with young kids. We've heard complaints from travellers about the poor availability of child-suitable foods even at the very best resorts.

Note that baby-food products are not on sale in resorts, so bring whatever you will need for the trip.

VEGETARIANS & VEGANS

Vegetarians will have no problem in resorts (although at cheaper resorts where there may be a set meal rather than a buffet spread, veggies will often be stuck with an unimaginative pasta dish or a ratatouille).

In general, resorts are well prepared for all types of diet, and in better resorts the chef may cook you a dish by request if what's on offer isn't appealing. Vegans will find Maldives quite a challenge, though soy milk is on offer in most resorts and the buffet allows each diner to pick and mix.

On inhabited islands things won't be so easy – fish and seafood dominate menus in the islands, so those who don't eat fish will have trouble. However, as vegan lifestyles become more and more normal, all high-end resorts will have choices suitable for plant-fuelled lifestyles.

Dining Etiquette

There's not a huge amount of etiquette to worry about if you eat in Male or resorts. If you're lucky enough to be entertained in a local house you should obey some basic rules. That said, Maldivians are very relaxed and as long as you show respect and enjoyment, they'll be glad to have you eating with them.

When going to eat, wait to be shown where to sit and wait for the *kateeb* (island chief) or the male head of the household to sit down before you do. Take a little of everything offered and do so only with your right hand, as the left hand is considered unclean by Muslims. Do ask for cutlery if you find it hard to roll your food into little balls like the Maldivians do; this is quite normal for foreigners.

What to Drink

The only naturally occurring freshwater in Maldives is rainwater, which is stored in natural underground aquifers beneath each island. This makes getting water quite a feat, and water conservation has always been extremely important in Maldivian culture, to the extent that Maldives Tourism Law states that no water resources may be diverted from an inhabited island to supply a resort.

All resorts have their own desalination plants to keep visitors supplied with enough water for their (by local standards incredibly wasteful) water needs.

Most resorts include a bottle or two of drinking water for each guest per day; though in many cheaper resorts, you'll need to pay for each one, which can add up quickly.

The main local drinks other than rainwater are imported tea and toddy tapped from the crown of the palm trunk at the point where the coconuts grow. Every village has its toddy man *(raa- very)*. The *raa* is sweet and delicious if you can get over the pungent smell. It can be drunk immediately after it is tapped from the tree, or left to become a little alcoholic (though not too much, for obvious reasons) as the sugar ferments.

Fermented *raa* is of course the closest most Maldivians ever get to alcohol; Maldives is strictly dry apart from the resorts. This may be a consideration if you're planning to travel independently in the country and stay in guesthouses on inhabited islands – your holiday will have to be totally dry, with alcohol available only by visiting a nearby resort, stepping aboard a live-aboard dive boat or swinging by the hotel near Male's international airport. Contraband alcohol is sometimes available on inhabited islands where there are many foreigners, but buying it is a bad idea and quality is rarely good.

Despite the ban on alcohol, nonalcoholic beer is very popular in Male and on inhabited islands. Soft drink, including the only Coca-Cola made from saltwater anywhere in the world (desalinated, of course), is available all over the country at prices much lower than in resorts.

Outside resorts the range of drinks is very limited. Teashops will always serve *bor feng* (drinking water) and, of course, *sai* (tea). Unless you ask otherwise, tea comes black, with *hakuru* (sugar). *Kiru* (milk) isn't a common drink and is usually made up from powder, as there are no cows in Maldives.

Plan Your Trip

Independent Travel

A mini-revolution has occurred in Maldivian travel in the past few years, stemming from the 2009 decisions of the Nasheed government to lift all travel restrictions on foreigners, allow the building of hotels on inhabited islands and create a national ferry network. These three factors have combined to mean that Maldives is for the first time open for business as an independent-travel destination. Despite the change of government since then – and the far less liberal approach to integration of tourists with the local population – the genie is now out of the bottle, and there seems to be no going back.

Highlights of Independent Travel in Maldives

Local Interaction

For all the luxury, resort guests can feel isolated from island life; but staying in a guesthouse puts visitors in the heart of local communities.

Island Hospitality

Hospitality is very important in Islam, and staying at an island guesthouse can feel like being a guest in a family home.

Real Maldivian cuisine

The finest Maldivian food is prepared not in resort kitchens but in family homes and rustic teashops.

Authentic Activities

In contrast to touristy excursions, guesthouses can arrange fishing trips with local fishermen and invitations to family homes and village social events.

Rethinking Island Tourism

Maldivian tourism developed in a very unusual way. From the inception of the first resorts in the 1970s, the government ensured that the devout and conservative local Muslim population was kept entirely separate from the alcohol-drinking, pork-guzzling, bikini-wearing Westerners frolicking on the beaches.

Amazingly, until 2009, a permit was needed for foreigners to stay overnight anywhere outside a resort island or the capital, meaning that the only contact that most island populations had with the outside world were the occasional tour group from a nearby resort visiting for an hour or two to buy souvenirs before disappearing back to the infinity pool. Now tourists are free to travel and overnight wherever they please – so options beyond the 100 or so resorts are enormous.

While this is exciting, it's not totally problem-free. Maldives isn't overflowing with great sights or cultural events – indeed, save the incredible underwater world and various water sports there's very little to do here except sunbathe and enjoy the beauty and tranquillity of the islands, and even this has to be done in accordance with fairly strict local customs. Yet for those who itch to enjoy the magnificent snorkelling, beaches, diving, surfing and fishing of Maldives, but can't imagine anything worse than being confined to a resort, your hour to visit the country has finally come.

Where to Go

While essentially the islands of Maldives are extremely similar to one another geographically and culturally, that doesn't mean that it's not going to make a difference where you go as an independent traveller. Many independent tourists head instinctively to popular traveller islands such as Maafushi, Thulusdhoo or Rasdhoo as they're relatively close to Male and easy to reach by speedboat. These are all good choices if you want a budget sun, sand and diving holiday with plenty of other travellers around, and lots of competition between hotels keeping prices low.

However, for a truly local experience it's far better to choose an island with a relatively small tourist presence, where you'll be as much of a novelty for the local population as they are for you, and where there aren't dozens of dive schools, water-sports centres and guesthouses touting for your business.

The best guesthouses will facilitate cultural interaction, often arranging for you to meet locals, perhaps inviting you into private houses or to various social events, such as a family meal or a fishing trip with locals. Indeed, many independent travellers who come to Maldives for beaches and diving often say that the human element is a real highlight of any backpacking trip here.

Popular Inhabited Islands

Maafushi (South Male Atoll; p92) The centre of the Maldivian independent travel scene with lots of accommodation options, a good bikini beach and low prices for diving and excursions.

Thulusdhoo (North Male Atoll; p75) A popular destination for surfers due to its access to two excellent breaks, this island is also easily accessible from Male.

Guraidhoo (South Male Atoll; p86) Little sister to Maafushi, Guraidhoo also has dozens of guesthouses and is a great base for diving and excursions.

Rasdhoo (North Ari Atoll; p98) Ari Atoll's most popular inhabited island, Rasdhoo heaves with guesthouses and has some superb beaches.

Thoddoo (North Ari Atoll; p100) Another friendly and popular island with a bikini beach and a growing guesthouse presence.

Dhigurah (South Ari Atoll; p100) Charming Dhigurah has a huge beach and sandbank, some lovely accommodation, and access to numerous superb dive sites.

Hanimaadhoo (Haa Dhaalu, Northern Atolls; p105) About as remote as you can get, this still totally undeveloped island is a great place to see life on a traditional Maldivian island.

Fuvahmulah (Gnaviyani, Southern Atolls; p128) An interesting combination of urban island and remote community, Fuvahmulah also has an excellent beach.

Gan (Laamu, Southern Atolls; p124) Connected to three other islands by a causeway and itself the largest single island in Maldives, Gan offers lots to see and do, and has a great diving guesthouse to boot.

Guesthouse Options

There is an ever-growing number of independently run guesthouses in the villages and towns that make up Maldives beyond the resorts. These are most prevalent in the atolls near to the capital, making a ferry ride from Male a maximum of three or four hours, although they can be found as far away as Haa Dhaalu Atoll, on the island of Hanimaadhoo, an hour's flight north of the capital.

In general the guesthouses are similar. They tend to be modest and fairly small (normally between three and six rooms), but comfortable, aiming at budget and midrange travellers. They generally offer full-board accommodation (usually as there are few or no other suitable eating options on the island) and a full list of excursions and activities to ensure that boredom doesn't ever encroach.

The latter is important, as there is often relatively little to do on a small, conservative island. In some cases, guesthouses are

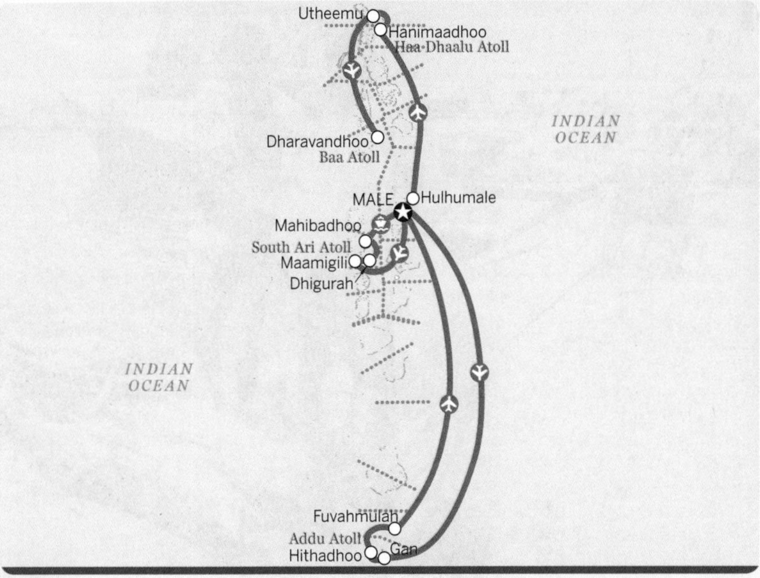

Utheemu
Hanimaadhoo
Haa Dhaalu Atoll
INDIAN OCEAN
Dharavandhoo
Baa Atoll
MALE
Hulhumale
Mahibadhoo
South Ari Atoll
Maamigili
Dhigurah
INDIAN OCEAN
Fuvahmulah
Addu Atoll
Hithadhoo
Gan

Maldives Beyond the Resorts

This grand tour of Maldives is for the independent traveller wanting to see beyond the infinity pool and the resort buffet. Start your journey by spending a couple of nights in **Male** (p58), the mercantile capital where over a third of the Maldivian population lives. While many visitors transit through the city, few bother to spend any time here. It's a curious place with a good museum, some fascinating markets and a few ancient mosques.

From Male take a flight south to the island of **Gan** (p129) in Addu Atoll. Spend a couple of nights on the island of **Hithadhoo** (p129) and visit its nature reserve and dive sites before taking a boat to **Fuvahmulah** (p129), a lone island in the middle of the Equatorial Channel. Here, you can visit a traditionally isolated place, enjoy its gorgeous beach and dive with tiger sharks at Tiger Zoo.

After a couple of nights here, fly back to Male, and take a connecting flight to Maamigili and an onward speedboat transfer to the beautiful island of **Dhigurah** (p100) in South Ari Atoll. Here you can enjoy the magnificent beaches and famous sandbank, and take an excursion to see whale sharks cruising the Dhidhdhoo Beyru. After three nights on this magical island, take a ferry to **Mahibadhoo** (p100), the atoll capital, for a night and then transfer by speedboat back to Male.

Spend a couple of nights on the island of **Hulhumale** (p72), the overspill island for Male and a taste of the future for Maldives. While it's hardly a beauty, it's fascinating to see how central planning has created a new island.

From here, fly north to **Hanimaadhoo** (p105), in Haa Dhaalu Atoll. Spend several days up here at the Barefoot Eco Hotel enjoying the beaches and the friendly town nearby. Take a day trip to the historically important island of **Utheemu** (p104), where you'll find the famous palace of Maldivian national hero Mohammed Thakurufaanu. From here, fly down to **Dharavandhoo** (p109) in Baa Atoll, a Unesco Biosphere Reserve famous for its incredible diving and superb resorts. Treat yourself to a few days in one of the atoll's amazing resorts if you can; if not, take a guesthouse on Dharavandhoo. Either way, be sure to go snorkelling with the manta rays at Hanifaru Bay to wrap up your trip.

1

2

1. Unloading fresh tuna at Male fish market **2.** *Undholi* on Rihiveli Island resort (p87) **3.** Traditional minaret used for call to prayer

Local Life

Life on local Maldivian islands is starkly different to that in a resort. Alcohol and bikinis are out, while calls to prayer from the mosque and landing the daily catch are in. Inhabited islands in Maldives are conservative and locals often shy, but visiting one is a unique cultural experience.

Call to Prayer

Island life is dominated by the call to prayer, which signals the arrival of dawn and then recurs four times throughout the day, its last one sounding just after the sun sets. Most men attend prayers at least once a day, while women pray at home.

Eating in a Teashop

Even the smallest of islands has a teashop or two, where locals go to drink tea, eat simple plates of 'short eats' (snacks) or bigger meals. They're the social hub of each island, and a great place to meet people and find out what's going on each day.

Swinging on an Undholi

Maldivians love to while away the heat of the day on their beloved *undholis*, a large swing chair that can fit several people. It's an ingenious way to create a cool breeze, can be found in almost any local home and many Maldivians will tell you they essentially grew up on one.

Catch of the Day

Most Maldivian islands don't have markets, and so instead fish is usually sold at the harbour as fishing boats return. You'll never know what fishermen might have caught, but you'll find a small crowd gathering when they do and see some interesting exchanges as any excess is quickly sold off.

AVOIDING OFFENCE ON LOCAL ISLANDS

When you decide to travel independently outside the resorts, it's important to realise that you're entering a very conservative Muslim country. Maldivians are tolerant people, but even if nothing is said overtly, dressing in ways that they consider immodest (particularly for women), will definitely cause offence or unease.

In places such as Maafushi, where the island is almost totally reliant on tourism, these strictures are not so absolute, but if you are staying on a small island with just one guesthouse, and are one of the few foreigners to visit, it's doubly important to be sensitive. This means that women should wear long skirts, cover their shoulders and avoid low-cut tops. Men can get away with shorts, but don't walk about bare-chested. Beaches on inhabited islands cannot be swum at in the normal way – when women swim at all, they do so fully clothed, and even men wear T-shirts, and you should follow their example.

Nowadays many inhabited islands with guesthouses have enclosed foreigner beaches (known universally as 'bikini beaches') where you can swim just as you would anywhere else in the world. Guesthouses on islands without bikini beaches often offer day trips to deserted islands where tourists can strip down without fear of offending.

Another thing to consider is the lack of alcohol, which may not gel with your idea of a relaxing holiday. No alcohol is available anywhere outside of the resorts and on live-aboard boats, and tourists are not allowed to import alcohol, even in hold luggage. If you stay on an inhabited island, your only option will be to negotiate access to an accommodating resort or a passing live-aboard boat.

very upmarket, with prices comparable to resorts and almost identical facilities minus the availability of alcohol.

Activities are pretty similar across the country: desert-island visits, beach barbecues, snorkelling, diving and fishing expeditions. Staff members at guesthouses tend to be a highlight. Young, enthusiastic and entrepreneurial, they are pioneers of local tourism and, for the most part, speak great English and have a real passion for showing foreigners the very best of their country.

The National Ferry Network

While there have always been public ferries connecting the islands, their timetables used to be largely guesswork and journeys achingly slow. Now there is a national ferry network based in Male and in the individual atoll capitals that somewhat regularly (but cheaply) connects all the inhabited islands in the country.

Timetables can still be unreliable and boats often break down, but as in most cases you'll be travelling from one guesthouse to another, staff will be able to tell you what time the ferries go and from where. Getting around by ferry can still be slow and it may take you 24 to 48 hours to reach far-flung destinations, often involving an overnight in Male or an atoll capital, depending on where you're heading.

While most places in the central atolls have connections to Male daily except Fridays, local ferries that connect inhabited islands within the atolls themselves normally only run every other day. Luckily, private speedboat transfers have appeared to take the strain, slashing journey times and making many remote islands far more accessible from Male and the airport.

Taking a local ferry is a fascinating cultural experience, and you'll often find yourself the only non-Maldivian on the creaking old dhonis and *vedhis* (large dhoni with square-shaped wooden superstructure) that make the journeys between islands and atolls – a great way to meet people and get a feel for local life.

Travelling by ferry is remarkably cheap. Short journeys within an atoll cost only Rf20, rising to Rf57 for longer journeys between atolls, while even huge inter-atoll trips will set you back only Rf200 (around US$15).

Ferry schedules for planning your journey into the atolls from Male can be found on the websites of Maldives Transport and Contracting Company (p178) and Atoll Transfer (p178).

Regions at a Glance

Male

History
Eating
Shopping

Mosques & Museums

Male has an array of historic mosques to check out, as well as a first-class National Museum. Don't miss the superb Old Friday Mosque with its intricate carvings.

Varied Dining

The capital has a great range of places to eat, and after being in a resort the low prices and wide choice will seem like thrills in themselves. Even on a budget there's plenty of choice: don't miss traditional Maldivian 'short eats' at any local teashop – delicious!

Shop Till You Drop

Male is all about trade and commerce, and its mercantile atmosphere is infectious. Don't miss the catch being hauled in and sold at the fish market, or the crowds at the produce market. For a real slice of the shopping action, head down Chandhanee Magu for souvenir shops and then wander the main avenue of the city, Majeedee Magu.

p58

North & South Male Atolls

Luxury
Surfing
Independent Travel

Superb Resorts

Few atolls have the concentration of excellent, world-class resorts that can be found in North and South Male Atolls. Whether it's small and romantic (Cocoa Island by COMO), super-glamorous (One & Only Reethi Rah) or back-to-nature luxury (Gili Lankanfushi) you're after, you'll find the right resort here.

Surf Breaks

North Male has several excellent surf breaks on the eastern side of the atoll. There are a few nearby resorts and guesthouses that cater to surfers, and the best thing of all is that surf season coincides with Maldivian low season!

Backpacker Hub

The small island of Maafushi in South Male Atoll has become the centre of Maldives' thriving independent traveller scene. Here you'll find scores of guesthouses, a bikini beach and cheap diving.

p71

Ari Atoll & Around

Wildlife
Island Hopping
Beaches

Whale Sharks & Hammerheads

There are two unique wildlife-watching opportunities in Ari, unfortunately at opposite ends of the atoll. In the south, swim with whale sharks, the largest fish in the world, while in the north, dive with hammerhead sharks at Hammerhead Point.

Paradise Found

Don't forget your PADI certification or at least your mask and fins for some snorkelling in North and South Ari Atolls. You'll see an incredible array of marine life on the reef, from sharks and moray eels to turtles and rays.

Mind-blowing Beaches

When it comes to beaches, you'll be spoiled for choice. Every single one of the dozens of resorts and guesthouses here has access to perfect white sand and an amazing turquoise lagoon with warm, clear water.

p94

Northern Atolls

Diving
History
Beaches

Pristine Underwater World

The lack of resorts and the Unesco Biosphere Reserve in Baa Atoll makes the north one of the best places to dive in the country. Liveaboard dive boats can take you to even remoter locations than the resorts.

Maldivian Heritage

Take a trip to Utheemu in the country's very far north if you'd like to see some real Maldivian cultural heritage. The island is home to Utheemu Palace, the perfectly preserved 16th-century mansion of Maldives' national hero.

Perfect White Sand

In the remote Northern Atolls are some of the most extraordinarily perfect beaches you'll ever come across. What's more, the relative lack of resorts means that even beyond your resort you'll find plenty of perfect uninhabited islands with equally brilliant sands.

p103

Southern Atolls

Snorkelling
Fabulous Resorts
Independent Travel

Fabulous Marine Life

Addu Atoll has some stellar snorkelling and dive sites including Manta Point, a busy cleaning station and the *British Loyalty* wreck, a torpedoes supply ship sunk in WWII. Do not miss diving in Gnaviyani, Laamu or Dhaalu atolls either.

Lap of Luxury

The Southern Atolls are home to some of the most impressive luxury resorts in Maldives, including Shangri-La Villingili, Six Senses Laamu, St Regis Vommuli and Niyama Private Islands, all setting new standards for pampering and style.

Local Life

For the truly intrepid independent traveller, the south is a great place to explore alone. Check out the island of Fuvahmulah with its two inland lakes and traditionally isolated community, or visit Maldives' second largest city, Hithadhoo.

p116

On the Road

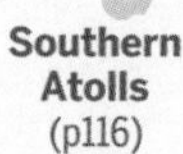

Male

POP 154,000

Includes ➡

Best Places to Stay

- Hotel Jen Male (p66)
- Sala Boutique Hotel (p66)
- Somerset Inn (p65)
- Novina Hotel (p65)
- LVIS Boutique Hotel (p65)

Best Places to Eat

- Sala Thai (p67)
- Newport (p67)
- Royal Garden Café (p67)
- Thai Wok (p67)
- Irudhashu Hotaa (p66)

Why Go?

The pint-sized Maldivian capital is the throbbing, mercantile heart of the nation, a densely crowded and fascinating place, notable mainly for its stark contrast to the laid-back pace of island life elsewhere in the country.

Male (*mar*-lay) offers the best chance to see the 'real' Maldives away from the resort buffet and infinity pool. Overlooked by tall, brightly coloured buildings and surrounded by incongruously turquoise water, Male is a hive of activity, the engine driving Maldives' economy and the forum for the country's saga-worthy political struggles.

Male is also pleasingly quirky – alcohol-free cafes and restaurants jostle with shops and lively markets and the general capital-city hubbub is very much present. This island city may not have a huge number of sights, but it offers a very real chance to get a feel for Maldives and to meet Maldivians on an equal footing.

When to Go

May–Nov Marginally cooler than the rest of the year, and not as sweaty during these months.

July Independence Day celebrations on 26 July see floats and dancing children in Republic Square.

November Parades and marches mark Republic Day on 11 November, when the capital celebrates.

History

Male has been the seat of Maldives' ruling dynasties since before the 12th century, though none left any grand palaces. Some trading houses appeared in the 17th century, along with a ring of defensive bastions, but Male didn't acquire the trappings of a city until the mid-20th century. Indeed, visitors in the 1920s estimated the population at only 5000, and much of the island was covered by trees. Despite this, Male has always been the heart of the nation – the name 'Maldives' derives from the city.

Growth began with the 1930s modernisation, and the first banks, hospitals, high schools and government offices appeared in the following decades. Only since the 1970s, with wealth from tourism and an expanding economy, has the city really burgeoned and growth emerged as a problem.

And a problem it has definitely become: despite extending the area of the city through land reclamation over the island's reef, Male is unable to extend any further, so expansion onto nearby Hulhumale has been the policy of successive governments since the 1990s. Overcrowding, difficulties with water supply, traffic gridlock and issues with the treatment and disposal of sewage are all problems Male residents are familiar with. This was underscored in late 2014, when the city's one desalination plant caught fire and the capital was left without running water for seven days – a real problem in a city with no freshwater sources.

In 2018, Male was connected by a mammoth bridge, the China-Maldives Friendship Bridge, to the airport island and Hulhumale, thus beginning the next chapter of this small island's story.

Male

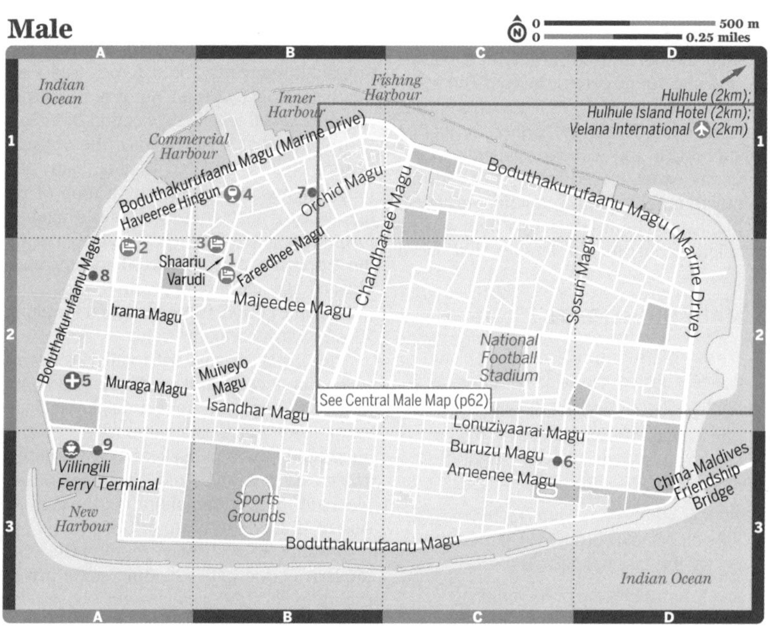

Male

Sleeping
1 LVIS Boutique Hotel B2
2 Marble Hotel A2
3 Somerset Inn B2

Drinking & Nightlife
4 Jazz Café B1

Information
5 Indira Gandhi Memorial Hospital A2
6 Island Sailors C3
7 Surfatoll B1

Transport
8 Maldivian A2
9 New Harbour A3

Sights

Male has a handful of worthwhile sights, and you won't be able to miss the **China-Maldives Friendship Bridge** (Map p73), connecting Male to the airport island of Hulhule. Unlike most other causeways in the country, this US$250m project goes over the open sea, meaning that vast concrete supports have been planted in the seabed.

★ Old Friday Mosque MOSQUE

(Hukuru Miskiiy; Medhuziyaarai Magu) This is the oldest mosque in the country, dating from 1656. It's a beautiful structure made from coral stone into which intricate decoration and Quranic script have been chiselled. Non-Muslims wishing to see inside are supposed to get permission from an official of the Ministry of Islamic Affairs. Most of the staff are officials of the ministry, however, and so if you are conservatively dressed and it's outside prayer times, you may well get permission to enter on the spot.

Even though an ugly protective corrugated-iron sheet now covers the roof and some of the walls, this is still a fascinating place. The interior is superb and famed for its fine lacquer work and elaborate woodcarvings. One long panel, carved in the 13th century, commemorates the introduction of Islam to Maldives. The mosque was built on the foundations of an old temple that faced west towards the setting sun, not northwest towards Mecca. Consequently, the worshippers have to face the corner of the mosque when they pray – the striped carpet, laid at an angle, shows the correct direction.

Overlooking the mosque is the solid, round, blue-and-white tower of the *munnaaru* – the squat minaret. Though it looks a bit neglected rather than particularly old, this minaret dates from 1675. To one side of the mosque is a cemetery with many elaborately carved tombstones. Stones with rounded tops are for females, those with pointy tops are for males and those featuring gold-plated lettering are the graves of former sultans. The small buildings are family mausoleums and their stone walls are intricately carved. Respectably dressed non-Muslims are welcome to walk around the graveyard; you don't require permission for this.

★ National Museum MUSEUM

(☎332 2254; Chandhanee Magu; adult/child Rf100/20; ⏲10am-4pm Sun-Thu) Maldives' National Museum may be a ferociously ugly building gifted by China, but it nevertheless contains a well-labelled collection of historic artefacts that serve to trace the unusual history of these isolated islands. Sadly the museum was broken into by a mob of religious extremists during protests against former president Nasheed in 2012, and its most precious items, some 30 ancient Buddhist coral stone carvings from the country's pre-Islamic period, were destroyed for being 'idols'. Security remains tight.

The display begins with galleries devoted to the ancient and medieval periods of Maldivian history. Items on display include weaponry, religious paraphernalia and household wares as well as many impressively carved Arabic- and Thaana-engraved pieces of wood commemorating the conversion of Maldives to Islam in 1153.

Upstairs is a display representing the modern period and including some prized examples of the lacquer-work boxes for which Maldives is famous, and various pieces of antique technology including the country's first gramophone, telephone and a massive computer. Quirkier relics include the minutes of the famous underwater cabinet meeting held under President Nasheed in 2009 and an impressive marine collection, the highlight of which is the 6m-long skeleton of the very rare Longman's Beaked Whale, which is yet to have been sighted alive in the ocean.

MALE HIGHLIGHTS

National Museum Discovering historic artefacts, a whale skeleton and other quirky relics at Maldives' best museum.

Old Friday Mosque Admiring the beautiful coral carved exterior of the oldest mosque in the country.

Fish Market (p62) Watching the morning's catch being brought in, gutted and sold at this fascinating daily market.

Irudhashu Hotaa (p66) Sampling delicious short eats at this authentic local hangout.

Maldive Victory (p64) Diving this wrecked cargo ship, which has been gathering coral and sea creatures since 1981.

China-Maldives Friendship Bridge Witnessing this impressive piece of newly complete Chinese engineering, the first bridge in Maldives crossing the open sea.

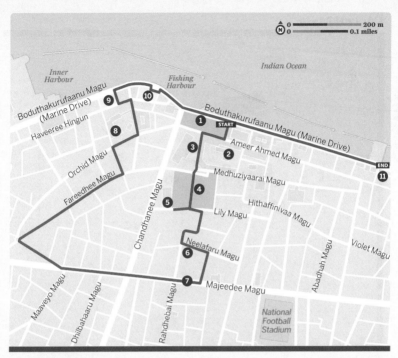

City Walk **Male**

START JUMHOOREE MAIDAN
END NEWPORT
LENGTH 3KM, ONE HOUR

Begin your exploration from the waterfront near ❶ **Jumhooree Maidan**, the main square, conspicuous for the huge Maldivian flag flying. This is where festivals and official ceremonies are often held, and has also been the site of political demonstrations in the past. All around here is the apparatus of government and you'll notice that it's a well-guarded place, with the police station on one side and the whit ❷ **National Security Service (NSS) Headquarters** to the south.

To the west of the NSS is the ❸ **Grand Friday Mosque** (p62). Walk down the gravel street past its main entrance and you'll arrive at the recently totally refitted ❹ **Rasrani Bageecha** (p63). This was once the grounds of the last sultan's palace and was known as Sultan's Park, but it has undergone a garish reincarnation as a pleasure ground for local families. Nearby is the ❺ **National Museum** to your right. Continue south from here through busy streets until you reach the ❻ **Tomb of Mohammed Thakurufaanu** (p63), honouring the man who liberated Maldives from the Portuguese in the 16th century.

Cut down to ❼ **Majeedee Magu**, the city's main thoroughfare, and head west to Fareedhee Magu and up to Orchid Magu, passing the striking ❽ **Theemuge**, previously the official residence of the president and now the seat of the supreme court.

Head north towards the fascinating ❾ **produce market** (p62) before heading down the seafront to the ❿ **fish market** (p62), the soul of the city. To end, wander back along the jetties on the seafront watching the crowds come on and off boats. Finish up with a cool drink at ⓫ **Newport** (p67) with a view of the harbour and the bustle of Male's main road.

Central Male

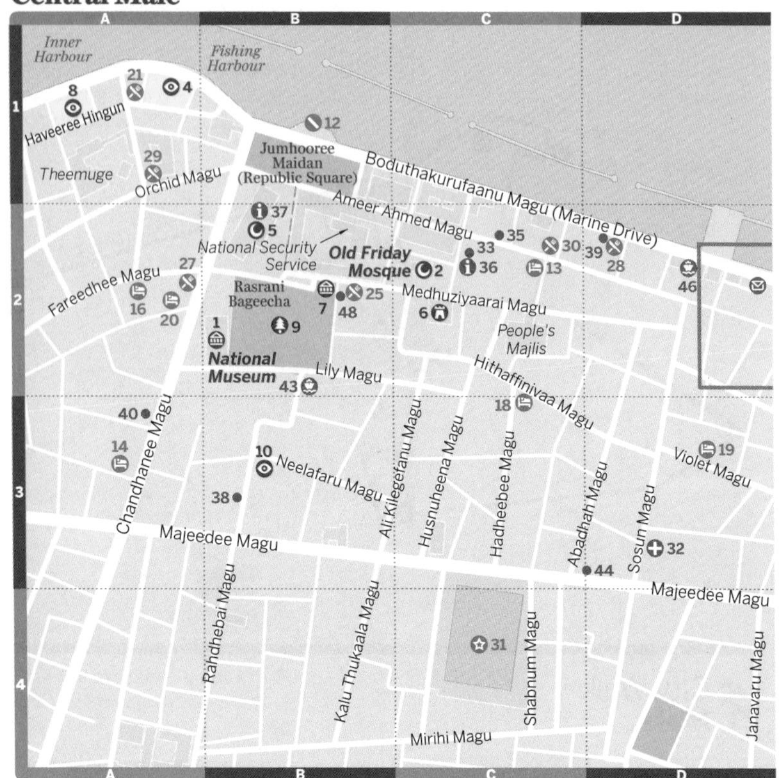

Fish Market
MARKET

(Boduthakurufaanu Magu; ⏲5am-7pm) Although the squeamish may well object to the buckets of entrails or the very public gutting of fish going on all around, the Fish Market should not be missed. This is the soul of Male – and it's great fun watching the day's catch being brought in from the adjacent fishing harbour. Look out for some truly vast tuna, octopus and grouper. Maldivian women don't usually venture into these areas, although foreign women walking around won't raise any eyebrows.

Produce Market
MARKET

(Haveeree Hingun; ⏲dawn-dusk) The busy produce market gives you an enjoyable taste of Maldives – people from all over the country gather here to sell home-grown and imported vegetables. Coconuts and bananas are the most plentiful produce, but look inside for the stacks of betel leaf, for wrapping up a 'chew'. Just wandering around, watching the hawkers and the shoppers and seeing the vast array of products on display is fascinating and as real a Maldivian experience as possible.

Grand Friday Mosque
MOSQUE

(Jumhooree Maidan) The golden dome of this impressive modern mosque dominates the skyline of Male and has become something of a symbol for the city. Opened in 1984 and built with help from the Gulf States, Pakistan, Brunei and Malaysia, the Grand Friday Mosque is striking in its plainness, built in white marble and virtually free from decoration. Set back off the main square, Jumhooree Maidan, it is the biggest mosque in the country.

Tourists wanting to enter the mosque can only visit between 9am and 5pm, and outside of prayer times. The mosque closes to all non-Muslims 15 minutes before prayers and for the following hour. Before noon and between 2pm and 3pm are the best times

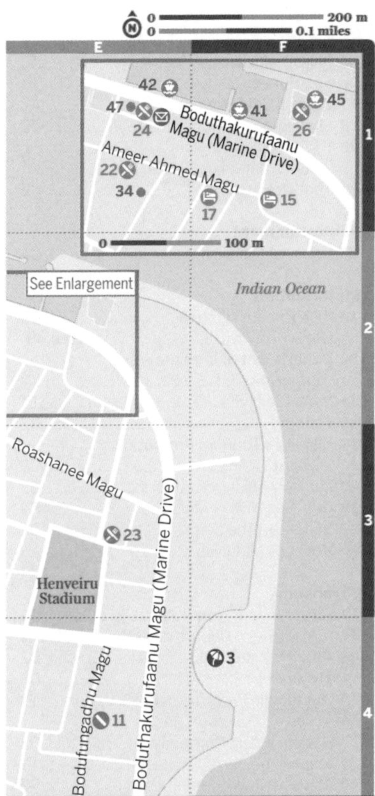

to visit. Invading bands of casual sightseers are not encouraged, but if you are genuinely interested and suitably dressed, you'll be welcomed by one of the staff members who hang out by the entrance. Men must wear long trousers and women a long skirt or dress. The main prayer hall inside the mosque can accommodate up to 5000 worshippers and has beautifully carved wooden side panels and doors, a specially woven carpet and impressive chandeliers.

Muleeaage & Medhu Ziyaarath PALACE

Muleeaage was built as a palace for the sultan in the early 20th century, though he was deposed before he could move in and the building was used for government offices for about 40 years. It became the president's residence in 1953 when the first republic was proclaimed. At the eastern end of the building's compound, behind an elaborate blue-and-white gatehouse, the Medhu Ziyaarath is the tomb of Abul Barakat Yoosuf Al Barbary, who brought Islam to Male in 1153.

National Art Gallery MUSEUM

(☎333 7724; www.artgallery.gov.mv; Medhuziyaarai Magu; ⏰9am-6pm Sun-Thu) FREE Under one roof you'll find the National Library, various cultural centres from countries around the world and this exhibition space, which has temporary displays of Maldivian art. There is sadly no permanent collection, so often there's nothing to see here if there's not an exhibit, but it's worth dropping by to check.

Tomb of Mohammed Thakurufaanu TOMB

(Neelafaru Magu) In the backstreets in the middle of town, in the grounds of a small mosque, is the tomb of Mohammed Thakurufaanu, Maldives' national hero who liberated the country from Portuguese rule and was then the sultan from 1573 to 1585. Thakurufaanu is also commemorated in the name of the road that rings Male, Boduthakurufaanu Magu (*bodu* means 'big' or 'great').

Artificial Beach BEACH

A sweet little crescent sand beach has been crafted from the breakwater tetrapods here where locals can swim and enjoy a day on the beach. There's a whole range of fast-food cafes nearby, though the construction of the massive new China-Maldives Friendship Bridge has rather robbed the area of any of the charm it once had.

Rasrani Bageecha PARK

(⏰9am-noon, 4-6pm & 8pm-midnight) Previously known as Sultan's Park and once part of the grounds of the now-demolished sultan's palace, this former green lung of Male was redeveloped and renamed Rasrani Bageecha in 2017. Instead of a much-needed, meditative and shady public space, it's now a neon-clad Dubai-style entertainment zone with various playgrounds, which will at least appeal to kids.

DANGERS & ANNOYANCES

Male is generally a very safe city. Indeed, the main danger is posed by the mopeds that seem to appear from nowhere at great speeds; cross roads cautiously. During times of political unrest, avoid protests and other public gatherings, as these have been violently suppressed in the past.

Central Male

Top Sights
1 National Museum ... B2
2 Old Friday Mosque ... C2

Sights
3 Artificial Beach ... F4
4 Fish Market ... A1
5 Grand Friday Mosque ... B2
6 Muleeaage & Medhu Ziyaarath ... C2
7 National Art Gallery ... B2
8 Produce Market ... A1
9 Rasrani Bageecha ... B2
10 Tomb of Mohammed Thakurufaanu ... B3

Activities, Courses & Tours
11 Sea Explorers Dive School ... E4
12 Whale Submarine ... B1

Sleeping
13 Hotel Jen Male ... C2
14 House Clover ... A3
15 Mookai Hotel ... F1
16 Novina Hotel ... A2
17 Real Inn ... F1
18 Sala Boutique Hotel ... C3
19 Skai Lodge ... D3
20 Somerset Hotel ... A2

Eating
21 Dawn Café ... A1
22 Good Life Enterprises ... E1
23 Irudhashu Hotaa ... E3
24 Newport ... E1
25 Royal Garden Café ... B2
Sala Thai ... (see 18)
26 Sea House ... F1
27 Seagull Café House ... A2
28 Shell Beans ... D2
29 STO People's Choice Supermarket ... A1
30 Thai Wok ... C2

Entertainment
31 National Stadium ... C4

Information
32 ADK Private Hospital ... D3
Crown Tours ... (see 39)
33 Department of Immigration & Emigration ... C2
34 Inner Maldives ... E1
35 Laundry ... C2
36 Maldives Tourism Promotion Board ... C2
37 Ministry of Islamic Affairs ... B2
38 Real Sea Hawks Maldives ... B3
39 Sultans of the Sea ... D2
40 Voyages Maldives ... A3

Transport
41 Airport Ferry Arrival Jetty ... F1
42 Airport Ferry Departure Jetty ... E1
43 Atoll Transfer ... B2
44 FlyMe ... D3
45 Hulhumale Ferry Terminal ... F1
46 Maldives Transport and Contracting Company ... D2
47 Maldivian ... E1
48 Mega Maldives Airlines ... B2

Activities

There is some excellent diving within a short boat ride of Male, even though the water here is not as pristine as it is elsewhere in the country. Some of the best dives are along the edges of Vaadhoo Kandu (the channel between North and South Male Atolls), which has two Protected Marine Areas. There is also a well-known wreck.

Maldive Victory — DIVING

(Map p42) This wreck is an impressive and challenging dive because of the potentially strong currents. This cargo ship hit a reef and sank on Friday, 13 February 1981; it now sits with the wheelhouse at around 15m and the propeller at 35m. The wreck provides a home for a rich growth of coral, sponges, tubastrea and large schools of fish.

Hans Hass Place — DIVING

(Map p42) This wall dive beside Vaadhoo Kandu in a Protected Marine Area has a lot to see at 4m or 5m, so it's good for snorkellers and inexperienced divers when the current is not too strong. There's a wide variety of marine life, including many tiny reef fish, sea fans and other soft corals. Further down, there are caves and overhangs.

Lion's Head — DIVING

(Map p42) A Protected Marine Area that was once famous for shark feeding, Lion's Head still sees numerous grey-tip reef sharks despite the practice being strongly discouraged these days. The reef edge is thick with fish, sponges, soft corals and the occasional turtle. Although it drops steeply with numerous overhangs to over 40m, there is still much to see at snorkelling depth.

Sea Explorers Dive School — DIVING

(Map p42; ☎331 6172; http://seamaldives.com.mv/; H. Asfaam 1st fl, Bodufungadhu Magu; dives per person from US$90) The Sea Explorers Dive School was the first dive centre in Male and is a very well-regarded operation that does dive courses and organises regular day trips to nearby dive sites. It also offers packages on its enormous and very impressive live-aboard, Ritrella Cruise Hotel, the biggest cruising yacht in Maldives.

Whale Submarine TOUR
(Map p42; ☎790 3939; www.whalesubmarine.com.mv; adult/child US$95/48) The Whale Submarine leaves four times a day year round, and while it's not useful for whale watching (as suggested by the name), it's still a very popular way for kids (three and over only) and non-divers to get a peek of life deep underwater. It is an expensive excursion, however, and definitely not for claustrophobes. Book online or by phone, and a free transfer to the embarkation jetty will be arranged for you.

Sleeping

Male makes Hong Kong look spacious, and as you'd expect on this densely populated island, space is at a premium. Compared to the rest of Asia prices are very high here, though a night in Male still costs peanuts compared to one in most resorts. One cheaper option is to stay on Hulhumale (p72), a 10-minute boat ride away from Male, and the place where Maldives' nascent backpacker scene is concentrated.

Skai Lodge GUESTHOUSE $
(☎332 8112; www.skailodge.com.mv; Violet Magu; r US$76; ❄📶) This attractive and well-maintained townhouse full of plants boasts 13 clean and well-maintained rooms (those upstairs are bigger and brighter) with good bathrooms, hot water, phone and TV; some even have balconies, which makes this a good deal by local standards.

Real Inn HOTEL $
(☎300 0822; hotelrealinn@gmail.com; off Ameer Ahmed Magu; s/d from US$35/40; ❄📶) Tucked away on a side street just a block back from the airport ferry, this place is the cheapest deal in town. The rooms are simple but have all you need, including fridge, cable TV and hot water. There are just two singles, so it's best to reserve in advance for these. Look for the 'rooms for rent' sign. Breakfast is not included.

★**Novina Hotel** HOTEL $$
(☎400 4004; www.intalhotels.com; Fareedhee Magu; r US$116; ❄📶) Brand new in 2017, the Novina is eight floors of sparking modernity that stands out for its delightful staff, convenient location and creature comforts. Aimed at those who seek luxury on a budget, it might not exactly be cheap, but there's an excellent price-quality ratio given Male's abundance of overpriced hotels. Bathrooms are tiny, but minibars are well stocked.

★**Somerset Inn** HOTEL $$
(☎332 2133; Kulhidhoshu Magu; r from US$95; ❄📶) This recent addition to Male's uninspiring hotel scene is a breath of fresh air. Run by the same team as the flashier Somerset Hotel (p66), the Somerset Inn offers excellent rooms that – despite the very reasonable price – have Nespresso machines, high-speed wireless and a decent breakfast included in the price. Complimentary airport transfers in both directions are also included.

LVIS Boutique Hotel BOUTIQUE HOTEL $$
(☎766 3223; www.lvishotels.com; Jahaamuguri Goalhi; r from US$70; ❄📶) The creation of four brothers whose initials give this hotel its unusual name, LVIS is an eight-room property on a side street in the heart of mercantile Male. Inside you'll find gleaming rooms, each with minibar, safe and flat-screen TV, making it a decent and stylish choice.

House Clover GUESTHOUSE $$
(☎300 5855; info@houseclovermaldives.com; Shaheed KTM Hingun, off Chandhanee Magu; s/d from US$79/81; ❄📶) Set over several floors of a high-rise building in the centre of the island, this 20-room guesthouse is sparklingly clean. The bright and spacious rooms have cable TV and decent bathrooms, while each floor shares basic kitchens and common areas. Staff members are super-helpful and reserving accommodation in advance is advised. A return airport transfer costs US$10.

Marble Hotel HOTEL $$
(☎330 2678; www.marble.mv; Kanba Aisa Rani Higun; s/d from US$63/96; ❄📶) On the far

SLEEPING PRICE RANGES

The following price brackets are used for hotels in Male. Prices are for the cheapest double room and include breakfast and bathroom unless otherwise stated.

$ less than US$80

$$ US$80–US$150

$$$ more than US$150

side of the island with some great views towards neighbouring Villingili from its higher rooms, Marble Hotel offers good-quality, spacious accommodation with TV and fridge. It's not particularly convenient for the airport ferry, but it's very handy for the Villingili Ferry Terminal if you're heading to the atolls. Breakfast is not included.

★Hotel Jen Male BUSINESS HOTEL **$$$**
(☎330 0888; www.hoteljen.com; Ameer Ahmed Magu; r from US$220;) By far Male's best hotel is this smart Shangri-La-run property a block back from the harbour. A little slice of glamour in the heart of town, this temple of orchids, doormen and minimalist furnishings has 117 slick and stylish rooms, a rooftop gym, a bar and a lap pool, a spa and a sumptuous breakfast buffet. Transfers from the airport are included.

★Sala Boutique Hotel BOUTIQUE HOTEL **$$$**
(☎334 5959; www.salafamilymaldives.com; Buruneege; r from US$175;) Set above Male's most celebrated restaurant, Sala Thai (p67), these six boutique rooms are of a very high standard, although like most Male non-high-rise hotels, there's little or no natural light in them. On the other hand there are real spring mattresses, mahogany furniture, flat-screen TVs, Nespresso machines and minibars. An excellent bet for a high-end experience with a superb breakfast.

Somerset Hotel BOUTIQUE HOTEL **$$$**
(☎300 9090; www.thesomerset.com.mv; Keneree Magu; s/d US$175/190;) This is the smarter of the two Somerset properties in Male, but there's little reason to pay twice the price for this one. It's not that much fancier: this being Male, the rooms are still rather cramped. The staff are delightful, however, breakfast in the downstairs cafe is excellent and the location is central. Transfers included.

EATING PRICE RANGES IN MALE

Male is the only place in Maldives where there are 'standard' restaurants. Prices represent the price for an average main course.

$ less than Rf100

$$ Rf100–Rf200

$$$ more than Rf200

Mookai Hotel HOTEL **$$$**
(☎333 8811; www.mookai.com.mv; Meheli Golhi; s/d US$138/171;) Overpriced and rather outmoded it may be – with a slew of fancy new hotels under construction nearby likely to raise the bar – but the Mookai does have a great location just seconds from the waterfront, small but clean and well furnished rooms, and a tiny but effective rooftop swimming pool to cool down in.

Eating

You'll eat decently in Male, with restaurants typically offering several different cuisines – most popular are Thai, Indian, Italian and American-style grills. Male restaurants don't serve alcohol, but many serve nonalcoholic beer. By contrast nearly every restaurant now has an espresso machine, and you can get a good cup of coffee almost anywhere.

Irudhashu Hotaa MALDIVIAN **$**
(Filigas Hingun; 'short eats' from Rf10; 7am-10pm) Our favourite 'short eats' place in town is this perennially busy meeting place by the Henveiru football field. After prayers at the next-door mosque, it's always jammed, and the spicy fish curries and selection of *hedhikaa* are delicious.

Dawn Café MALDIVIAN **$**
(Haveeree Hingun; 'short eats' from Rf10; 24hr) This is one of the best teashops in the area, and due to its fish-market location it's popular with fishermen and open around the clock. You can get a brilliant and very cheap meal here. Try it on Friday afternoon when people come in after going to the mosque.

Good Life Enterprises MALDIVIAN **$**
(Ameer Ahmed Magu; 'short eats' from Rf10; 7am-11pm, from 1pm Fri) A popular place right in the centre of things, this friendly and somewhat upmarket teashop serves up a delicious selection of 'short eats'.

Shell Beans INTERNATIONAL **$**
(☎333 3686; www.shellbeans.com; Boduthakurufaanu Magu; mains Rf75-110; 8am-11.30pm Sun-Thu, 3pm-12.30am Fri;) This useful spot on the seafront serves up tasty sandwiches, full breakfasts, burgers, good coffee and pastries. It's a great spot for lunch on the run, although there's seating both upstairs (which includes a great balcony with harbour views) and downstairs for a less hurried meal. It delivers all over the city.

VISITING A TEASHOP IN MALE

Maldivians don't have a particularly rich culinary history, due to obvious limitations to what's available on this isolated group of islands. The standard local eatery is known as a teashop, where little morsels known as *hedhikaa* ('short eats') are served up; Male is full of them.

Teashops are frequented by Maldivian men, and while it's not the done thing for local women to visit one, foreign women accompanied by men will not normally raise eyebrows. Some traditional teashops have in recent years broadened the menus, installed air-conditioning and improved service – you should feel quite comfortable in these places and they're a great way to meet locals. A bigger and slightly fancier teashop might be called a 'cafe' or even a 'hotel'.

Teashops have their goodies displayed on a counter behind a glass screen, and customers line up and choose, cafeteria style – if you don't know what to ask for, just point. Tea costs around Rf2 and the *hedhikaa* range from Rf4 to Rf10. You can easily fill yourself for under Rf30. At meal times teashops normally also serve bigger dishes such as soups, curried fish and *roshi* (unleavened bread). A full meal costs anything from Rf20 to Rf50.

Teashops open as early as 5am and close as late as 1am, particularly around the port and market area where they cater to fishermen. During Ramazan they're open till 2am or even later, but closed during the day.

Sea House INTERNATIONAL **$**
(☎333 2957; Boduthakurufaanu Magu; mains Rf50-180; ⏲24hr, closed 10am-1pm Fri) This breezy (and sometimes downright windy) place above the Hulhumale ferry terminal has expansive harbour views and a large menu that runs from pizza and sandwiches to full meals. It's a popular meeting place, and while the food won't amaze you (avoid the decidedly average breakfast, for example), it's a reliable option that's well located for transit passengers.

★ **Newport** INTERNATIONAL **$$**
(www.newport.mv; Boduthakurufaanu Magu; mains Rf130-250; ⏲6am-1am; 📶) This cool spot on Male's busy seafront road is a godsend to anyone travelling through Male. Sleek and minimalist, Newport feels very different to Male's other restaurants, and the food is excellent. The iPad menus are enormous and run from good breakfasts to falafel, seared tuna cubes, sandwiches, giant prawns and burgers. There's also good coffee.

Royal Garden Café INTERNATIONAL **$$**
(☎332 0288; Medhuziyaarai Magu; mains Rf70-180; ⏲8am-1am Sun-Thu, from 2pm Fri; 📶) This great little place, with a charming garden and an air-conditioned, stylish dark-wood interior, is housed in a rare surviving example of a *ganduvaru,* a nobleman's house. The menu is a combination of Italian, Indonesian, American and Indian cuisines – try the delicious satay chicken or the nasi goreng.

Thai Wok THAI **$$**
(☎331 0007; Ameer Ahmed Magu; mains Rf100-180; ⏲noon-3.30pm Sun-Thu, 7pm-midnight daily; 📶) The Thai food here is good value and authentic, though the best reason to visit is for the thrice-weekly buffet (R140 per person), where you can take your pick of lots of great dishes. The interior of the place is rather charmless, and it can be absolutely packed with tour groups, but the food makes it worth the trip.

Seagull Café House INTERNATIONAL **$$**
(☎332 3792; cnr Chandhanee Magu & Fareedhee Magu; mains Rf80-200; ⏲9am-midnight Sun-Thu, 4pm-midnight Fri; 📶) The Seagull boasts an impressively designed space complete with a charming downstairs garden and a first-floor terrace with a tree growing through it. The menu is extensive and includes sandwiches, burgers, curries, wraps, pasta, fish and grills. There's also a popular gelateria attached, serving up the city's best ice cream – perfect for dessert.

★ **Sala Thai** THAI **$$$**
(☎334 5959; www.salafamilymaldives.com; Buruneege; mains Rf150-200; ⏲noon-midnight Sat-Thu, 5-11.30pm Fri; 📶) This smart, beautifully designed restaurant is generally held to be the best on the island, and it's busy most

nights of the week. The Thai menu is sumptuous and thoroughly authentic, with a huge choice of soups, noodles and curries. Meals are served al fresco in a charming walled terrace, or inside in a plush dining room.

Drinking & Nightlife

Alcohol is not available in Male and you'll need to take the airport ferry and visit the bar at the Hulhule Island Hotel (p74) if you feel a burning need to drink while you're in the city. There's also very little in the way of nightlife in Male. Instead of carousing, locals love to stroll in groups along the seafront and Majeedee Magu until late. Thursday and Friday nights are the busiest, after prayers at sundown.

Jazz Café LIVE MUSIC
(Haveeree Hingun; ⏲8am-midnight Sat-Thu, from 2pm Fri) This friendly cafe takes a thoroughly un-Maldivian concept (jazz) and marries it to another (good coffee) to create one of the capital's nicest hangouts. It offers a full menu as well as good pastries, to be enjoyed to the taped (and sometimes live) jazz accompaniment.

Entertainment

Football or cricket matches can sometimes be seen at the **National Stadium** (Majeedee Magu). Tickets cost Rf15 to Rf50 and can be bought at the stadium gates. Otherwise, Male is a city with very little in the way of entertainment. There are no theatres, concert venues or nightclubs and musical performances are rare. Maldivians tend to be very family oriented and a typical evening will be spent at home or wandering with family or friends along the waterfront.

Shopping

Shopping is at the frenetic heart of the Male experience, and sometimes it seems as if locals do nothing else – a walk down Majeedee Magu, the city's main avenue and shopping street, will reveal an endless parade of clothes, shoes and bag shops, although there's generally little that will excite international travellers here.

Shops selling imported and locally made souvenirs, which are aimed at tourists, are on and around Chandhanee Magu. Many of the tourist shops have a very similar range of tatty stock, and it's hard to recommend any in particular. Male is definitely the best place to shop for more unusual antiques and Maldivian craft items – come here for old wooden measuring cups, coconut graters, traditional lacquer boxes, ceremonial knives and finely woven grass mats. The best places to find such items are along Chandhanee Magu, behind the Grand Friday Mosque.

BUYING PROVISIONS

Maldives has plenty of well-stocked supermarkets for buying provisions and supplies, though alcohol is one thing you will not find on the shelves. **STO People's Choice Supermarket** (Orchid Magu; ⏲9am-10pm Sat-Thu, 2-10pm Fri) has possibly the best selection of imported food and drinks for sale in the entire country.

Information

EMERGENCY

Ambulance	☎102
Fire	☎118
Police	☎119

INTERNET ACCESS

All hotels offer free wireless connections to their guests, as do most smarter restaurants and cafes. SIM cards can be bought at any mobile-phone store for as little as US$2 and used in your mobile phone for cheap data. Simply present your passport.

LAUNDRY

Nearly all hotels will take care of your laundry for a couple of dollars per item. Another option is **Laundry** (Ameer Ahmed Magu; ⏲8am-1pm & 2-7pm), where you can drop off clothes and pick them up the next day. It also offers a four-hour express service and dry cleaning.

LEFT LUGGAGE

There are no dedicated left-luggage facilities in Male itself. The only option is taking a day room at a hotel, or asking nicely at reception if you can leave your bags. There is a left-luggage service at the airport that costs US$5 per item, per 24 hours.

MEDICAL SERVICES

There are two main hospitals in Male, the **Indira Gandhi Memorial Hospital** (☎333 5211; www.mhsc.com.mv; Buruzu Magu) and the **ADK Private Hospital** (☎331 3553; www.adkhospital.mv; Sosun Magu), and together they are the best facilities in the country. At the time of writing, the Indira Gandhi Memorial Hospital was building a brand new 20-storey skyscraper by the New Harbour, which will be a state-of-the-art facility once it's complete. Both hospitals have doctors trained to do a diving medical check. There are many well-stocked chemists outside both establishments.

MONEY

International banks line the waterfront Boduthakurufaanu Magu near the airport ferry dock. All have ATMs that accept international cards. Credit cards are accepted widely in the city – nearly all hotels and restaurants will allow you to pay this way.

More local banks are clustered near the harbour end of Chandhanee Magu and east along Boduthakurufaanu Magu. There are also change facilities and ATMs at the airport.

Do note that you cannot change Maldivian Rufiya into foreign currencies unless you have a receipt from a change bureau showing how you obtained the Rufiya. If you take out money on a credit card, you will not be able to exchange it when you leave the country.

POST

Main post office (☎331 5555; Boduthakurufaanu Magu; ⏰9am-7.30pm Sun-Thu, 10am-3.30pm Sat). There's a post office at the airport too.

TELEPHONE

Anyone staying in Maldives for a while will save a lot of money by getting a local SIM card for their mobile phone. You can buy these from any mobile-phone shop; just bring along your passport.

TOILETS

The most conveniently located public toilets (Rf2) are on the backstreet between Bistro Jade and the small mosque on Ameer Ahmed Magu. However, you can also pop in and use the toilets of most cafes or restaurants; the owners are almost universally polite and don't seem to mind.

TOURIST INFORMATION

The airport has a tourist information desk, which is supposedly open when international flights arrive, but sometimes this isn't the case. Even when it's not staffed, look on the shelf out the front for some useful booklets. Otherwise, the best places to start are the following websites:

www.lonelyplanet.com/maldives/male For planning advice, author recommendations, traveller reviews and insider tips.

www.visitmaldives.com The country's official tourism portal.

Non-Muslims wishing to enter any of Male's mosques should contact the **Ministry of Islamic Affairs** (☎332 2266; www.islamicaffairs.gov.mv; Grand Friday Mosque, Orchid Magu) inside the Grand Friday Mosque.

MALE FOR CHILDREN

Male isn't particularly child-friendly to get around. The narrow streets and rush of moped traffic make walking with kids or pushing a pram a fairly stressful experience; however, most hotels above two storeys have lifts and some restaurants have changing facilities.

Whale Submarine (p65) will appeal to kids of all ages (although be aware that those under three aren't allowed). The **Artificial Beach** (p63) is also a great place to swim, and older kids might be able to join in soccer or cricket matches with local children at the recreational areas nearby. The **Rasrani Bageecha** (p63) is the city's main leisure area and has rides and other activities for children.

TRAVEL AGENCIES

Few travellers use a travel agency in Maldives, as most people book their holidays from home and have little need to arrange anything in the country. Even independent travellers can usually book everything themselves. However, the following are experienced Male-based travel agencies that can make arrangements throughout the country, and they can often unlock good deals on resorts, guesthouses, domestic flights and transfers. A full list of Male travel agents can be found at www.visitmaldives.com/travel-agents.

Crown Tours (☎332 9889; www.crowntoursmaldives.com; 5th fl, Fasmeeru Bldg, Boduthakurufaanu Magu)

Elysian Maldives (Map p73; ☎773 8889; www.elysianmaldives.com; Villingili)

Inner Maldives (☎300 6886; www.innermaldives.com; Ameer Ahmed Magu)

Island Sailors (☎333 2536; www.islandsailors.com; Janavary Hingun)

Sultans of the Sea (☎332 0330; www.sultansoftheseas.com; ground fl, Fasmeeru Bldg, Boduthakurufaanu Magu)

Surfatoll (www.surfatoll.com; M Bolissafaru, 2nd Floor, Orchid Magu)

Voyages Maldives (☎332 2019; www.voyagesmaldives.com; Chandhanee Magu)

Getting There & Away

AIR

Nearly all international flights to Maldives arrive at Male's **Velana International Airport** (p176), which is on a separate island, Hulhule, about 2km east of Male island. Domestic flights with **Maldivian**

HOUSE NAMES

Street numbers are rarely used in Male, so most houses and buildings have a distinctive name, typically written in picturesque English as well as in the local Thaana script. Some Maldivians prefer rustic titles like Crabtree, Forest, Oasis View and Banana Cabin. Others are specifically floral, like Sweet Rose and Luxury Garden, or even vegetable, like Carrot, or the perplexing Leaf Mess. There are also exotic names like Paris Villa and River Nile, while some sound like toilet disinfectants – Ozone, Green Zest, Dawn Fresh. Some of our quirkier favourite house names include Hot Lips, Subtle Laughter, Remind House, Pardon Villa, Frenzy, Mary Lightning and Aston Villa.

(p176) and **FlyMe** (p176) and seaplane transfers to resorts also use the airport, although the seaplane terminal is on the far side of the island, involving a free five-minute bus ride around the runway.

Male is linked by direct flights to Abu Dhabi, Bangalore, Bangkok, Beijing, Chennai, Cochin, Colombo, Doha, Dhaka, Dubai, Frankfurt, Hong Kong, Istanbul, Kuala Lumpur, London, Moscow, Paris, Seoul, Shanghai, Singapore, Tokyo, Trivandrum, Vienna and Zurich.

BOAT

Male is the boat transport hub for the entire country, and it's possible to connect by boat from here with all neighbouring atolls and many nearby islands. However, it's important to know where your speedboat or dhoni will leave from, especially since many services are rather ad hoc.

All long-distance public ferry services depart from the **New Harbour** (☎799 8821, 300 1463; Boduthakurufaanu Magu) on the southwest corner of Male, including those to nearby Villingili, which leave from the **Villingili Ferry Terminal** (New Harbour; Boduthakurufaanu Magu). The New Harbour is fairly chaotic and you'll need to buy your tickets on the dhoni as you board. It's a good idea to get here at least half an hour before the scheduled departure time as it can take a while to locate the boat you need. Timetables can be found at www.mtcc.com.mv/content/comprehensive-transport-network.

The **Hulhumale Ferry Terminal** (Boduthakurufaanu Magu) is on the city's northeastern corner. Various other private services go from different jetties along the waterfront between the Hulhumale Ferry Terminal and the produce market, so always check exactly where the ferry you're supposed to be taking leaves from. Jetties are numbered and well signed, and if you're taking a speedboat transfer to an inhabited island, these services normally leave from here. Your guesthouse will provide you with all the information you'll need to catch your speedboat transfer from Male to whichever island you're heading to. **Ferries to the airport** (Boduthakurufaanu Magu) depart from outside the main post office on Boduthakurufaanu Magu.

In terms of reaching resorts, the airport harbour functions as the biggest transport hub in the country. In general, if you want to travel by boat to a resort from Male, you'll usually need to take the airport ferry and get a transfer from the airport, as this is where speedboats to resorts arrive and depart. You'll need to book your accommodation and the transfer in advance – it's not generally possible to take transfers to resorts without planning to stay there.

Safari boats and private yachts usually moor between Male island and Villingili, or in the lagoon west of Hulhumale. Safari-boat operators will normally pick up new passengers from the airport or Male and ferry them directly to the boat.

Getting Around

TO/FROM THE AIRPORT

Dhonis shuttle between the airport and Male all day and most of the night, departing promptly every 10 minutes. At the airport, dhonis leave from the **jetties** (Map p73; Rf10) just in front of the arrivals hall for Male's **airport ferry arrival jetty** (Boduthakurufaanu Magu). In Male they arrive and depart from the **landing** (p70) at the east end of Boduthakurufaanu Magu. The crossing costs Rf10 per person, or US$1 if you don't have any local cash.

TAXI

The numerous taxis in the city offer a few minutes of cool, air-conditioned comfort and a driver who can usually find any address in Male. Many streets are one way and others may be blocked by construction work or stationary vehicles, so taxis will often take roundabout routes.

Fares are Rf20 for any distance, rising to Rf25 after midnight. Some drivers may charge Rf10 extra for luggage. You don't have to tip. There are various taxi companies; your hotel will happily call you a taxi, or try calling **Dialacab** (☎332 3132), **Loyal Taxi** (☎332 5656) or **New Taxi** (☎332 5757).

North & South Male Atolls

Includes ➡

Best Resorts

- One & Only Reethi Rah (p83)
- Cocoa Island by COMO (p90)
- Gili Lankanfushi (p82)
- Jumeirah Vittaveli (p90)
- Rihiveli Beach Resort (p87)

Best Guesthouses

- Coke's Beach (p85)
- Kaani Village & Spa (p92)
- Crystal Sands (p93)
- Arena Beach Hotel (p93)
- Canopus Retreats Thulusdhoo (p85)

Why Go?

North and South Male Atolls are home to many of the country's most famous and best established resorts, and all the islands here are within easy reach of the capital city and Velana International Airport. South Male Atoll is also home to Maafushi, the biggest success story of Maldives' opening up to independent tourism on inhabited islands, where there are now more than 50 guesthouses and multiple dive and water-sports centres, although concerns about overdevelopment abound.

Both atolls have a wealth of natural draws too: excellent dive sites pepper both sides of Vaadhoo Kandu, the channel that runs between North and South Male Atolls, while Gaafaru Falhu Atoll, north of North Male Atoll, has at least three diveable shipwrecks. Some of Maldives' best surf breaks can be found in North Male Atoll, which is home to a small, seasonal surfer scene, and the beaches are superb almost everywhere.

When to Go

Jan–Apr Divers will experience the best visibility in the water at these times.

May–Nov The best months to surf North and South Male's excellent breaks.

Dec–Mar High season brings the best weather, with almost unbroken sunshine common for weeks at a time.

Around Male

With Male bursting at the seams, several surrounding islands are being developed to relieve the housing pressure on the capital. The following islands are worth a visit from Male by local ferry.

Hulhumale

Hulhumale is Maldives' brave new world, an overflow island for Male's population that has been planned in great detail and now measures several times its original size following land reclamation projects that have even swallowed up a second island.

Built 2m above sea level to protect against sea-level rises, this large island is mainly of interest to travellers as a place to overnight cheaply when transiting Male, though anyone interested in urban planning will find walking around Hulhumale fascinating.

The centrepiece to the island is its huge mosque – the golden glass dome of which is visible from all over the southern part of North Male Atoll.

There's even a surprisingly attractive artificial beach on the eastern side of the island, as well as shopping malls, guesthouses, restaurants and all the other trappings of urban life.

NORTH & SOUTH MALE ATOLLS HIGHLIGHTS

Maafushi (p92) Joining the backpacking crowd on Maldives' busiest inhabited island and the closest thing it has to a tourism capital.

Thulusdhoo (p75) Surfing the breaks at this friendly inhabited island, one of the fastest developing in the country.

Manta Point (p75) Snorkelling or diving with these magnificent creatures at this busy cleaning station surrounded by corals.

Helengeli Thila (p75) Witnessing thriving life on this exceptional reef on the northern edge of North Male Atoll.

Shark Point (p75) Diving with white-tip and grey-tip reef sharks at this excellent site located inside a Protected Marine Area.

Sleeping

Most hotels here offer airport pick-ups with advance notice.

Le Vieux Nice Inn GUESTHOUSE $
(335 7788; www.levieuxniceinn.com; Nirolhu Magu; r from US$70;) One block back from the beach, this friendly place is remarkably popular for its relatively low prices, good restaurant and excellent location in the middle of Hulhumale's chilled-out backpacker zone. Rooms are comfortable and modern, and the welcome is warm. They will pick you up by car from the airport if you give them notice.

Planktons Beach GUESTHOUSE $
(335 0344; www.planktonsbeach.com; Dhigga Magu; r from US$75;) The best of the budget guesthouses on Hulhumale's beach, Planktons has enviably sleek, well-equipped rooms with a minimalist feel and a white decor with bright tropical colour accents. Breakfast is served right on the beach, and water-sports equipment is available for those who have some time to kill. Staff are friendly and professional.

★**Hotel Ocean Grand at Hulhumale** HOTEL $$
(335 5077; www.oceangrandmaldives.com; Kaani Magu; r from US$150;) The most upmarket hotel in Hulhumale, the Ocean Grand overlooks the seafront and has some great lagoon views from its front rooms. This is a good choice for transiting Male in comfort, with free airport transfers in both directions and very professional staff who seem to make a real effort to ensure guests are happy. Don't miss the charming roof terrace.

Eating

Family Room Cafe CAFE $
(Dhigga Magu; 8am-11pm Sat-Thu, 2-11pm Fri;) This rather cool place on the seafront is a bit of a change of pace for Hulhumale, which doesn't really do much in the way of hipster spots. The main reason to go – as well as to witness Maldivian youth culture in its fullest flow – is for the excellent coffee (roasted on site), delicious smoothies, cakes and snacks.

Ravin's INTERNATIONAL $
(Nirolhu Magu; mains Rf50-200; 9am-midnight Sat-Thu, 1.30pm-midnight Fri;) Ravin's is a popular lifeline for foreigners living on Hulhumale and also with a younger, local crowd

Around Male

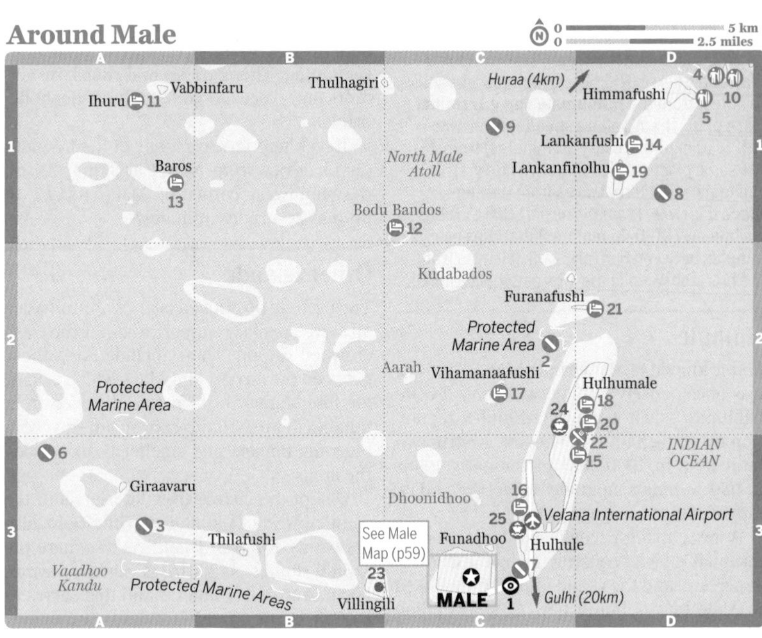

Around Male

Sights

1 China-Maldives Friendship Bridge C3

Activities, Courses & Tours

2 Banana Reef C2
3 Hans Hass Place A3
4 Honky's D1
5 Jailbreaks D1
6 Lion's Head A3
7 Maldive Victory C3
8 Manta Point D1
9 Okobe Thila C1
10 Sultan's D1

Sleeping

11 Angsana Ihuru A1
12 Bandos Island Resort C1
13 Baros A1
14 Gili Lankanfushi D1
15 Hotel Ocean Grand at Hulhumale D3
16 Hulhule Island Hotel C3
17 Kurumba Maldives C2
18 Le Vieux Nice Inn D2
19 Paradise Island Resort & Spa D1
20 Planktons Beach D2
21 Sheraton Maldives Full Moon Resort & Spa D2

Eating

Bombay Darbar .... (see 15)
Family Room Cafe .... (see 20)
22 Ravin's D3

Information

23 Elysian Maldives B3

Transport

FlyMe .... (see 25)
24 Hulhumale-Male Ferry C2
25 Male Ferry C3
Trans Maldivian Airways .... (see 25)

who appreciate the international cuisine. As well as Indian curries, there's steak, noodles and rice dishes on the menu, plus decent coffee. It's one block back from the beach.

Bombay Darbar INDIAN **$$**
(www.newtowninn.com/facilities/; Nirolhu Magu; mains Rf135-250; ⌚10am-midnight; 📶🌶) On the ground floor of the Newtown Inn, this multi-coloured Indian restaurant is one of the best on the island, with a large menu of cooking from all over the subcontinent. Try the excellent prawn masala or perhaps the traditional Tangdi kebab from the tandoori oven.

Getting There & Away

To visit Hulhumale from Male, take the Hulhumale-Male Ferry (Rf5.50, 20 minutes, every 15 minutes) from the **Hulhumale Ferry Terminal** (Map p73). There's also a speedboat service (Rf25, 10 minutes, every 30 minutes) from the same place for travellers in a hurry. From Hulhumale, the ferry leaves from the same **place** it arrives. From the airport there's a bus to Hulhumale (Rf20, 15 minutes) that runs every 30 minutes between 6am and 1am. It leaves from the bus stop outside the international terminal.

Hulhule

Better known as the airport island, Hulhule was once densely wooded with very few inhabitants – just a graveyard and a reputation for being haunted. The first airstrip was built here in 1960, and in the early 1980s it had a major upgrade to accommodate long-distance passenger jets.

A new, much-needed and long overdue terminal is being constructed by the Chinese at present, and the island is also being linked to Male by the brand new US$150 million China-Maldives Friendship Bridge (p60). Hulhule also accommodates the seaplane terminal on the lagoon on the east side of the island. Everyone passes through on their way in and out of the country, but it's not a place where most people spend any time.

There are a few passable eating options in and around the airport, but your best option for a good meal is to go to the **Hulhule Island Hotel** (333 0888; www.hih.com.mv; Hulhule island; r from US$325;), where you can eat well and also enjoy alcohol at the bar, the only place in Male where this is legal.

Until the completion of the China-Maldives Friendship Bridge, the easiest option from Male is the airport ferry (p70) (Rf10, 10 minutes) which runs every five minutes or so. For Hulhumale, buses (Rf10) leave from the bus stop just outside the airport terminal building, looping around the runway and along the main road of Hulhumale before circling back to the airport.

Villingili

Just 1km from the western shore of Male is the little island of Villingili – also known as Vilimale – the fifth district of the capital. The short boat ride here takes you into a different world, though; far more relaxed than Male proper, Villingili has something of a Caribbean feel, with brightly painted houses and a laid-back pace. Male residents come here to enjoy some space, play soccer and go swimming. There are several shops, restaurants and places to go for a (non-alcoholic) drink.

To get here just catch one of the frequent dhoni ferries from New Harbour (p70) on the southwest corner of Male (Rf3.25, 10 minutes, every five minutes).

Other Islands

The usefully positioned islands around Male all serve auxiliary support roles for the overcrowded capital. These include **Funadhoo**, between the airport and Male, which is used for fuel storage – it's a safe distance from inhabited areas, and convenient for both seagoing tankers and smaller boats serving the atolls.

One of the fastest-growing islands in the country, west of Villingili, is **Thilafushi**, also known as 'Rubbish Island' as it's where the capital dumps its garbage. Slightly further north, **Aarah** is a small island that serves as a government retreat.

North Male Atoll

Tourism is well developed in North Male Atoll, which includes the tiny single-island atolls of Gaafaru Falhu and Kaashidhoo to its north.

Maldivian tourism began here with the resort of Kurumba opening its doors in 1972, and many of the resorts in North Male are grand dames in the scope of the country's relatively recent conversion to luxury travel destination. As well as having many of the best known resorts, these days there are many inhabited islands that are now home to thriving guesthouse scenes.

Despite Male being the national capital of Maldives, it is not actually the atoll capital, as it's considered to be its own administrative district. Instead, the atoll capital is Thulusdhoo, on the eastern edge of North Male Atoll, a charming island with dozens of hotels and guesthouses on it that is particularly beloved by Italians and surfers.

Sights

The following islands are all less than an hour from Male. For transfers, either contact Atoll Transfer (p178) to arrange a speedboat (fares range from US$29 to US$40 one way) or head to Male's New Harbour (p70) and take public ferry 308, which leaves daily except Monday and Friday at 2.30pm, bound for Huraa, Thulusdhoo and Dhiffushi. Ferries back to Male leave early in the morning.

Thulusdhoo has traditionally been an industrious island, known for manufacturing of *bodu beru* (big drums), for its salted-fish warehouse and for its Coca-Cola factory, the only one in the world that makes the drink with desalinated water. Today, there some 30 guesthouses here, plus a bikini beach and a bridge link to a smaller island.

Himmafushi is famous for its main street selling some of the least expensive souvenirs in the country, such as carved rosewood manta rays, sharks and dolphins; the backstreets are more traditional. Seek out the cemetery with its coral headstones. A sand spit has joined Himmafushi to neighbouring Gaamaadhoo, where there used to be a prison – hence the name of the local surf break, Jailbreaks.

The island of **Huraa** is well used to tourists visiting from nearby resorts, but it retains its small-island feel, with several guesthouses and a buzzing surfer scene with 15 breaks within easy reach. The mosque here was built by Huraa's own small dynasty of sultans, founded in 1759 by Sultan Al-Ghaazi Hassan Izzaddeen.

Dhiffushi is an appealing inhabited island, with around 1000 inhabitants, three mosques and two schools. Mainly a fishing island, it has lots of greenery, grows tropical fruit, and is home to a couple of guesthouses.

Activities

Diving

North Male Atoll has some superb dive sites. Some are heavily dived, however, especially in peak seasons, due to the many resorts in the atoll.

★Helengeli Thila DIVING

Famous for its prolific marine life, Helengeli Thila, also called Bodu Thila, is a long narrow thila on the eastern edge of the atoll. Reef fish and pelagics (fish that inhabit the open sea) are common, including sharks, tuna, rays and jacks. Soft corals are spectacular in the cliffs and caves on the west side of the thila at about 25m.

★Shark Point DIVING

Also called Saddle, or Kuda Faru, Shark Point is in a Protected Marine Area and is subject to strong currents. Lots of white-tip and grey-tip reef sharks can be seen in the channel between a thila and the reef, along with fusiliers, jackfish, stingrays and some impressive caves, making this one of the area's most exciting dives.

★Manta Point DIVING

(Map p42) The best time to see the mantas for which Manta Point is famous is from May to November. Coral outcrops at about 8m are a 'cleaning station', where cleaner wrasse feed on parasites from the mantas' wings. Cliffs, coral tables, turtles, sharks and numerous reef fish are other attractions, as are the nearby Lankan Caves.

Surfing

Surfing is also a major draw, with islands along the atoll's eastern edge enjoying access to some of the best sites in the country between May and November. Here's a summary of the top breaks.

Jailbreaks (Map p42) A right-handed barrel reef break best surfed between June and August, named for the local prison.

Coke's (Map p42) A famous and challenging right-hander that can be surfed at any time between March and October, close to the islands' Coca-Cola factory.

Pasta Point (Map p42) This very popular reef break is a consistent left-hander that's best between May and August.

Sultan's (Map p42) Best from March to October, Sultan's is a consistent right-hander that never closes out.

Chickens (Map p42) A long left-hander, named for a local poultry farm, that is famously fast during July and August, but good from May right through to October.

Honky's (Map p42) A long left off the island of Thamburudhoo, loved by connoisseurs for its consistency and length; best surfed at low tide between March and October.

Lohi's (Map p42) Off the island of Lohifushi, near Adaaran Select Hudhuranfushi (p82), Lohi's is a long left-hander best surfed between May and October.

Sleeping

Resorts

Asdu Sun Island RESORT $

(☎664 5051; www.asdu.com; Asdhoo; full board r US$150; 📶) Perhaps the least self-conscious resort in the country, laid-back Asdu Sun Island is about as far away from the country's famous luxury resorts as can be imagined.

North Male Atoll

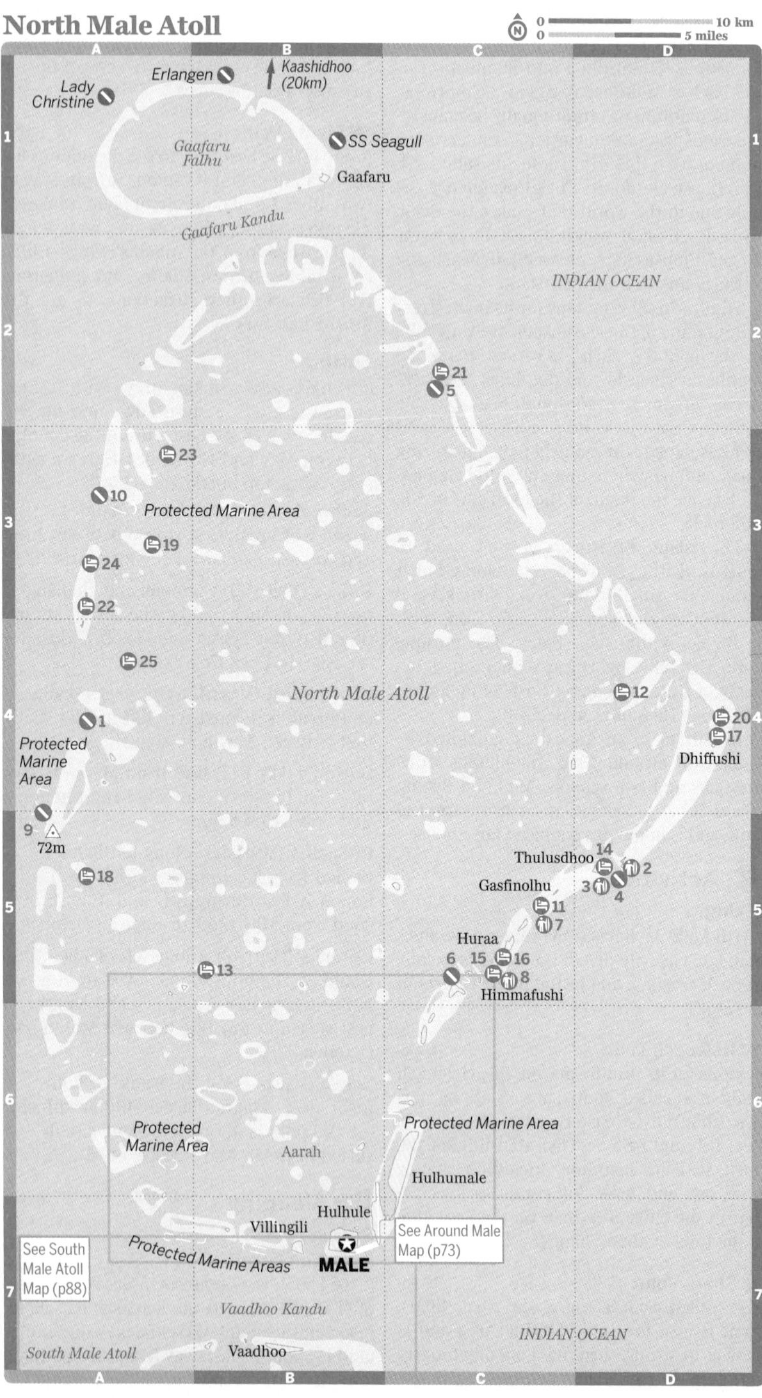

0 10 km
0 5 miles
Kaashidhoo (20km)
Erlangen
Lady Christine
Gaafaru Falhu
SS Seagull
Gaafaru
Gaafaru Kandu
INDIAN OCEAN
21
5
23
10
Protected Marine Area
19
24
22
25
North Male Atoll
12
20
17
Dhiffushi
1
Protected Marine Area
9
72m
14
Thulusdhoo
2
3
4
Gasfinolhu
18
11
7
Huraa
6
15
16
8
13
Himmafushi
Protected Marine Area
Protected Marine Area
Aarah
Hulhumale
Hulhule
Villingili
See Around Male Map (p73)
See South Male Atoll Map (p88)
Protected Marine Areas
MALE
Vaadhoo Kandu
INDIAN OCEAN
South Male Atoll
Vaadhoo

North Male Atoll

Activities, Courses & Tours

1 Bodu Hithi Thila A4
2 Chickens D5
3 Coke's D5
4 Colosseum D5
5 Helengeli Thila C2
6 HP Reef C5
7 Lohi's C5
8 Pasta Point C5
9 Rasfari A5
10 Shark Point A3

Sleeping

11 Adaaran Select Hudhuranfushi C5
12 Asdu Sun Island D4
13 Banyan Tree Vabbinfaru B5
14 Canopus Retreats Thulusdhoo D5
15 Cinnamon Island Dhonveli C5
Coke's Beach .... (see 14)
16 Four Seasons Resort Maldives at Kuda Huraa C5
17 Happy Life Maldives Lodge D4
18 Huvafen Fushi A5
19 Makunudu Island A3
20 Meeru Island Resort & Spa D4
21 OBLU by Atmosphere at Helengeli C2
22 One & Only Reethi Rah A3
23 Smartline Eriyadu A3
24 Summer Island A3
25 Vivanta by Taj Coral Reef A4

Beloved by Italian holidaymakers, many of whom repeat-visit, it's a great spot for divers with few needs beyond a pristine house reef, cheap diving and somewhere to enjoy a beer come sundown.

All the staff on the island are members of owner Ahmed's family, whose quarters are not hidden away out of sight as is the norm in Maldives, but instead enjoy equal status on the island to those of the guest rooms. Chickens run around freely and you'll feel almost like you're on a local island here, while also enjoying some of the perks of life in a resort.

The tiny island is thickly forested and has a stunning white beach around much of it, and excellent diving opportunities abound nearby.

Accommodation is in aging two- and three-unit white-painted concrete huts, all terribly simple and rather worn, free of air-con, TV, hot water and glass windows, but clean.

Food is not a highlight, however, with simple pasta and fish served up for all meals, so dining can get boring here rather quickly. If you're looking for a cheap diving holiday while maintaining access to alcohol, though, this remains an excellent choice.

OBLU by Atmosphere at Helengeli RESORT **$$**

(959 6001; www.oblu-helengeli.com; Helengeli; all-inclusive r from US$390;) Right on the northern tip of North Male Atoll, Helengeli is a remote, long and thin island that has recently been transformed from a quiet budget diving resort to an impressively run, midrange all-inclusive family resort by the Atmosphere group. With a superb house reef and huge choice of nearby dive sites, the resort remains a diver favourite.

There are now 116 villas on the island in four categories. These start with the 48-sq-m Beach Villas and go up to the 191-sq-m Beach Suites with Pool, which boast their own 20m pool. All are spotless and breezy, with warm tropical colour accents and attractive furnishings including driftwood desks, outdoor bathrooms and attractive and private outdoor areas.

The villas are quite tightly packed together and while the beaches are good, there are rocks in many places that make swimming a little challenging.

Atmosphere Aqua Club runs daily dives all over the north of the atoll and also take care of water sports, many of which are free. The all-inclusive packages include a sunset fishing trip and a visit to an inhabited island for every guest during their stay, plus there are dozens of chargeable daily activities.

For relaxation and pampering there's the gorgeous Garden Spa, while for food there's a busy buffet that has a very good variety of dishes as well as live cooking stations. The bar here is lively with regular live music and guests on all-inclusive packages that include free non-brand-name drinks, ensuring that the atmosphere is always sociable.

Overall this is a great resort for families and couples interested in having lots to do and no final bill to worry about.

Vivanta by Taj Coral Reef RESORT **$$**

(664 1948; www.tajhotels.com; Hembadhu; r from US$665;) Heart-shaped Taj Vivanta is a glamorous resort that still manages to feel laid-back and unpretentious.

Although cheaper than its sister resort Taj Exotica in South Male, it's not a large step down in service and quality. All 62 rooms are very plush, including 32 water villas with large terraces and direct access to excellent snorkelling in the lagoon.

Rooms feel thoroughly modern and smart, if a bit anonymous and Ikea-like in their art choices. There are great touches such as outside showers, though no private plunge pools, save in the very top room category. The resort centres on the large Latitude restaurant, which has a great beachside position and serves up three buffet meals per day.

Nearby, there is a pizza station and a teppanyaki bar next to the large infinity pool. The beach here is somewhat narrow, rocky in part and held in place by wired rocks, though the sand is wonderfully soft elsewhere.

Other facilities include Jiva Spa, which focuses on Indian massage, Ayurvedic therapies and other treatments and pampering from the subcontinent. You'll find a water-sports centre and a dive school, and snorkelling around the island is excellent (and equipment is free). A reliable number of manta rays turn up at 5pm every day to be fed: an incredible spectacle and one that visitors from nearby resorts sometimes come over to see.

Overall, Taj Vivanta is a recommended choice for small, smart luxury without any fuss.

Meeru Island Resort & Spa RESORT **$$**
(☎664 3157; www.meeru.com; Meerufenfushi; full board r from US$574; ❄📶🏊) Meeru is a long, verdant stretch of island with a dazzling white beach.

The third-largest resort in the country, it's also massively popular and offers almost every conceivable activity. Indeed, so spread out is the resort that for convenience there are two receptions and two buffet restaurants, to avoid guests overexerting themselves on the way to dinner.

Rooms come in a startling number of categories, from cosy, prefab timber-clad self-contained units to the 87 water villas. The latter range from rustic-style older rooms in bright colours with open-air bathrooms and Jacuzzis to newer, sleeker but perhaps less charming water villas, all in dark wood and with extra luxuries such as espresso machines and direct water access.

All non-motorised water sports are included here. There are two excellent spas, one of which is entirely over water, and two swimming pools. Other amenities include a nine-hole golf course, two tennis courts, a gym and a golf driving range.

Even more unusual is the extraordinary blue whale skeleton on display in the middle of the island, and a small but rather neglected museum of Maldivian history and traditions above the barnlike main reception.

The house reef can only be reached by boat and these leave every two hours to take snorkellers and divers off to the outer reef, where the aquatic life is fantastic. Fishing trips are offered, and there is of course a diving school, plus a vast lagoon perfect for learning sailing and windsurfing.

Overall, Meeru gets great reviews from guests. It caters to a wide variety of interests

MORE NORTH MALE ATOLL DIVES

There are many other rewarding dive sites in North Male Atoll. Consider the following:

Banana Reef (Map p42) A Protected Marine Area with a bit of everything: dramatic cliffs, caves and overhangs, brilliant coral growths, prolific reef fish and big predators such as sharks, barracuda and grouper. Also good for snorkellers.

Bodu Hithi Thila Prime manta territory from December to March, with healthy soft corals, and good snorkelling.

Rasfari (Map p42) Slopes and thilas frequented by grey-tip reef sharks, barracuda, eagle rays and trevally.

Colosseum (Map p42) A cliff-backed amphitheatre, where sharks and barracuda take centre stage.

HP Reef (Map p42) A narrow channel with abundant soft blue corals and pelagics, plus a swim-through chimney.

Okobe Thila (Map p42) Shallow caves full of prolific reef fish, including big Napoleon wrasse.

and budget levels – it's a big resort but it's not crowded and has retained its personal, friendly feel.

Kurumba Maldives RESORT **$$**

(☎664 2324; www.kurumba.com; Vihamanafushi; r from US$495; ❄📶🏊) Established in 1972, Kurumba Maldives was the first resort in the country and one that has gone through many changes over five decades. Today it is a high-quality place that continues to be extremely popular, combining a huge range of facilities, ease of access from the airport, family friendliness and quality accommodation to very successful effect.

Some may feel the overly manicured gardens and relentlessly modern architecture make the resort feel a little sterile; others, however, will like its grand country-club style – golf buggies rule the roads here and the resort is big enough for this to be justifiable.

Kurumba is the closest resort to Male, and as such it regularly caters for business conferences and conventions as well as day-trippers from the capital, who come for the renowned restaurants.

There are eight restaurants to choose from (more than any other resort island in the country), and these are a highlight, including Indian, Italian, Arabic, Thai and Japanese outlets.

The rooms come in a huge range of categories, the pool villas being especially impressive, each with its own pool in a private back garden. There are no water villas here, and few villas have direct beach access, but it's never too far to the water. There's no end to the facilities available, from a huge and well-equipped dive school to a water-sports centre, tennis courts, babysitters, a gorgeous spa, two gyms and two pools.

Kurumba is a place for scale and grandeur and not for hiding away on a desert island, and it remains a hugely popular choice for both couples and families.

Sheraton Maldives Full Moon Resort & Spa RESORT **$$**

(☎664 2010; www.starwoodhotels.com; Furanafushi; r from US$541; ❄📶🏊) Magnificently laid out with real style and class, this resort has the ambiance of an upscale country club rather than a remote tropical island. This is in part due to its proximity to the capital, but everything else here is aimed at the urban sophisticate, from the understated public areas to the luxurious spa, housed on its own island.

While lavish, Sheraton Maldives offers affordable luxury in its 176 refurbished rooms, including its smart water villas and beachfront deluxe rooms, all of which feature thatched roofs, shuttered windows, plunge pools and private gardens or terraces.

For dining, there's a choice between a Thai restaurant; the al fresco Sand Coast, which serves up international cuisine; and the beachfront Sea Salt, where steaks and seafood are the order of the day. Feast, the main restaurant, also serves high-quality buffets three times a day, while T-For Tea House is a poolside dim sum and noodle restaurant.

A full range of facilities is squeezed onto this small island, including tennis courts, a gym and an inviting swimming pool that has its own waterfall. There are no motorised water sports, and the lagoon isn't suitable for snorkelling, but sailing, windsurfing and snorkelling trips are offered. There's a full and well-run dive centre, and big-game fishing is also available.

Best of all, it's easy to reach Male and the airport, making it a great weekend choice or somewhere where you can transit the capital in style.

Angsana Ihuru RESORT **$$**

(☎664 3502; www.angsana.com; Ihuru; r from US$478; ❄📶) 🍃 With its canopy of palm trees and surrounding gorgeous white beach, Angsana conforms exactly to the tropical-island stereotype and often features in photographs publicising Maldives. The house reef forms a near-perfect circle around the island, making it brilliant for snorkelling and shore dives, while the relatively low prices here make this a much more affordable way to enjoy Maldives.

The 45 rooms circle the island, each with direct access to a slice of beach. Each is decorated in bright colours, with black furniture, lime-green fabrics and simple outdoor bathrooms. They are rather closely packed together, however, and lack excessive charm, but they are comfortable and clean.

The sand floor restaurant serves buffet meals, though most guests prefer to eat dinner on the deck overlooking the sea. The Thai spa consists of eight treatment rooms, almost all doubles, perfect for romantic pampering.

All non-motorised water sports are free, including all snorkelling equipment. The resort works passionately to conserve its healthy reef, and offers guests the opportunity to help out with various marine biology projects. While there is some decent shore diving to be done, the best dive sites are some distance away on the edges of the atoll. Dive boats head out each morning and afternoon.

One benefit of staying here is the boat that goes back and forth to next-door sister property Banyan Tree every two hours, meaning that Angsana guests can enjoy the facilities there as well.

Bandos Island Resort RESORT **$$**
(☎664 0088; www.bandosmaldives.com; Bandos; r US$360;) One of the largest resorts in the country, Bandos has developed and expanded enormously since it opened as the second resort in Maldives in 1972. The island is highly developed and resembles a well-manicured town centre rather than a typical tropical island.

Many love it for that reason, though it's perhaps not ideal for travellers seeking rustic escapism.

Bandos has it all, from a conference centre, several restaurants and a nightclub to tennis courts, a billiard room, a sauna, a gym, and a beauty salon. The child-care centre is free during the day, and babysitters are affordable in the evening, so in general the resort is one of the most child-friendly in the country.

Fine if rather narrow beaches surround the island, and the house reef is handy for snorkelling and diving. Lots of fish and a small wreck can be seen here. The dive centre does trips to about 40 dive sites in the area, and even has a decompression chamber – one of the only ones in the country.

Rooms are modern, with red-tiled roofs, white-tiled floors, and minibar, though they're far from luxurious. The much fancier water villas, which include services such as a private butler, are a lot more expensive.

Overall this is a great option for families and those who like lively resorts where there's potential to meet lots of new people and to have a huge range of activities available.

Makunudu Island RESORT **$$**
(☎664 6464; www.makunudu.com; Makunudu; half board r from US$468;) Makunudu Island is a favourite of many romantics who return again and again for its utter simplicity, gorgeous beaches, thick vegetation and a surrounding reef so big that it's hard for speedboats unfamiliar with the island to find their way into the dock.

The no-frills and rustic approach will charm many, but it's not for travellers seeking particular luxury.

Just 2.4 hectares in area, the tiny island almost looks like it might sink under the sheer weight of lush vegetation on it – and the low-key rooms are hard to spot at first, with individual thatched-roof bungalows hidden amid the jungle-like foliage. All rooms face the beach and feature natural finishes, varnished timber, textured white walls and open-air bathrooms, and have all the expected facilities except the deliberately excluded TV.

The service and food are both excellent. Breakfast and lunch are buffets, while most dinners are a choice of thoughtfully prepared set menus, served in the delightful open-sided restaurant.

There are excellent dive sites in the area, the house reef is great for snorkelling, and the dive school is very experienced at running dives from the island. Windsurfing and sailing are free, as are shorter excursions.

This unaffected place won't appeal to travellers wanting pampering, water villas or cutting-edge design, but if a small, exclusive, natural-style resort appeals, Makunudu is one of the best choices in Maldives.

Paradise Island Resort & Spa RESORT **$$**
(☎664 0011; www.villahotels.com; Lankanfinolhu; r from US$429;) Paradise Island is huge and offers some great deals for people seeking a wide range of facilities and services at a reasonable price. The beaches are gorgeous, the lagoon an incredible colour even by local standards and the whole place is well run and friendly. It's a great choice if you like numerous activity options and plenty going on.

The atmosphere, though, is hardly intimate: you're crowded onto one of the country's biggest island resorts. If you want seclusion and true escape, go elsewhere. Rooms are simple, with white tiles, white walls and satellite TV. They are absolutely fine, but unlikely to be places where you'll want to spend much of your time.

By contrast, the 62 high-end rooms in the Haven development, a sort of resort within a resort, come in four categories. They are very sleek, stylish and rather minimalist, the higher categories coming with enormous slate pools and all having large sun terraces with direct access to the water. However, given that Haven's prices are comparable to other more intimate, less mass-market resorts, its appeal is perhaps limited.

NON-EXCLUSIVE SURFING

With so much in Maldives being exclusive, the decision of the government in 2014 to end the policy of exclusivity for surf breaks was welcomed by locals and surfers around the world alike. Until then, surf breaks near to resort islands were deemed to be property of the resorts, meaning that only guests of each property were able to surf these waves, even when they were some distance from the island proper. This created tensions between locals (many of whom love to surf) and hotel managers, with the law at first firmly on the side of the resorts. However, in a decision welcomed by people across the surfing, guesthouse and tourism industry, since 2014 – provided you can get there – you're now free to surf at any break in the country.

Packages with meals at the resort are definitely worth it: you get a decent buffet for every meal and the other three restaurants are not a massive step up, so you won't find yourself wanting to eat elsewhere that much.

Guests staying at the Haven have two restaurants for their exclusive use. The island is well landscaped and has good beaches and a swimming pool. Some rooms are a long way from the restaurant, and many don't have much of a view, however. The Dive Oceanus dive centre is very friendly and offers boat dives to the many excellent dive sites nearby.

Smartline Eriyadu RESORT **$$**
(☎664 4487; www.smartlineeriyadu.com; Eriyadu; s/d from US$360/430; ❄📶🏊) Smartline Eriyadu is a fully renovated midrange resort popular with divers who come here for the uncrowded waters that surround this remote island. It's also a wonderfully mellow place where you're generally left to your own devices.

The oval-shaped island suffers from beach erosion, but the beaches are still attractive, with a beautiful sandbank sometimes created by the changing current.

The island is full of repeat visitors and children are warmly welcomed with a kids clubs and plenty of activities during the day. There's a good reef that is great for snorkelling, with turtles and dolphins regular visitors just metres from the beach. There's a lovely pool, a water-sports centre, a spa specialising in Thai and Ayurvedic treatments, and diving is good value.

The rooms are divided into two categories: standard and deluxe. Most are in two-room units on the beach, each with its own sea-facing patio, though views can be blocked by the island's thick foliage. Rooms have polished timber floors, TVs and minibars and have bright tropical decor.

The island is quite heavily developed, but the buildings are interspersed with lots of shady trees and shrubbery. The sand-floor restaurant serves most meals in buffet style, with a varied selection of European dishes, curries and seafood.

The usual water sports and excursions are available, as is some low-key evening entertainment, but this economical resort is mainly for diving, snorkelling and relaxing on the beach.

Cinnamon Island Dhonveli RESORT **$$**
(☎664 0055; www.cinnamonhotels.com; Kanuhuraa; s/d from US$350/440; ❄📶🏊) This well-run if rather crowded resort boasts a great pool, some lovely beaches, its own surf break and tennis courts. There are six categories of room catering for everyone from honeymooners and keen divers to groups of surfers who come here in big numbers from June to September for the break at nearby Pasta Point (p75).

The charming-looking water villas are painted blue, have thatched roofs and Indian-style carved wood frames, while inside they are sparkling clean and have mottled walls and bright tropical accents. Better value are the simple but attractive cheaper rooms on the island itself.

While it has some great beaches, the island is quite sparse in places, and beach erosion is a problem, with some unsightly sandbags in view. The beach on the north side of the island is great for swimming and sunbathing, and is safe for children. All meals are buffet style and feature a fair selection of good food. All in all, there's a lot going for Dhonveli, as it offers a good standard of service and facilities for the price.

Adaaran Select Hudhuranfushi RESORT **$$**
(☎664 1930; www.adaaran.com; Lohifushi; r from US$355; ❄📶🏊) Adaaran Select Hudhuranfushi is a good choice for a family holiday

where activities are laid on in bucket loads. Run by the Sri Lankan Adaaran group, this large and high-quality resort is set on an almond-shaped island fringed by gorgeous white-sand beaches and centred on a huge hangar-like reception surrounded by restaurants, bars and a great pool.

The rooms are bright and tasteful with a rustic feel, despite being well-equipped and featuring outdoor showers in the higher categories. There's a gym, a spa, water sports and dive centres and a choice of two restaurants and two bars. It's a perfect destination for comfortable but unpretentious romance, family holidays and diving.

Summer Island RESORT **$$**

(☎664 1949; www.summerislandmaldives.com; Ziyaaraifushi; r incl full board from US$450;) Following a complete renovation in 2015 during which 90% of the resort was rebuilt from scratch, Summer Island is now looking superb and is easily one of the best-value midrange choices in the country. The resort, Maldivian village in style, has somehow gained almost 50 rooms, an infinity pool and a second restaurant without losing any of its charm.

As the international hotel conglomerates circle the country, it's refreshing that Summer Island remains 100% Maldivian owned. It's also helmed by a local female general manager, the first of her kind in Maldives. The island itself is very pleasantly vegetated, with hammocks strung up between palm trees and chickens running around, just like on an inhabited island. There's even a mosque (and a call to prayer) for the staff, which is integrated into the resort rather than hidden away.

The new-look rooms are all superb, though the family room stands out with its own small pool and tasteful decor and fittings. All rooms on the island have outdoor bathrooms, while the new water villas enjoy private sun terraces and direct water access. The standard beach villas are in blocks of four, of which the upstairs 'vista' rooms are the best. There are good beaches along one side of the island.

Summer Island has two restaurants – the main canteen serves up a large buffet three times a day, while the fancier Hiya is reserved for people staying in the water villas and guests on premium packages only. There's a Serena spa for pampering as well as a dive and water-sports centre. Environmental credentials are strong here: as well as heating all hot water by means of solar power, the resort is also planning to print 3D moulds for coral to build its own reef with, something that's never been attempted elsewhere in the country.

All in all, this is a great value and progressively run option for divers and anyone seeking relaxed romance.

★Gili Lankanfushi RESORT **$$$**

(☎664 0304; www.gili-lankanfushi.com; Lankanfushi; r from US$1830;) Astonishingly impressive Gili Lankanfushi is the original pioneer of barefoot luxury in Maldives, where the 'no shoes, no news' philosophy reigns supreme and few visitors come away anything but amazed. Each of the palatial two-floor villas is built over water: they're extraordinary rustic-meets-sophisticated timber creations that are as open to the elements as possible.

The 45 villas range from the 'standard' Villa Suite, which has two rooms as well as a sea garden, a sun deck and a bed on the enormous roof terrace for stargazing, to the vast Private Reserve, a free-standing lagoon complex sleeping nine people in the lap of luxury, a short boat ride from the main island.

All the buildings are made from natural materials – most woods are imported from sustainable forests elsewhere in Asia – and the attention to detail is incredible, with luxurious treats hidden away under natural fibres in what is one of Maldives' most environmentally conscious resorts.

The resort has not changed massively since it was built almost 20 years ago, but the concept has proven strong enough to remain competitive in the age of mega-luxurious six-star resorts, and it retains many repeat visitors.

The island itself is small but very pretty and is criss-crossed with sand paths, along which guests can cycle to the main communal areas: the infinity pool overlooking the beach, the charming overwater bar and the beachside restaurant, where elaborate buffets and à la carte menus are equally impressive.

Foodies will appreciate the wine cellar, a sumptuous subterranean space for private degustation dinners and wine tasting around a huge driftwood table, although By The Sea, an evenings-only Japanese restaurant is hands down the top table on the island.

Every room comes with a 'Man Friday' – a butler whose job it is to bring you anything you need. This is certainly not a good place for those who don't like to be fussed over: with a staff-to-guests ratio of 3:1 – one of the highest in Maldives – staff glide out of nowhere and appear magically to know your name.

As well as a dive school, a gym and a water-sports centre (where all non-motorised equipment is free to borrow) there's a brand new marine biology centre with information and lectures for guests on the creatures of the reef.

The island is very convenient for the airport, with the journey taking just 10 minutes by speedboat, and yet you will still feel wonderfully remote at this intelligently luxurious place. If you can afford it, this is a wonderful choice for a truly luxurious yet thoroughly rustic and unpretentious holiday.

★One & Only Reethi Rah RESORT **$$$**
(☎664 8800; www.oneandonlyresorts.com; Reethirah; r from US$2426; ❄📶🏊) One & Only Reethi Rah is still king of the Maldivian resorts. There may be resorts that cost more, but none have surpassed this extraordinary and ambitiously designed place, which is all about glamour and style, and shamelessly so. Indeed, if you aren't comfortable with almost mind-boggling pampering and luxury, this probably isn't the place for you.

The palatial Balinese-influenced rooms are some of the most enormous in the country, with high ceilings and beautifully furnished interiors. Some – but far from all – have their own pools, but those that don't enjoy direct access to the lagoon or beach. Though you would never guess it, much of the vast island is the result of land reclamation and has been landscaped for optimum beach space.

The island's atypical geography is clearly apparent from the air, where you can see an unusual number of perfect crescent beaches around the island. From its original 15.8 hectares, the island now stands at an incredible (for Maldives, at least) 44 hectares, which gives the island a spread-out feel, meaning plenty of privacy, empty beaches and guaranteed tranquillity.

The island is too large to be covered comfortably on foot, so guests get around by bicycle, though club cars can be called from reception as well. Other unique features include a canal that was built for the sea to flow through the island (a unique example of this in Maldives), a sumptuous black slate lap pool built out over the ocean and a reception unsurpassed in grandeur anywhere else in the country. Vegetation is thick and the spotless white-sand beaches are truly alluring.

There are now six restaurants on the island, including Tapasake for Japanese cuisine, Fanditha for Middle Eastern cooking and two recent additions: Botanica for outdoor organic meals and Rabarbaro for divine Italian. There's a huge ESPA-run spa that focuses on Asian treatments, including Balinese and Thai massage, a gym, two tennis courts and a pro-tennis trainer, a superb diving school, a kids club and a full water-sports program.

All in all, if you can afford it, One & Only Reethi Rah is easily one of Maldives' most impressive and sumptuous private island experiences.

★Huvafen Fushi RESORT **$$$**
(☎664 4222; www.huvafenfushi.com; Nakatchafushi; r from US$2100; ❄📶🏊) Huvafen Fushi set a new standard for stylish, sophisticated luxury when it opened in 2005 and has inspired countless imitators elsewhere in Maldives and beyond. Understated and more than a little fabulous, Huvafen Fushi is all about unfussy luxury and hassle-free glamour, making the most of its gorgeous beaches and reef, its superb restaurants and world-class water villas.

The villas are thoroughly modern, with clean lines, lots of space and all featuring their own plunge pools, 40-inch plasma-screen TVs, Bose surround systems, media centres, espresso machines and remote-control everything. The water villas that have been so widely copied remain some of the most impressive in the country, each with its own plunge pool and enclosed deck overlooking the sea, with access to the lagoon down a staircase.

Despite this, the atmosphere within the resort is informal and relaxed, with no reception and most things being arranged by the thakuru (butler) in-room. There's an impressive array of dining options: Celsius for international, Feeling Koi for izakaya-style Japanese cooking and Forno for Neapolitan pizza and pasta. There's also Vinum, one of the largest wine cellars in Maldives, and the funky sand-floored UMBar by the enormous infinity pool.

The gorgeous Lime Spa has an amazing underwater treatment room, so you can be massaged while schools of fish swim by the windows.

There's also a gym, diving and water-sports centres, plus three individually designed dhonis moored in the lagoon that guests can book to stay on for a night or two during their visit.

Manta rays show up at 5pm each day for feeding: an unforgettable sight!

Four Seasons Resort Maldives at Kuda Huraa RESORT **$$$**
(☎664 4888; www.fourseasons.com/maldiveskh; Kuda Huraa; r from US$1485;) The smaller of the two Four Seasons properties in Maldives, Four Seasons Kuda Huraa is also the more intimate and laidback. The style here is that of a luxurious Maldivian village, and after its refurbishment a few years ago, it's now looking superb. The beaches on the island are lovely and there are two gorgeous pools.

The charming rooms range from beach bungalows with quaint brick walls and high thatched roofs to glamorous water villas on the far side of the resort. The furnishings combine tropical luxury with modern design and are sleek and attractive, while all room categories now have private plunge pools.

The highlight of the resort is its sublime food, with four superb restaurants, two bars serving small plates and both in-villa and private dining experiences. The exquisite Indian cuisine served at Baraabaru and the delicious clay-oven-baked pizzas at Reef Club should absolutely not be missed.

The spa is on a smaller island a short boat ride across the lagoon. The trip is done on a mini-dhoni that goes back and forth whenever guests want to get there. A kids club and a teens club are both free and children are generally welcomed and made a fuss of wherever they go on the island, so this is a great option for a high-end family holiday.

All non-motorised water sports are free, some 40 dive sites are visited by the dive school and the gym is excellent.

GREEN GASFINOLHU

Tiny Gasfinolhu island, just south of North Male Atoll's capital Thulusdhoo, was the country's first carbon-neutral resort island, becoming so in 2015 to a flurry of press interest. It managed this through the installation of 6500 sq m of solar panels, allowing it to run on 100% solar power, which it produces at almost two times the amount needed to meet peak demand. While the island retains a diesel generator to step in during excessive periods of overcast skies and bad weather, it normally uses them very sparingly. Plans for the future include a zero-waste management system and reuse of chilled water in the island's air conditioning, both important innovations in Maldives' notoriously environmentally unsustainable resorts. While its environmental credentials are impressive, the resort – Mahureva – is exclusively booked out by Italian travel agents.

Baros RESORT **$$$**
(☎664 2672; www.baros.com; Baros; r from US$1112;) Understated, sophisticated class jumps out at you from the moment you arrive and see Baros' impressive fine-dining restaurant and cocktail bar Lighthouse, which has a shapely circus-tent roof and the feel of an exclusive yacht club. This is the centrepiece of the resort and the calling card for a place that offers classic relaxation and superb service.

Other dining can be had at the far less formal Cayenne Grill overlooking the reef, where you can have your food cooked any way you choose by the fleet of chefs, or the all-day poolside Lime Restaurant, where buffet breakfasts and à la carte lunch and dinner are served. All guests are on a bed-and-breakfast basis, allowing them to enjoy the variety of eating opportunities throughout their stay (although this does add up quickly, of course).

The atmosphere is intimate and quiet, with children under six not allowed. There's 'gentle' jazz and Maldivian music three times a week, and that's about the scope of the nightlife. There is diving, snorkelling and swimming, and a Serena spa that is popular with couples. The three room categories on the island are all beautiful. Even the standard 'deluxe villa' is a refined 89-sq-m structure with a sumptuous outdoor shower and garden, while the 30 water villas are excellent. Many villas now have plunge pools, and all enjoy direct access to the lagoon and a sun terrace.

Baros is one of many upmarket resorts that has made a conscious decision not to have a swimming pool. It's an excellent resort and has rightly earned a loyal following. This is a great choice for a luxurious, tranquil and romantic getaway.

Banyan Tree Vabbinfaru RESORT $$$
(☎664 3147; www.banyantree.com; Vabbinfaru; r from US$950;) Banyan Tree's only Maldives resort boasts beautiful wide beaches on a lovely circular island far enough from Male to feel like a true desert island experience. The island offers a refreshing take on the top-end experience, a combination of romantic destination, escape and ecotourism project that is extremely quiet and popular with honeymooners and couples.

While certainly aimed at the luxury market, Banyan Tree is not at the heady heights of some of its competitors who charge at least twice as much for a room. In fact, given that many packages are either full board or all inclusive, this works out as relatively good value for money.

There's good snorkelling on the house reef and good diving a short distance away on the atoll edge, as well as a gym and a water-sports centre. Banyan Tree was one of the first resorts to have a marine laboratory on the island, and guests are able to help out in various capacities – including planting their own coral in the coral garden and monitoring the juvenile sharks and turtles kept under observation in cages just off the island shore.

The restaurant and bar are both casually elegant, open-sided spaces with sand floors and quality furniture, and the buffet meals cater to all tastes, though lack of choice in dining options might annoy some. For special meals, in-villa dining and sandbank dining are both available.

A spa with Thai-trained therapists offers a full range of exotic treatments, and all 48 villas have plunge pools, although there is no main pool. Angsana Ihuru, Banyan Tree's 'little sister' resort, is just across a small channel next door – a boat goes back and forth every two hours, allowing guests at each resort to enjoy the other's facilities.

Guesthouses

★**Coke's Beach** GUESTHOUSE $
(☎760 2232; www.cokesbeach.com; Thulusdhoo; s/d from US$96/110;) This five-room guesthouse right on the beach is perfectly located for two of the country's best surfing spots (best between March and September), one of which, the eponymous Coke's (p75), is quite literally on the doorstep. The rooms are simple but spotless and there's a large dining table for communal meals and a friendly backpacker vibe to the whole place.

Canopus Retreats Thulusdhoo GUESTHOUSE $
(☎987 8833; www.canopusretreats.com; Thulusdhoo; r from US$115;) A popular and innovative guesthouse on the surfing island of Thulusdhoo, Canopus Retreats makes an effort to help its guests mix with locals and make sure they see more than just the beach on the doorstep. The 12 rooms are comfortable and stylish with modern bathrooms. Most have sea views and balconies and breakfast is served on the beach.

Happy Life Maldives Lodge GUESTHOUSE $
(☎977 4151; www.happylifemaldives.com; Dhiffushi; s/d US$66/92;) On one of North Male Atoll's most pleasant inhabited islands, this friendly guesthouse has four comfortable rooms, all of which have open-air bathrooms and one of which enjoys sea views. The beach is a short walk away, and it's bikini, meaning you can swim without offending local sensibilities. Meals are good, and there's an impressive list of activities.

Getting There & Away

Nearly all resorts in North Male Atoll collect their guests from the airport by launch, as even the furthest island is less than an hour away. All the inhabited islands are connected by public ferry from Male's **Villingili Ferry Terminal** (p70) as well as private services that leave from the jetties along the island's northern edge.

Kaashidhoo

The island of Kaashidhoo is way out by itself, in a channel north of North Male Atoll. The island has a clinic, a secondary school and over 1800 people, which makes it one of the most populous in Kaafu. Some of the ruins here are believed to be remains of an old Buddhist temple.

Local crops include watermelon, lemon, banana, cucumber and zucchini, but the island is best known for its raa – the 'palm toddy' made from the sap of a palm tree, drunk fresh or slightly fermented.

Local boats going to or from the Northern Atolls sometimes shelter in the lagoon in Kaashidhoo in bad weather. Dive boats on longer trips might stop to dive at Kaashidhoo East Faru, a good place to see large pelagic marine life. There's one guesthouse on the island at present, and more are planned.

To reach Kaashidhoo, take public ferry 307, which leaves Male's New Harbour (p70) at 11am Sunday, Tuesday and Thursday, arriving in Kaashidhoo at 5pm.

From Kaashidhoo, boats leave for Male every Saturday, Monday and Wednesday at 7am and arrive in Male at 1pm.

Gaafaru Falhu

This small atoll has just one island, also called Gaafaru, with a population of 1100 and a couple of guesthouses. The channel to the north of the atoll, Kaashidhoo Kuda Kandu, has long been a shipping lane, and several vessels have veered off course and ended up on the hidden reefs of Gaafaru Falhu.

There are three diveable wrecks – *SS Seagull* (1879), *Erlangen* (1894) and *Lady Christine* (1974). None is anywhere near intact, but the remains all have good coral growth and plentiful fish.

Dive trips are possible from the nearby resorts of Oblu by Atmosphere at Helengeli (p77) and Smartline Eriyadu (p81), as well as from Gaafaru itself and from live-aboard dive boats.

To reach Gaafaru, take public ferry 307, which leaves Male's New Harbour (p70) at 11am Sunday, Tuesday and Thursday, arriving in Gaafaru at 2.45pm. From Gaafaru, boats leave for Male every Saturday, Monday and Wednesday at 9.15am and arrive in Male at 1pm.

South Male Atoll

Crossing the Vaadhoo Kandu, the choppy channel between North and South Male Atolls, you'll notice that South Male Atoll has a very different feel from its busy northern neighbour.

This is partly due to the lack of people – there are only three inhabited islands here, all of which have relatively small populations – and partly to do with the fact that the uninhabited islands are spread out, giving an immediate sense of remoteness.

This is not likely to be the case for long, however, with the massive new Crossroads development under construction at the time of writing. This US$680 million project will create eight new interconnected resorts on a chain of man-made islands reclaimed from the Embudhoo Lagoon.

Already boasting the most successful guesthouse island in the country, Maafushi, South Male Atoll, it seems, is also going to be home to Maldives' first mega-resort.

Sights

From Male's New Harbour (p70), public ferry 309 leaves daily except Monday and Friday at 3pm bound for Guraidhoo and Gulhi. Ferries back to Male leave early in the morning.

Guraidhoo ISLAND

Guraidhoo enjoys good anchorage and is a busy port used by both fishing dhonis and passing safari boats. Sultans from Male sought refuge here during rebellions from as early as the 17th century; today it's popular with budget travellers who stay at the cheap guesthouses, and with visitors from nearby resorts – it's actually possible to walk across the lagoon to the island resort of Kandooma at low tide!

Gulhi ISLAND

The island of Gulhi, north of Maafushi, is not large but is inhabited by around 900 people. Fishing is the main activity, and there's also a small shipyard and a couple of guesthouses.

Activities

Diving

Some of the best dive sites are around the Vaadhoo Kandu, which funnels a huge volume of water between the North and South Male Atolls.

Embudhoo Express DIVING

(Map p42) Embudhoo Express is a 2km drift dive through the Embudhoo Kandu, which is a Protected Marine Area. With the current running in, rays, Napoleon wrasse and sharks often congregate around the entrance. The current carries divers along a wall with overhangs and a big cave. The current strength can make for a demanding dive, but the rewards are worth it.

Kuda Giri DIVING

(Map p42) The attraction of Kuda Giri is the hulk of a small freight ship, deliberately sunk here to create an artificial reef. Sponges and cup corals are growing on the wreck, and it provides a home for large schools of fish. Sheltered from strong currents, this is a good site for beginners and for night dives.

Velassaru Caves DIVING

(Map p42) The rugged Velassaru Caves and overhangs, on the steep wall of the Vaadhoo Kandu, have very attractive coral growth. You may see sharks, turtles and rays on the bottom at around 30m. This dive is not for beginners, but if the current isn't too strong there's excellent snorkelling on the reef edge.

Surfing

There is also some excellent surfing here, with four stand-out breaks to test your virtuosity.

Twin Peaks (Map p42) An unpredictable left-hand break that can only be reached by boat, rarely busy and with some of the biggest swell in the atoll.

Natives (Map p42) Also called Foxys, this 150m-long spot just off the side of Kandooma is a fast right-hand wave that breaks over the reef.

Rip Tides (Map p42) A challenging and fast right-hander breaking for 150m on a reef in the middle of a channel south of Guraidhoo; come by boat for excellent shortboarding and longboarding.

Guru's (Map p42) Just off the island of Gulhi, Guru's is a fun little left-hander where aerials are sometimes possible depending on the conditions.

Sleeping

South Male Atoll is the centre of Maldives' independent tourism industry, with Maafushi hosting over 50 guesthouses and still more being built. But that's far from all: there are also around 20 resorts here, including some of the very best and longest-established in the country.

Resorts

Embudu Village RESORT $
(☎664 0063; www.embudu.com; Emboodhoo; full board s/d from US$178/295; ❄📶) Embudu Village is a very popular budget resort with a heavy focus on divers and couples. It's as relaxed as its sand-floor reception suggests, and has a thoroughly unpretentious atmosphere. This is one of the best-value resorts in the country, and while it's not particularly charming or rustic, it does have lots going for it as a budget destination.

The island itself has some gorgeous beaches, is thickly vegetated and has a very accessible house reef. Best of all is the deep and wide sandbank at one end of the island, which is lapped by the turquoise lagoon. All accommodation is on a full-board basis, with buffet meals that manage to be varied and of good quality even at this price.

The standard beach villas were recently renovated and now have air-con and hot water as well as attractive if simple furnishings. There are also 16 water villas, which are pleasant and spacious, though now a little in need of refreshment since they were built over a decade ago. There's a Serena spa and water-sports equipment is available.

Diverland runs the popular diving program here, with over 90 different sites in the nearby area. Diving is excellent value and there are discounts for multidive packages. If you're not looking for luxury but an unpretentious and affordable beach-and-diving holiday with access to alcohol and no worries about covering up for locals, Embudu Village is an excellent choice.

Biyadhoo Island Resort RESORT $
(☎333 6611; www.biyadhoo.com; Biyadhoo; full board s/d US$316/322; ❄📶) Attractive Biyadhoo has thick foliage, high palms and lovely beaches in parts. It attracts a crowd of loyal divers, many of whom are repeat visitors and love the good deals for full-board packages and diving available here. It's also a popular day-trip destination for independent travellers staying on Maafushi who want some alcohol and a change of scene.

All 96 rooms are standards, housed in 16-room, two-storey blocks. All have minibars, little patios and dark wooden furniture, but don't expect any feeling of luxury. Request a room on the west side of the island for beach proximity – beaches on the east side have been badly affected by erosion and as such are not good for sunbathing, often visibly covered in sandbags. While the main beach on the west side is wide and flat, it can get crowded as the small island accommodates a lot of visitors.

The in-house dive operation charges guests at the end of their stay for the best overall package based on the number of dives they did, so there's no need to book anything in advance. Most people here are on full-board deals, with buffets served up for each meal in the resort's one restaurant. Other facilities include a football pitch, badminton and volleyball, and a spa.

The resort has a friendly and relaxed feel and won't disappoint anyone looking for a good-value base for diving.

★ **Rihiveli by Castaway Hotels & Escapes** RESORT $$
(☎664 1994; www.rihivelimaldives.com; Mahaana Elhi Huraa; r US$396; 📶) One of Maldives' less mainstream resorts, Rihiveli has almost nothing in common with islands pitched at package tourists, and remains true to the spirit of its French founder, who set the

South Male Atoll

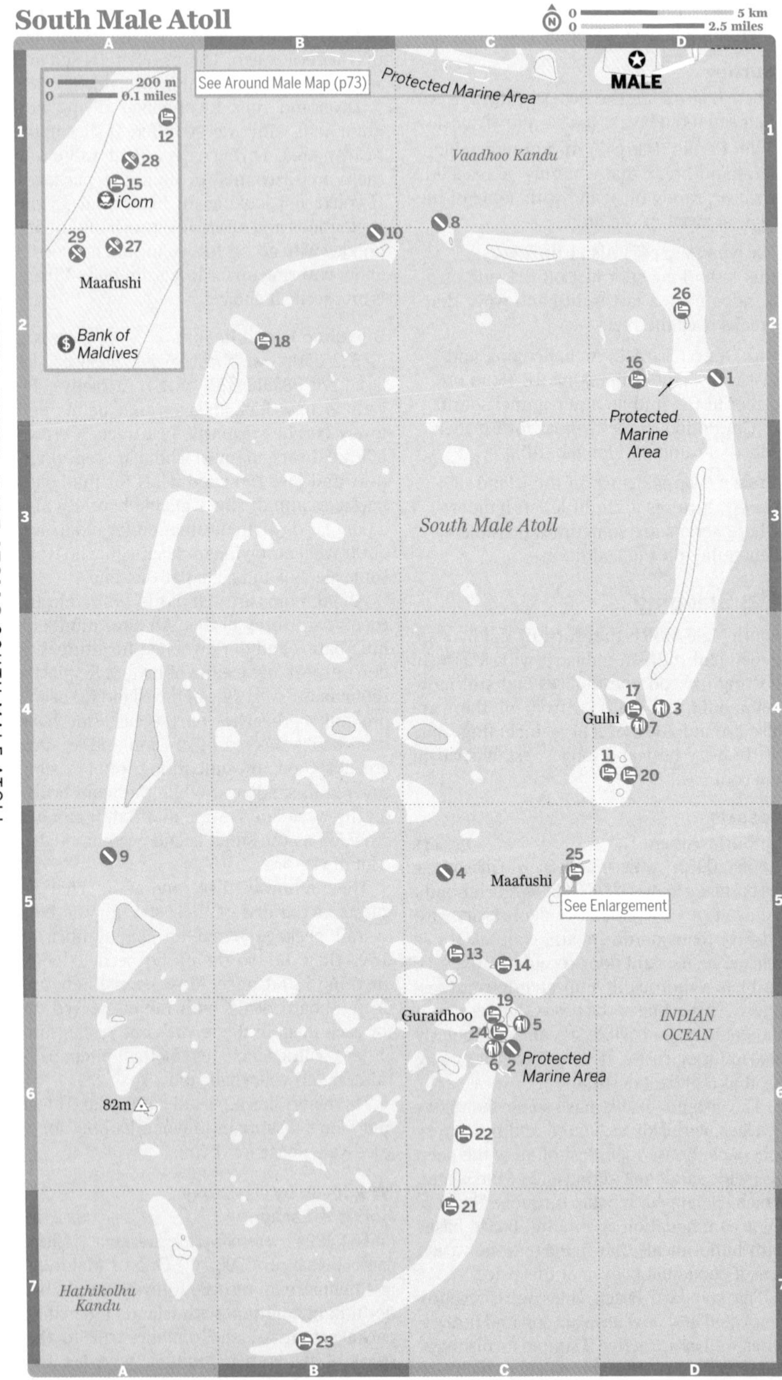

0 5 km
0 2.5 miles
0 200 m
0 0.1 miles
See Around Male Map (p73)
Protected Marine Area
MALE
Vaadhoo Kandu
12
28
15
iCom
29
27
Maafushi
Bank of Maldives
10
8
26
18
16
1
Protected Marine Area
South Male Atoll
17
3
Gulhi
7
11
20
9
25
4
Maafushi
See Enlargement
13
14
19
Guraidhoo
5
24
6
2
Protected Marine Area
INDIAN OCEAN
82m
22
21
Hathikolhu Kandu
23

South Male Atoll

Activities, Courses & Tours		17 Gurus Maldives	D4
1 Embudhoo Express	D2	18 Jumeirah Vittaveli	B2
2 Guraidhoo Kandu	C6	Kaani Village & Spa	(see 15)
3 Guru's	D4	19 Medhufaru Inn	C6
4 Kuda Giri	C5	20 Naladhu Private Island	D4
5 Natives	C6	21 Olhuveli Beach & Spa	C7
6 Rip Tides	C6	22 OZEN by Atmosphere at Maadhoo	C6
7 Twin Peaks	D4	23 Rihiveli by Castaway Hotels & Escapes	B7
8 Vaadhoo Caves	C1	24 Rip Tide Vacation Inn	C6
9 Vaagali Caves	A5	Shadow Palm Hotel	(see 12)
10 Velassaru Caves	B2	25 Stingray Beach Inn	C5
Sleeping		26 Taj Exotica	D2
11 Anantara Dhigu & Anantara Veli	D4	**Eating**	
12 Arena Beach Hotel	A1	27 FineBake by Suzy	A2
13 Biyadhoo Island Resort	C5	28 Pizza & Pasta Mamma Mia	A1
14 Cocoa Island by COMO	C5	29 Summer Kitchen & Bakery	A2
15 Crystal Sands	A1		
16 Embudu Village	D2		

place up in the 1980s as a refuge. This was the first resort to use the now ubiquitous 'no news, no shoes' phrase, and you'll quickly understand why.

Accommodation consists of just 48 sea-facing bungalows, all built in a rustic style from coral stone and with traditional thatched roofs. They have all the basics for comfort such as hot water, but nothing considered superfluous, such as air-con, fridges, phones or a TV. This is the secret of its success and also the reason Rihiveli will never be overrun. That said, it has a loyal crowd of repeaters, many who have been coming for years.

The open-air bar has a sand floor and shady trees overhead, while the restaurant is built over the lagoon and has a lovely view as well as simple but tasty food. A conch shell is blown to call guests to meals, and everyone is invited to take tea with the staff daily at 5.30pm: yes, this is not your typical Maldivian resort!

The usual water sports and tennis are all included in the room price, as is a daily excursion, so there's no chance of boredom here. You can wade across the lagoon to two uninhabited islands where the resort organises regular barbecue lunches. Frequent boat trips to other reefs make up for the lack of snorkelling sites next to the resort. The main diving destinations are around nearby Hathikolhu Kandu, and there's a small wreck to explore.

With its relaxed ambience, perfect white-sand beaches and natural appeal, Rihiveli is a unique and special resort for those who appreciate the simple things in life and want a totally laidback and unfussy beach-and-activities holiday.

Olhuveli Beach & Spa RESORT **$$**

(☎664 2788; www.olhuvelimaldives.com; Olhuveli; all-inclusive r from US$550; ❄ 📶 🏊) Olhuveli is a big, midrange resort that somehow manages to feel very intimate. This is mainly due to the relatively large size of the island, which accommodates its 129 rooms without feeling crowded, but also due to the clever use of space.

The beaches on both sides of the island are very attractive, and Olhuveli understandably has many repeat visitors.

The rooms are spread along the beaches in free-standing two-level blocks, one room below and one above. They are tastefully done, furnished throughout with dark-wood four-poster beds, all featuring balconies or patios that lead straight out to the sea. There are also two rings of quietly stylish water villas stretching over the lagoon.

Snorkelling is excellent off the end of the jetty, at the edge of the reef, where turtles are common. The dive school runs drift dives in nearby channels, as well as wreck and night dives.

Food is served at the main restaurant buffet, but there are also alternatives such as pan-Asian restaurant Four Spices, the poolside Island Pizza and the beachfront Lagoon Restaurant.

Overall, Olhuveli offers excellent value. It's a great compromise between budget prices and high standards, and between romance and activities.

★**Jumeirah Vittaveli** RESORT **$$$**
(☎664 2020; www.jumeirah.com; Bolifushi; r from $1139; ❄📶🏊) Meaning 'vastness of space' in Dhivehi, Jumeirah Vittaveli is actually half created from reclaimed land, though you'd never guess that from looking at it. It's a beautiful place, with sumptuous white beaches and plentiful thick vegetation. However, its real draw is its rooms, which are nothing short of astonishingly palatial and gorgeously decorated, bringing the best of Dubai to Maldives.

Even the starting category, the Beach Villa, is a vast 184 sq m, and all rooms have their own private swimming pools as standard, up to and including the 800-sq-m Presidential Suite, which is astoundingly luxurious.

The most notable rooms are the Ocean Suites, six of which stand independent of each other over the reef, and can only be reached by dhoni.

These are popular with those seeking total privacy, though arguably the Beach Villas on the main island are more charming, surrounded as they are by a swimming pool moat on three sides. As well as being spacious, rooms are tall, with wonderful beamed ceilings, marble floors and distinctive thatched roofs, while decor combines timeless tradition with modern touches such as flat-screen TVs, media centres and rain showers.

The island enjoys gorgeous stretches of beach, while the public areas are also impressive, all crafted in timber and sublimely decorated.

Facilities on the island include the magnificent over-water Talise Spa, a gym, a water-sports centre and a very smart diving centre. The resort has two L-shaped communal pools, one for families, the other restricted to adults, so there's peace and quiet even though children are more than welcome on the island, as the excellent kids club shows.

There are three restaurants to choose from: Swarna for Indian cuisine; Mediterranean at Fenesse; and steak and seafood at the candlelit MU Beach Bar & Grill. Altogether this is one of the smartest and luxurious resorts in the country, and is a perfect choice for a high-end romantic break.

★**Cocoa Island by COMO** RESORT **$$$**
(☎664 1818; www.comohotels.com/cocoaisland; Makunufushi; r from US$1775; ❄📶🏊) This wonderful place was an early Maldivian resort, and since its lavish refit at the hands of COMO, Cocoa Island has consistently impressed with its style and service. Indeed, this is one of the very few resorts that manages to get everything so right with such little fuss: a combination of perfect beaches, beautiful rooms, excellent food and superb staff.

First of all, the small island has no rooms on it at all – they're all built over water in a shape that mirrors that of the island itself. And what rooms they are – built in the shape of traditional Maldivian dhoni boats – all clean lines, white cotton and dark wood. Newer two-floor loft villas are clad in white timbers and are even more stunning. Other great touches include outdoor showers, direct sea access from the rooms, and gorgeous COMO Shambhala bathroom products.

On the island proper there is nothing superfluous. A large infinity pool, cracking beaches the entire way around, a gorgeous à la carte restaurant with a large range of dishes, a smart cocktail bar, a sumptuous spa, a gym, and the excellent and friendly dive centre. Everything is totally luxurious, but nothing is over the top.

All in all, a great recommendation for unpretentious and low-key luxury that will keep even the most demanding guests happy.

Taj Exotica RESORT **$$$**
(☎664 2200; www.tajhotels.com; Emboodhu Finolhu; r from US$1120; ❄📶🏊) Within easy striking distance of the airport, yet still feeling wonderfully secluded and exclusive, this

MORE SOUTH MALE ATOLL DIVES

There are many other rewarding dive sites in South Male Atoll. Consider the following:

Vaagali Caves (Map p42) A good unexposed dive, with caves at around 15m, filled with sponges and soft corals, and abundant fish atop the reef.

Vaadhoo Caves (Map p42) Small caves, plus a bigger one with a swim-through tunnel, home to excellent soft corals, gorgonians, jackfish and the odd eagle ray.

Guraidhoo Kandu (Map p42) Split into two channels, with numerous reef fish, larger pelagics near the entrance and mantas when the current is running out.

elegant, understated resort is the flagship of the Indian Taj Group in Maldives and is all about quiet luxury and indulgence. Its super-stylish public areas and gorgeous rooms make it perfectly suited to romantic beach holidays, and as such it is very popular with honeymooners.

The island here is long and thin, with a beach on the lagoon side and water villas on the atoll edge. All categories of rooms are very smart and are decorated with Asian flair and colour, nearly all of them with their own plunge pools overlooking one of the white-sand beaches.

The public areas include a library, a well-stocked games room, a gorgeous infinity pool and, at the far end of the island, the Jiva Spa. There's a gym and free yoga classes each morning.

Taj Exotica was one of the original pioneers of fine à la carte dining in Maldives and it's safe to say you'll eat excellently here, with everything ordered and individually cooked from a sumptuous and expensive menu. This is one place where full board would come in handy – the meals here are far from budget – but with four fabulous restaurants to choose from, you'll almost certainly never get bored.

Overall this small but beautifully realised island is a real treat for honeymooners or couples looking for a perfect high-style but utterly tranquil escape.

OZEN by Atmosphere at Maadhoo RESORT **$$$**
(☎400 2222; www.ozen-maadhoo.com; Maadhoo; all-inclusive r US$1950; ❄📶🏊) The smartest of the three OZEN resorts that have recently opened in Maldives, Maadhoo really means what it says when it terms itself a luxury all-inclusive – once you've paid your hefty hotel room price, everything is free, including the generously stocked minibar whose contents you choose. It's a fabulous place, with gorgeous rooms, lovely beaches and superb restaurants.

While luxury all-inclusives have never quite worked in Maldives, this one is perhaps the best one yet. However, a lot here depends on whether you're staying four nights or more, after which lots more becomes free, including a spa treatment and diving.

Luxury treatment starts with the airport transfer, which is done on an impressively plush speedboat fitted out like a private jet. On arrival in your room, you're given a foot massage, and things just get better from there on in.

People who like to eat and drink a lot will probably find this an ideal place to come, as not only do you get endless cocktails and food, but you can even tell your personal butler which spirits and wines to place in your minibar each day – all at no extra cost. The resort is centred on its large infinity pool and busy bar area, though if you want peace and quiet, take a dip in the far more private pool at the glamorous spa.

The rooms are wonderful; both beach villas and water villas are imaginatively designed, stuffed full of tasteful *objets d'art* and enlivened by bright fabrics. All the beach villas and half of the water villas have plunge pools. They all feature Segafredo coffee makers, vast bathrooms and direct sea access.

Food is definitely a highlight here: there's the buffet & à la carte–combined main restaurant The Palms, IndoCeylon serving South Asian specialities and Peking, a high-style Chinese restaurant.

There's also fine dining underwater at M6m, a seafood restaurant that has a seven-course set menu for lunch and dinner. It's massively popular and most guests will need to reserve before arriving at the resort to guarantee getting a table.

The kids club here is fabulous and is the only one we've ever seen with its own beach as well as a pool. Best of all, much of the island is still rather wild and as yet undeveloped, giving you the luxury of long walks along the beach.

Overall, it's hard to fault this impressive place with its fantastic staff, generous all-inclusive plans and sumptuous rooms.

Naladhu Private Island RESORT **$$$**
(☎664 4105; www.naladhu.anantara.com; Naladhu; r from US$1625; ❄📶🏊) Naladhu is the most exclusive of three resorts run by Thai group Anantara on three separate islands around a stunningly beautiful lagoon.

You get the best of both worlds here; while you're totally secluded on a private island with just 18 villas on it, you also have the option to use the facilities of the other, far larger **resorts** (☎664 4100; www.anantara.com; Dhigu & Veli; r from US$615; ❄📶🏊).

The concept here is simple: this is an exclusive refuge for those who want to remain unseen and totally private. The villas are sumptuous, with huge private pools and either lagoon access in the six beach houses or views to the ocean in the ocean houses. The top-category room here is the two-bedroom residence, a totally private mansion for utter seclusion.

The island has its own large pool, a spa and the smart Living Room restaurant on the beach, but if you want to explore different restaurants, swim on different beaches, go diving or use any of the other facilities you'd associate with bigger resorts, you can simply walk across the bridge to Veli, or take a boat to Digu, the other two islands run by Anantara here. Needless to say, the bridge to Veli is for the exclusive use of Naladhu guests, and accommodates one-way traffic only.

Consistently given awards, this secluded bolthole gets rave reviews from its loyal band of glamorous customers.

Guesthouses

Medhufaru Inn GUESTHOUSE **$**
(☎777 6934; www.medhufaruinn.com; Guraidhoo; r from US$67; ❄📶) Possibly the most charming accommodation on Guraidhoo, the Medhufaru Inn is a stylish house with a balcony running along its first floor overlooking a quiet sand-floored courtyard. Decoration is thoughtful and interesting with some almost boutique-hotel touches in the six rooms; the owner is exceptionally friendly and helpful. Beaches on Guraidhoo aren't amazing, but excursions are also available.

Gurus Maldives GUESTHOUSE **$**
(☎783 9160[]; www.gurusmaldives.com; Gulhi; r US$105; ❄📶) The best choice on the charming island of Gulhi is this wonderful bolthole, which is just metres from a shimmering white-sand bikini beach. The rooms are simple, clean and comfortable with satellite TV and minibars, and guests are welcome to use the guesthouse kitchen themselves, or they can just order meals. A great alternative to Maafushi.

Rip Tide Vacation Inn GUESTHOUSE **$**
(☎777 6272; www.guesthouses-in-maldives.com; Guraidhoo; s/d US$52/57; ❄📶) The first guesthouse established on Guraidhoo is this seven-room place on the beach facing a resort across a shallow lagoon. The rooms are comfortable with large bathrooms and satellite TVs, and there's a pleasant sand-floored restaurant. It remains good value, despite all the competition from the dozens of other guesthouses that have proliferated here in the past few years.

ℹ Getting There & Away

All resorts in South Male Atoll collect their guests from the airport by speedboat, as even the furthest island is only an hour away. All the inhabited islands can be reached by public ferry from Male's **Villingili Ferry Terminal** (p70). Ferries go in both directions every day except Friday. There are also private speedboat services offered to all three islands from both Male and the airport. These also run on Fridays.

Maafushi

POP 3030

The centre of Maldives' independent travel scene, the island of Maafushi has undergone seismic change since the first guesthouses opened here in 2010, and it now has over 50 hotels and guesthouses. It is easily Maldives' most cosmopolitan and progressive inhabited island, and there's a bikini beach and a very competitive diving and excursions market.

You can even leave the island to drink alcohol on floating bars just outside the harbour, or take a day trip to one of the many nearby resorts that welcome day guests in search of alcohol, pork and a more relaxed attitude to semi-clad sunbathers.

Maafushi may not be the most attractive island, with only a few good beaches that tend to get crowded, but it's well located for dozens of day trips and, quite frankly, the sheer amount of guesthouse competition keeps prices affordable. Welcome to Maldives for backpackers.

Activities

Maafushi has some of the most competitively priced activities in the country on offer, from cheap diving, snorkelling trips and windsurfing to sports fishing, kitesurfing and dolphin-watching trips. There's a huge number of outlets concentrated around the northern end of the island near the beaches, and all guesthouses arrange activities.

Sleeping

★**Kaani Village & Spa** HOTEL **$**
(☎911 3626; www.kaanivillage.com; Maafushi; r US$124; ❄📶🏊) This sleekly put together place is impressive, and unique mainly for its great courtyard pool, which allows guests to swim without offending local sensibilities, something almost no other guesthouse on Maafushi can do. The rooms, over two stories facing the pool, are stylish, comfortable and

modern with good bathrooms. There's even a small spa here too: it's almost a resort!

Crystal Sands HOTEL $
(☎779 0660; www.crystalsands.mv; Maafushi; r from US$99; ❄📶) This three-storey building is right opposite the port where you arrive on Maafushi, and it's very much a sleek hotel rather than a guesthouse. The 18 large, bright and impressively designed rooms, complete with rain showers and walk-out balconies with sea views, are a glamorous and comfortable place to relax. There's also a fabulous roof terrace for sunbathing.

Downstairs the Symphony Lagoon restaurant has a big menu with international cuisine and does a buffet dinner each night.

Arena Beach Hotel HOTEL $
(☎793 3231; www.arenabeachmaldives.com; Maafushi; r from US$205; ❄📶) The cream of the crop on Maafushi, this high-rise place has an enviable location within the screened-off confines of the bikini beach, where you're free to frolic semi-clad without offending. The 19 rooms all have balconies (many enjoying great views), safes, minibars and TVs. Staff are friendly and there's a decidedly laid-back vibe to the beach restaurant outside.

Stingray Beach Inn GUESTHOUSE $
(☎778 1068; www.stingraybeachinn.com; Maafushi; s/d incl breakfast US$55/65; ❄📶) Stingray Beach was the first guesthouse in Maafushi, and this rustic and quiet courtyard place remains one of the best deals on the island. There are 10 timber-floored rooms here built around a sandy courtyard and while they're on the small side and are a little dark, they do have large beds and share use of a Jacuzzi.

Shadow Palm Hotel GUESTHOUSE $
(☎910 0109; www.shadowpalm.com; Maafushi; r from US$85; ❄📶) This great-value spot is just moments from the beach and has a very friendly backpacker vibe to it. Tile floored rooms are sparklingly clean and have bright fabrics and wall decorations. The hotel specialises in snorkelling trips – which it also offers to nonguests – and these are some of the best available on the island.

Eating

A number of boats with alcohol licenses regularly visit the island and weigh anchor just outside the harbour and will collect visitors who want to come for a drink. You'll often be given a flyer on the main road.

Summer Kitchen & Bakery INTERNATIONAL $
(Maafushi; mains Rf60-180; ⏲7am-midnight; 📶) This friendly Maldivian-Chinese place offers a choice of outdoor dining in a relaxed sandy area facing the harbour, or a brightly lit interior where you can watch your food being prepared and choose desserts and cakes from a well-supplied display counter. The menu is predominantly Chinese and is very tasty, though there's also a smaller Western menu. Portions are big.

FineBake by Suzy BAKERY $
(www.bysuzy.com; Maafushi; snacks from Rf20; ⏲7am-7pm Sat-Thu, 2-7pm Fri) This lovely little locally run bakery is the brainchild of Suzy, who learned how to bake in Sri Lanka. It's a simple, cheap and unfussy place on Maafushi's main street, and is a great spot to get a simple lunch or afternoon snack.

Pizza & Pasta Mamma Mia ITALIAN $
(Maafushi; pizza Rf50-120; ⏲9am-midnight) This simple sand-floor place does surprisingly excellent wood-fire-oven pizza in a range of flavours. It also has a coffee shop on one side of it, run by the same people.

Information

MONEY

There is a **Bank of Maldives** bank (Map p88) with two ATMs on the island.

Getting There & Away

Maafushi is well connected to both Male and the airport. The cheapest option to get between the two is the daily public ferry (Rf 30, 1½ hours) leaving Maafushi every morning except Friday at 7.30am.

The same ferry leaves Male's **New Harbour** (p70) at 3pm each afternoon except Friday. There's a second sailing in each direction on Monday, Wednesday and Saturday – this leaves Male at 10am and Maafushi at 12.30pm.

Private speedboat transfers (Rf385, 40 minutes) connect Maafushi to both Male's northern jetties (as opposed to the less conveniently located New Harbour) and then with the airport, making them a very popular and far faster way to make the journey.

There are multiple departures throughout the day, including on Friday. Enquire at your guesthouse as there are multiple companies, or just buy tickets from **iCom** (☎790 2069; www.icomtours.com) near the Maafushi dock.

Ari Atoll & Around

Includes ➡

Best Resorts

- W Maldives (p95)
- Mirihi (p101)
- Kandolhu Maldives (p97)
- Conrad Maldives Rangali Island (p101)
- Constance Halaveli Maldives (p97)

Best Guesthouses

- Boutique Beach (p102)
- Beach Villa Ukulhas (p98)
- Casa Mia (p98)
- Thoddoo Retreat (p100)
- Liberty Guest House (p102)

Why Go?

Centred on a vast, sumptuous and inviting oval lagoon dotted with reefs, Ari Atoll sits to the west of the capital and is famed for its superb diving and stellar beaches. The nutrient-rich water that flows out to the open sea through large channels between the islands attracts many ocean-going creatures and divers from all over the world.

South Ari Atoll, a Protected Marine Area, remains one of the best places in the world to see whale sharks, which are spotted year-round on the outer reef, while North Ari Atoll is famous for its hammerhead sharks, although these are far more elusive and require deep diving to see. The small natural atoll of Rasdhoo, to Ari Atoll's northeast, and the single island of Thoddoo both host vibrant, growing guesthouse scenes that attract budget travellers looking for an affordable diving holiday.

When to Go

May–Dec The best time to dive or snorkel with amazing whale sharks.

Jan–Mar High season coincides with European winter; expect blue skies and high temperatures.

Dec–Apr This is prime hammerhead shark-spotting season in northern Ari Atoll.

North Ari Atoll

The top half of giant Ari Atoll, North Ari is a huge lagoon boasting alluring resorts and inhabited islands with fast-growing guesthouse scenes, as well as pristine desert islands. While there's no airport in this part of the atoll, it's well connected by speedboat and seaplane charter to Male. The islands of **Ukulhas** and **Mathiveri** are popular with backpackers and divers who want to spend time amid local communities.

Activities

North Ari has some great dive sites with prolific fish life. Top dives include:

Fish Head Also called Mushimasmingali Thila, this steep-sided coral outcrop has multi-level ledges and caves adorned with sea fans and black corals; prolific fish life includes fusiliers, large Napoleons, trevally, barracuda and plentiful grey-tip reef sharks.

Ellaidhoo House Reef Only accessible to Ellaidhoo Maldives guests, this excellent reef has a long wall just 25m from the beach, with sea fans, whip corals, schools of bannerfish, Napoleons, stingrays and morays and even a small wreck.

Orimas Thila Overhangs, caves, crevices, canyons and coral heads, with good growths of soft corals and sea fans, anemones and clown fish; also good for snorkellers.

Maaya Thila A classic round thila known for its resident white-tip reef sharks; caves and overhangs around it have lots of gorgonians, soft corals and schools of reef fish.

Fesdu Wreck A 30m trawler with a good covering of corals at a depth of 18-30m. Moray eels and grouper live inside the hull, which is easily entered and has good growths of soft corals and sponges.

Halaveli Wreck This 38m cargo ship was deliberately sunk in 1991 to provide a haven for reef fish, including friendly stingrays enticed here by regular feeding.

ARI ATOLL HIGHLIGHTS

Dhidhdhoo Beyru (p100) Swimming with giant whale sharks as they cruise along the surface of Ariadhoo Kandu.

Manta Reef (p100) Witnessing enormous alien-like rays at a giant feeding area and cleaning station between December and April.

Hammerhead Point (p98) Starting the day before dawn with a dive to see these magnificently weird creatures in Rasdhoo Atoll.

Fish Head Discovering Mushimasmingali Thila, one of Maldives' top dive sites, with dozens of sharks, amazing corals and impressive topography.

Dhigurah (p100) Yearning to get off the beaten track? Try this gorgeous inhabited island full of great guesthouses and superlative beaches.

Ukulhas Exploring one of Maldives' loveliest, best-looked-after and ecologically conscious inhabited islands.

Sleeping

Resorts

Ellaidhoo Maldives by Cinnamon RESORT **$**
(666 0669; www.cinnamonhotels.com; Ellaidhoo; r from US$336;) Ellaidhoo is the most hardcore diving destination in Maldives, with over 100 dive sites within a half-day trip. It has what many consider to be the country's finest house reef (quite an accolade given the competition!), with a 750m wall, lots of caves, corals, rich marine life and a small shipwreck. It's hard to choose a better base for divers.

There's also plenty for non-divers. The smart villa-style accommodation and large two-storey water villas are good deals for this price range. They're bright and well maintained, though all fairly simple, as you'd expect in a diving resort. Dining is by buffet and most guests are on all-inclusive or full-board packages.

With a fairly small beach, the island isn't the most picturesque in the country by a long shot, but it offers enough of an all-round holiday to attract non-divers and divers alike.

★**W Maldives** RESORT **$$$**
(666 2222; www.wretreatmaldives.com; Fesdhoo; r from US$1570;) W Maldives is sleek and imaginative, a boutique luxury island loaded with more casual cool than any other in the country. W manages to get it right on all levels – staff are informal and friendly, and the resort itself is stunning.

Tiny Fesdhoo island is simply gorgeous, with superb white-sand beaches and a great house reef packed with turtles, rays and reef

Ari Atoll & Around

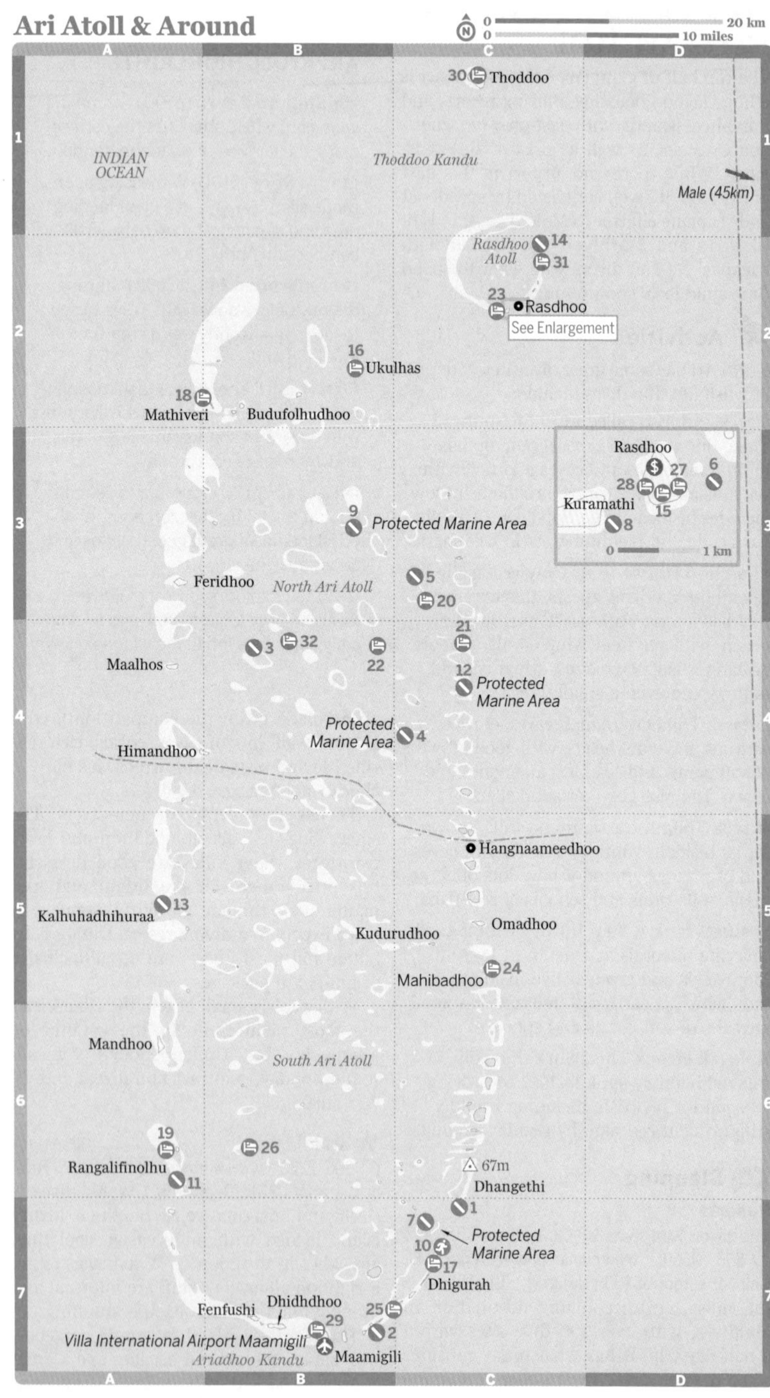

0 20 km
0 10 miles
A
B
C
D
1
2
3
4
5
6
7
30 Thoddoo
INDIAN OCEAN
Thoddoo Kandu
Male (45km)
Rasdhoo Atoll
14
31
23
Rasdhoo
See Enlargement
16
Ukulhas
18
Mathiveri
Budufolhudhoo
Rasdhoo
27
6
28
Kuramathi
15
8
0 1 km
9
Protected Marine Area
5
Feridhoo
North Ari Atoll
20
21
3
32
22
Maalhos
12
Protected Marine Area
Protected Marine Area
4
Himandhoo
Hangnaameedhoo
13
Kalhuhadhihuraa
Omadhoo
Kudurudhoo
24
Mahibadhoo
Mandhoo
South Ari Atoll
19
26
67m
Rangalifinolhu
11
Dhangethi
1
7
Protected Marine Area
10
17
Dhigurah
Fenfushi
Dhidhdhoo
25
29
2
Villa International Airport Maamigili
Ariadhoo Kandu
Maamigili

Ari Atoll & Around

Activities, Courses & Tours

1 Broken Rock ... C7
2 Dhidhdhoo Beyru ... B7
Ellaidhoo House Reef ... (see 21)
3 Fesdu Wreck ... B4
4 Fish Head ... C4
5 Halaveli Wreck ... C3
6 Hammerhead Point ... D3
7 Kudarah Thila ... C7
8 Kuramathi House Reef ... D3
9 Maaya Thila ... B3
10 Maldives Whale Shark Research Programme ... C7
11 Manta Reef ... A6
12 Orimas Thila ... C4
13 Panetone ... A5
14 Veligandu Kandu ... C2

Sleeping

15 Acqua Blu Rasdhoo ... D3
16 Beach Villa Ukulhas ... B2
17 Boutique Beach ... C7
18 Casa Mia ... A2
19 Conrad Maldives Rangali Island ... A6
20 Constance Halaveli Maldives ... C3
21 Ellaidhoo Maldives by Cinnamon ... C4
Island Vista Inn ... (see 16)
22 Kandolhu Maldives ... B4
23 Kuramathi Island Resort ... C2
24 Liberty Guest House ... C5
25 LUX* Maldives ... B7
26 Mirihi ... B6
27 Ras Beach Inn ... D3
28 Rasdhoo Island Inn ... D3
29 Shamar Guesthouse & Dive ... B7
30 Thoddoo Retreat ... C1
31 Veligandu Island Resort & Spa ... C2
32 W Maldives ... B4

sharks. On the island itself are the standard rooms – and even in the starting categories they're wonderful – each with its own private plunge pool and, perhaps their most charming feature, a thatched-roof 'viewing deck' above the room, complete with daybeds. Higher categories are over water, culminating in four vast suites that would satisfy even the most demanding Saudi prince. All rooms are staggeringly cool, with clean lines, Bose surround-sound systems, private plunge pools and huge private terraces.

The activities and facilities are just as good, from free non-motorised water sports and an excellent diving school to a superb spa that looks a world away from any other in Maldives. There's also the 15 Below nightclub (one of the few in the country and definitely the best looking). Add to this three excellent restaurants, three glamorous bars, a vast swimming pool and even a private desert island for guests to use, and it's easy to see why this is the choice of the discerning, wealthy and cool.

★Kandolhu Maldives RESORT **$$$**
(☎333 2200; www.kandolhu.com; Kandholhudhoo; r from US$1450; ❄📶🏊) This gorgeous addition is a refreshingly tiny place – there are just 30 villas – but it already has an army of honeymooners and romance-seekers as fans.

The circular island has beaches all the way around and is perched on top of an excellent house reef, making it ideal for luxurious relaxation. There are 11 water villas, four of which come with their own pools. The villas are gorgeous creations with huge bathrooms and big private terraces with direct water access. On the island itself are another 21 rooms, many of which either have their own pools or jacuzzis. Furnishings are contemporary and somewhat neutral, but feature clean lines and crisp linens. Nice touches include free GoPros left in each room so guests can record the amazing marine life while they snorkel.

Despite Kandolhu's diminutive size, there are four à la carte restaurants; choose from international all-day restaurant The Market, modern Mediterranean with a view at the raised Olive, and gorgeous sushi and sashimi at Banzai. The Ultimate Inclusions package allows guests to use any restaurant they choose for each meal, which makes it a good deal if you don't want to fret about extra costs adding up. Elsewhere on the island there's a dive school, water-sports centre, wonderful spa and a full range of excursions.

Constance Halaveli Maldives RESORT **$$$**
(☎666 7000; www.halaveli.com; Halaveli; r incl half board from US$1200; ❄📶🏊) This supremely luxurious resort is one of Ari Atoll's most popular honeymoon spots, and it's looking superb following a full renovation a few years ago. The small island has gorgeous white-sand beaches all around it, but its most obvious feature is the chain of water villas – larger than the island itself – protruding over the turquoise lagoon.

This is a romantic luxury resort, with lavish accommodation largely in 57 huge water villas, each of which has wood and marble flooring and traditional thatched roofs, plus a large plunge pool in black slate. There are also beach villas – which range in size and facilities – on Halaveli itself. The island suffers from bad erosion, and stone wavebreaks have been placed around the edges, which can rather detract from the idyll in parts.

The main buffet restaurant is supplemented by Jing, an overwater restaurant serving up Asian-European fusion, and Meeru, which offers simple grilled dishes on the beach. You'll also find a sumptuous spa, dive school, gym, tennis court, water-sports centre and kids club.

Guesthouses

★ **Beach Villa Ukulhas** GUESTHOUSE $
(☎789 4462; www.beachvillaukulhas.com; Ukulhas; r from US$325; ❄ 📶) These villas, just moments from the beach on gorgeous Ukulhas (p95), are a real step up from the usual guesthouse offerings, with vast rooms that are beautifully and originally decorated with lots of natural wood furnishings. The villas are set amid well-tended gardens where the excellent meals are taken. The family running the place is also incredibly professional and warm.

★ **Casa Mia** GUESTHOUSE $
(☎966 4412; www.casamiamaldives.com; Mathiveri; r incl full board from US$245; ❄ 📶 🏊) This sleek and upmarket place is about as good as guesthouses in Maldives get. Indeed, the feel is far more that of a boutique hotel; Casa Mia is on its own private beach at one end of lovely Mathiveri (p95) and has 10 stylish and spacious rooms surrounding a swimming pool. Its unique selling point is the availability of alcohol from a safari boat moored just off the shore, a legal way of drinking without having to stay at a resort.

★ **Island Vista Inn** GUESTHOUSE $
(☎748 4045; www.islandvistainn.com; Ukulhas; r from US$125; ❄ 📶) This boutique-leaning guesthouse is one of the smartest options on the beautiful island of Ukulhas (p95), with stylish and spacious rooms, some of which have outdoor bathrooms. There's a lovely walled garden here for guests to relax in, and the magnificent bikini beach is a short walk away. A private 3D cinema and a chef creating ambitious menus are other drawcards.

Getting There & Away

Most resorts fly their guests to North Ari using seaplane charter flights from Male. By contrast, most independent travellers get here by using either speedboat transfers from Male or the far cheaper (but far slower) public ferries. For timetables check the **MTCC** (p178) website, and for tickets on private speedboats, contact **Atoll Transfer** (p178).

Rasdhoo Atoll

The small atoll of Rasdhoo lies off the north-eastern corner of Ari Atoll. The atoll's main island, also called **Rasdhoo**, is the administrative capital of North Ari Atoll, despite not being within the natural atoll itself.

Rasdhoo is an attractive little town with a secondary school, a health centre, several mosques and a growing number of guesthouses and souvenir shops. There are traces here of a Buddhist society pre-dating the arrival of Islam.

Today it's a big backpacker destination, with great beaches nearby, excellent and affordable diving and some of the better guesthouse accommodation in the country.

Activities

Rasdhoo is a great spot to dive, with a reputation for reliable sightings of hammerheads, mantas and other large pelagics. Top dives include:

Hammerhead Point Also known as Rasdhoo Madivaru, this is a great spot to see hammerhead sharks, mantas and other large pelagics that gather where the reef drops off into deeper water.

Veligandu Kandu A channel connecting Rasdhoo's lagoon to the open ocean, sloping gently from 10m to 25m and rich with coral outcrops and abundant reef fish. Manta rays can often be seen here in season.

Kuramathi House Reef Accessible from Kuramathi's shore, and good for beginner divers and snorkellers; sea fans and feather stars decorate the reef wall. Watch sharks, stingrays and turtles cruise, and see the dhoni and the 30m freighter that have been sunk as artificial reefs.

Sleeping & Eating

Resorts

Kuramathi Island Resort RESORT $$
(☎666 0527; www.kuramathi.com; Kuramathi; r incl full board from US$642; ❄ 📶 🏊) Kuramathi is one of the biggest resorts in the country, with 290 rooms. The island itself – 1.8km long – is huge by Maldivian standards, and has the luxury of thick vegetation and plenty of undeveloped areas, making it ideal for

long walks along the perfect beaches. This is a solid upper-midrange resort.

The rooms are all contemporary and furnished in an elegant and understated style with four-poster beds and stylish outdoor bathrooms. The nine categories run from the 45-sq-metre beach villas to the Honeymoon Pool Villas, which measure 310 sq metres and include their own 10m lap pools.

For dining, there's a huge choice including the Reef seafood restaurant, Thai at Siam Garden, a pizzeria, and Indian food at Tandoor Mahal. The island's list of activities is enormous – it has a huge spa, several swimming pools, a gym, a dive school, a water sports centre and the excellent Bageecha children's club. There's also a dedicated Eco Centre, which runs projects such as a hydroponic garden (from which the restaurants' salads come) and has a resident marine biologist.

Veligandu Island Resort & Spa RESORT **$$$**
(666 0519; www.veliganduisland.com; Veligandu; r incl full board from US$878;) Fringed with white beaches and featuring a huge 80m sandbank at one end, Veligandu is a popular and smart option with good accommodation for this price range. Rooms are comfortable and stylish; nearly all of them are over water. The island is famous for its great beaches and is located on a beautiful lagoon.

The Jacuzzi Beach Villas are the starting category, nestled among the trees on the beach; the smarter Jacuzzi Water Villas have outdoor jacuzzis, semi-open-air bathrooms and steps down into the lagoon.

The main Dhonveli restaurant serves up buffets three times a day and has a good Maldivian night each Friday, showcasing local food. The à la carte Madivaru restaurant is open in the evenings for a quieter, more romantic dinner.

The edge of the house reef is not very accessible and isn't great for snorkelling, though there are a couple of excellent nearby dive and snorkelling sites reachable by boat; hammerhead shark sightings are common.

Guesthouses

Rasdhoo Island Inn GUESTHOUSE **$**
(986 2014; www.rasdhooislandinn.com; Rasdhoo; s/d US$82/98;) Right on Rasdhoo's bikini beach, Rasdhoo Island Inn couldn't be better located. Rooms have lovely touches such as outdoor showers, sandy terraces and traditional furnishings; children are welcome to sleep on the daybed in each room. There's an excellent on-site restaurant and excursions and activities are available. Owner Hasan and his team make visitors feel immediately at home.

Acqua Blu Rasdhoo GUESTHOUSE **$**
(777 5711; www.acquablurasdhoo.com; Rasdhoo; s/d US$66/77;) This eight-room guesthouse is just a couple of blocks from Rasdhoo's bikini beach and offers comfortable, modern and spacious quarters to its guests. There's a decent in-house restaurant that serves three meals a day. The various multiday full-board packages available are good value and include snorkelling, activities and excursions to other islands.

Ras Beach Inn GUESTHOUSE **$**
(755 3000; www.rasbeachinn.com; Rasdhoo; r from US$72;) This friendly, laid-back guesthouse just a short walk from a private beach offers different types of simple rooms, each with their own minifridge and sparkling modern bathroom. The house is enclosed in a sandy courtyard where thatch umbrellas protect guests from the sun. A full array of activities, including diving, is on offer.

Information

There is a **Bank of Maldives** (Rasdhoo) with an ATM on Rasdhoo where you can take out cash in rufiya using a foreign credit or debit card.

Getting There & Away

Guests at resorts in Rasdhoo arrive by seaplane charters from Male's **airport** (p176).

RECOMPRESSION CHAMBERS

Maldives has two hyperbaric chambers on hand to treat people suffering from decompression sickness (also known as 'the bends'), which can affect divers who surface too quickly after a dive, causing nitrogen bubbles to form in the bloodstream. However, they are far apart, one on **Bandos** (p80) in North Male Atoll, and a second on **Kuramathi** (p98) in North Ari Atoll. If you follow official diving regulations and take a decompression stop in the water at the end of each dive, you should never have to use either, but they're there for emergencies. For more information, see Diving Health & Safety (p181).

For independent travellers, there are two speedboat connections in both directions between Male and Rasdhoo every day (US$45, one hour). Book seats online with **Atoll Transfer** (p178).

A cheaper and slower option is to take the public ferry from Male's **New Harbour** (p70) to Rasdhoo every Monday and Thursday (Rf57, 3½ hours); the same boat makes the trip in the opposite direction every Sunday and Wednesday. Rasdhoo is also connected by ferries to Thoddoo (Rf25, 1¼ hours, Saturday and Tuesday) and to Ukulhas (Rf25, one hour, Monday, Wednesday, Thursday and Sunday) in Ari Atoll. See the **MTCC** (p178) website for timetables.

Thoddoo

Though administratively part of Ari Atoll, Thoddoo is actually a single, separate, oval island about 20km from the northern edge of the main atoll. It's about 1km across, and has a population of 1350 fishermen and their families. Thoddoo is known for its fertile soil, its dancers, and for being the biggest producer of watermelons in the country.

Thoddoo is believed to have been occupied since ancient times; a Buddhist temple here contained a Roman coin minted in 90 BC, as well as a silver bowl and a fine stone statue of Buddha. Today, Thoddoo is a backpacker favourite with around a dozen guesthouses and a bikini beach.

Sleeping & Eating

★Thoddoo Retreat GUESTHOUSE $

(☎762 5265; www.thoddooretreat.com; r from US$88; ❄️📶) Our personal choice on the island, Thoddoo Retreat is a friendly and well-run place with a team of locals who welcome guests like family members. The seven atmospheric rooms here are Maldivian in style, with wooden slatted wardrobes and traditional long-slung beds; bathrooms are modern. Meals, served al fresco in the sandy courtyard, are superb and varied.

Getting There & Away

There's no airport on the island, but there are daily speedboats from Male to Thoddoo at 3pm (US$50, 1⅓ hours) and from Thoddoo to Male daily at 7am. Contact **Atoll Transfer** (p178) for tickets. For those on a budget, there's a public ferry from Male's **New Harbour** (p70) to Thoddoo on Monday and Thursday each week. It leaves Male at 9am and arrives in Thoddoo at 4.25pm (Rf57, 7½ hours). In the other direction, ferries leave Thoddoo at 6.30am on Sunday and Wednesday. In addition, there's a ferry to and from nearby Rasdhoo (Rf25, 1¼ hours) on Saturday and Tuesday. Check **MTCC** (p178) for timetables.

South Ari Atoll

South Ari is famous for its year-round population of whale sharks, which cruise the outer atoll channel gorging themselves on plankton just south of **Maamigili**.

Mahibadhoo, with around 2000 inhabitants, is the atoll capital and has a growing guesthouse scene. Maamigili, on the atoll's southern tip, is the most populous island here with 2300 people, many of whom work in nearby resorts. The island also has the only airport in Ari Atoll and is a popular base for divers. Between the two, **Dhigurah**, with a population of around 600, is a charming local island with a massive sandbank and a growing number of guesthouses.

Activities

★Dhidhdhoo Beyru DIVING

From May to September, whale sharks cruise almost continually along the 10km-long Dhidhdhoo Beyru on the southwestern edge of the atoll, which extends from Ariadhoo Kandu north to the tip of Dhigurah island. Even out of season there are consistent whale shark sightings here, which increase during a full moon when the currents become faster.

★Manta Reef DIVING

Also called Madivaru, Manta Reef is at the end of a channel where powerful currents carry plankton out of the atoll during the northeast monsoon (December to April) – fast food for manta rays. Mantas also come to be cleaned. Reef fish include Napoleon wrasse, snapper and parrotfish, while pelagics such as turtles, tuna and sharks visit the outer reef slope.

Sleeping & Eating

As well as numerous resorts, South Ari Atoll has seen an explosion of guesthouses on local islands, especially on Mahibadhoo, Dhigurah and Maamigili.

Resorts

★Mirihi RESORT $$$

(☎668 0500; www.mirihi.com; Mirihi; r from US$1115; ❄️📶) Named for a small yellow flower, Mirihi is remarkable for making the most of a small island without overdeveloping it.

THE GENTLE GIANTS OF MALDIVES

Ari Atoll is the best place in Maldives to spot the whale shark (*Rhincodon typus*), the world's largest fish. These gentle, plankton-eating giants can grow more than 12m in length, and some 200 are known to habitually return to these waters every year, attracting divers and snorkellers from all the surrounding resorts.

While whale sharks live on plankton and small fish that they filter from the water with their giant mouths, their sheer size means that divers need to exercise caution around them and avoid blocking their path or touching them. Note that snorkelling is generally thought to disturb whale sharks less than diving.

The **Maldives Whale Shark Research Programme** (www.maldiveswhalesharkresearch.org; Dhigurah) (www.maldiveswhalesharkresearch.org) has been monitoring whale sharks here for more than a decade, and they have openings for volunteers to help with research at their base on Dhigurah in South Ari Atoll. Contact the organisation for more information.

It's equally attractive as a stylish luxury resort, a rustic romantic retreat or a top-end dive island. The wonderful beach that rings the thick vegetation in the centre of the island and the fantastic house reef beyond are both first class.

Following a full refurbishment a few years ago, Mirihi is looking better than ever. While the island is tiny, 30 of the resort's rooms are built over the water, so the island itself doesn't feel too crowded. The newly renovated beach villas, of which there are just six, have polished timber finishes, white linen furnishings, rich orange-and-yellow accents and every conceivable amenity, including espresso machines. The water villas are essentially the same, with the addition of water views and very private sundecks; the top category room is the Two Bedroom Overwater Suite, which is good for families.

The main restaurant Dhonveli offers a good-quality buffet, while fine dining – grills and seafood are served – can be had at Muraka on a jetty over the water. Elsewhere Mirihi manages to pack in a gym, a small spa and activities such as windsurfing, snorkelling and kayaking. Divers come here for access to sites all over South Ari Atoll. The island's yacht, the *Mirihi Thari*, goes out frequently for whale-shark-spotting on the atoll edge – an unforgettable experience.

Conrad Maldives Rangali Island RESORT **$$$**
(☎666 0629; https://conradhotels3.hilton.com; Rangalifinolhu & Rangali; r from US$990; ❄📶🏊) Sumptuous barefoot luxury is the name of the game at the Hilton Group's longstanding Maldivian resort. Famous throughout the country for its unique two-island set-up and Maldives' first undersea restaurant, Conrad Maldives is an excellent choice for couples and families wanting to escape in style, while still having a huge choice of activities, cuisine and beaches.

The property immediately looks unique: it's housed on two islands that are connected by walkway across a broad lagoon, a great touch that offers both a large choice of beaches (all superb) and plenty of space. The heart of the resort – with the main lobby, restaurants, bars, water sports, dive centres and 100 beach villas – is on Rangalifinolhu; the second island, Rangali, is only for adults and has two further restaurants plus a bar, separate reception area and 50 water villas.

The rooms are varied and attractively conceived in all 11 categories; even the standard beach villas check in at a spacious 150 sq metres. All rooms have private sun terraces and outdoor bathrooms as well as sea views from the bath. The spectacular water villas all enjoy their own private outdoor areas, gorgeous wooden interiors and, in the more luxurious ones, glass floors.

With seven restaurants running the gamut of cuisines from Maldivian to Japanese and European, you have plenty of choice. Most impressive is the glass-domed, underwater Ithaa Undersea Restaurant, the first example in Maldives of a trend that has since been emulated at other resorts. Diving, water sports, excursions and a fantastic kids club are all also on offer, as are three spas (including one exclusively for children!).

LUX* Maldives RESORT **$$$**
(☎668 0901; www.luxresorts.com; Dhidhoofinolhu; r from US$960; ❄📶🏊) This long island is one of the bigger resorts in Maldives, but feels intimate and easily manageable on foot

through good design. It boasts beautiful beaches that wrap around the entire island, a stellar house reef with passing whale sharks, and impressive architecture that combines fashionable minimalism with island chic.

Rooms range from the thatched-roof beach pavilions – a good size at 65 sq metres – and go up to the giant 360-sq-metre LUX* villa. There's a large set of water villas off each side of the island; they're quite some distance from the island itself, which can either make you feel like you have a long walk to the main restaurant, or that you're lucky to enjoy some seclusion. While only half of the water villas have plunge pools, you'll find them at all the cheaper beach pool villas, making these rooms good value for money.

The island has seven restaurants, multiple bars, a spa, a PADI five-star dive centre, a full water sports centre and the usual host of excursions.

The lagoon is wide and a good place to learn windsurfing or catamaran sailing. There's no snorkelling to be had from the shore but you can take one of the free boat trips (which depart every afternoon) to the reef edge. The island has always been popular with divers, with whale shark encounters common from May to November, and visiting mantas from December to May.

MORE SOUTH ARI ATOLL DIVES

There are many other stunning dive sites in South Ari. Consider these:

Kudarah Thila A very demanding but exciting dive; currents rush past gorgonians, whip corals, black corals and a whole field of sea fans, surrounded by sharks and trevally from the open sea.

Broken Rock A canyon in the mouth of the Dhigurashu Kandu, Broken Rock, 10m deep and 3m wide and rich in sea fans and coral formations; extreme care must be taken when following the channel to avoid damaging the marine life.

Panetone On the north side of Kalhuhadhihuraa Faru, with strong currents that encourage soft coral growth. Good for giant trevally, barracuda, turtles, sharks (from March to November) and mantas outside the channel from December to April.

Guesthouses

★ **Liberty Guest House** GUESTHOUSE $
(330 0618; www.libertyguesthouse.mv; Mahibadhoo; r from US$75;) Our top choice on South Ari's capital island of Mahibadhoo (p100), Liberty Guest House stands out for the quality of its charming and professional staff, the likes of whom are sadly rarely seen in Maldives. The six rooms are bright and modern, with outdoor areas in each. The in-house dive centre makes it an ideal base for a diving holiday.

Shamar Guesthouse & Dive GUESTHOUSE $
(793 3404; www.sha-mar.com; Maamigili; r from US$89;) Passionate divers Shamoon and Markus run this Maldivian-German diving guesthouse surrounded by fields of crops on a relaxed corner of Maamigili (p100) island. There's a handful of clean and spacious rooms, a chilled-out communal area in the front garden, and meals and drinks for guests between daily dives. An excellent choice for an affordable diving holiday.

★ **Boutique Beach** BOUTIQUE HOTEL $$
(973 9663; www.boutiquebeach.club; Dhigurah; all-inclusive r US$360;) This innovative six-room place is moments from Dhigurah's (p100) bikini beach. All-inclusive packages include high-standard accommodation, superb meals and diving. Rooms are huge, with four-poster beds, a balcony and outdoor bathrooms with Molton Brown products. British owner and passionate diver Romney ensures a warm welcome.

Getting There & Away

Resorts in South Ari Atoll usually fly their guests in by seaplane charter, though in some cases they'll lay on a speedboat transfer from Male's **Velana International Airport** (p176). Another option is flying guests from Male to the small **airport** (p117) on the island of **Maamigili** (p100), which is served by several **FlyMe** (Map p73; 301 3000; www.flyme.mv; Velana International Airport) flights a day, after which speedboat transfers are used.

For independent travellers, there are ferry connections from Male's **Villingili Ferry Terminal** (p70) to the South Ari capital of **Mahibadhoo** (p100) (Rf53, 4¼ hours), which continue to Maamigili (Rf53, seven hours). These leave Male at 9am on Saturday, Monday and Wednesday and return from Maamigili (8am) and Mahibadhoo (10.30am) on Sunday, Tuesday and Thursday.

Northern Atolls

Includes ➡

Best Resorts

- ➡ Four Seasons Landaa Giraavaru (p112)
- ➡ Amilla Fushi (p111)
- ➡ Soneva Fushi (p113)
- ➡ Anantara Kihavah Villas (p112)
- ➡ Kanuhura (p115)

Best Guesthouses

- ➡ Barefoot Eco Hotel (p105)
- ➡ Three Hearts Guesthouse (p114)
- ➡ Aveyla Manta Village (p114)
- ➡ Villa Kamadhoo (p114)
- ➡ Palm Villa Guesthouse (p107)

Why Go?

The Northern Atolls – the least-developed region of Maldives – remain scarcely known to foreigners, which makes them a great place to experience traditional Maldivian life. Maldivian history owes much to this part of the country: national hero Mohammed Thakurufaanu, the man who drove the Portuguese out of Maldives in the 16th century, was born on the island of Utheemu in Haa Alifu Atoll. The island is today a place of pilgrimage for Maldivians, who come to see his small wooden palace (p104).

There's huge diving and snorkelling potential throughout the region; there are wrecks along the western fringe of the atolls – many only now being properly explored – while Baa Atoll, a Unesco World Biosphere Reserve, boasts pristine waters, diverse marine life and the famous manta ray feeding ground, Hanifaru Bay (p109). With just a handful of resorts and guesthouses, you'll often feel like you have the Northern Atolls to yourself.

When to Go

Jan–Mar Peak season coincides with the best weather in the north (and European winter).

Jun–Nov Manta ray spotting season attracts keen divers and snorkellers.

May–Sep Low season doesn't mean the weather is any worse; room prices are at their lowest.

Haa Alifu

Haa Alifu is Maldives' northernmost atoll and contains **Utheemu**, by far the most historically interesting island in the Northern Atolls. The birthplace of Sultan Mohammed Thakurufaanu – who, with his brothers, overthrew Portuguese rule in 1573 – the island is centred around a memorial to this Maldivian hero, and there is a gorgeous beach and a couple of guesthouses.

Elsewhere in the atoll is the capital island **Dhidhdhoo**, which offers good anchorage for passing yachts, and three remote resorts. At the very top of Haa Alifu, **Uligamu** is the 'clear-in' port for private yachts arriving in Maldivian waters. It has health and immigration officers, and yachts are able to complete all entry formalities there.

Sights

Utheemu is a shrine to Maldivian national hero Mohammed Thakurufaanu, who, alongside his brothers, overthrew Portuguese rule in 1573. His childhood home, the **Utheemu Ganduvaru** (Rf25; 9am-6pm Sun-Thu) palace, is open to visitors on escorted tours led by museum staff; inside you can see fascinating 500-year-old wooden interiors, including swing beds (used to keep cool in the heat), lamps that burn coconut palm oil and elaborate wooden carvings.

The young freedom fighter prayed at the nearby **Kandhuvalu Mosque**, a tiny wood-and-stone place with a beautiful teak interior that can be glimpsed from the entrance. Sadly, entry is not possible for non-Muslims. Thakurufaanu's father is buried in the cemetery here.

NORTHERN ATOLLS HIGHLIGHTS

Hanifaru Bay (p109) Snorkelling with the magnificent manta rays gliding around this famous plankton feeding ground in enormous numbers.

Utheemu Ganduvaru Discovering the childhood home of Maldivian national hero Mohammed Thakurufaanu, one of Maldives' best historical experiences.

Shipyard (p115) Diving two wrecks located within a mere 50m of each other, amid formidable corals and in the company of nurse sharks.

Shark Nursery (p109) Coming face-to-face with dozens of juvenile white-tip and grey-tip reef sharks in this picturesque basin behind a big reef.

Kandhuvalu Mosque Glimpsing the gorgeous carved teak interior of this ancient mosque on Utheemu.

Sleeping

Hideaway Beach Resort & Spa RESORT $$$
(650 1515; www.hideawaybeachmaldives.com; Dhonakulhi; r from US$840;) Hideaway is certainly true to its name, located about as remotely as you can imagine in Maldives' most northerly atoll, attracting those seeking true escape and unpretentious luxury.

Covered in thick jungle and set on a gorgeous crescent-shaped island with beaches 1.5km long on both sides, Hideaway is breathtaking. A long string of water villas stretches over the lagoon; these are impressive, spacious structures, each coming with its own 18-sq-metre plunge pool and boasting total privacy.

The rooms on the island itself share a rustic style with Maldivian decor and contemporary fittings. All have huge outdoor bathrooms and many have infinity pools. They're enclosed by thick vegetation, and most enjoy their own direct beach access.

There is a choice of four restaurants on the island, including fine dining at Matheefaru and Asian fusion at the overwater Samsara. The pristine reefs around the island provide superb snorkelling, and the untouched sites further afield make diving another great reason to come here.

The resort is totally child-friendly and has a great kids club; many of the villas can accommodate entire families, so space isn't a problem. If you're travelling by yacht, Hideaway has its own marina.

Getting There & Away

There is no airport in Haa Alifu, but northern Maldives' main airport – **Hanimaadhoo International Airport** (p176) – is just a short distance away in Haa Dhaalu. Resorts arrange for their guests to take scheduled **Maldivian** (Map p59; 333 5544; www.maldivian.aero; Dhaarul-Emaan Bldg, Majeedhee Magu, Male) flights to Hanimaadhoo, then collect them by launch.

Public ferries 101, 102, 103, 104, 105, 106 and 107 connect the inhabited islands of Haa Alifu with each other. Many of them also connect to towns in next-door Haa Dhaalu. See the **MTCC** (p178) website for routes and timetables.

Haa Dhaalu

Haa Dhaalu is an administrative district spread over 14 inhabited islands and made up of South Thiladhunmathee Atoll and the far smaller Maamakunudhoo Atoll. The atoll capital, **Kulhuduffushi**, is the most populous island, home to around 8200 people, with a hospital, secondary school, plenty of shops and a few guesthouses. Planes land on nearby **Hanimaadhoo**, which has one of Maldives' best guesthouses.

Maamakunudhoo Atoll is the graveyard of several ships, including the English ships *Persia Merchant,* wrecked here in 1658, and the *Hayston,* which ran onto a reef in 1819. In each instance, survivors were rescued by local people and treated with great kindness, a source of much local pride.

Sleeping

★**Barefoot Eco Hotel** GUESTHOUSE **$**

(☎652 9000; www.thebarefoot.com; Hanimaadhoo; r from US$260;) This excellent place is spread out along a gorgeous 1km-long white-sand beach on Hanimaadhoo's remote northern shore. It's perhaps the closest melding of guesthouse ethos with resort facilities in the country. This is a fantastic choice for visitors who'd like a very comfortable beach holiday but also want to have contact with Maldivian culture.

The large and charming rooms are arranged in stylish two-storey blocks of four facing the sea, meaning that nearly all have wonderful sea views from their patios or balconies. There's a big buffet, very attractive public areas and a dive centre.

As the hotel is located some distance from the population on Hanimaadhoo, there's no problem stripping down to speedos or a bikini on either the beach or by the gorgeous lap pool, which is lined with coral stones rescued from old buildings.

The Barefoot also lives up to its 'eco' name – it has an excellent program that includes the use of solar power, the purchase of local produce for the restaurant and the organisation of various community educational program. Just don't expect to be able to drink alcohol and you'll love it here.

Getting There & Away

The main **airport** (p176) in the northern Maldives is on **Hanimaadhoo** in Haa Dhaalu. There are five flights a day between Hanimaadhoo and Male (US$195, one hour), as well as regular flights to **Ifuru Airport** (p109) in Raa Atoll and **Dharavandhoo Airport** (p114) in Baa Atoll. There is also a direct service to Trivandrum (US$210, 1½ hours) in India from here each Monday and Thursday. All flights are operated by **Maldivian**.

Ferries connect the inhabited islands in Haa Dhaalu and also run to islands in neighbouring Haa Alifu and Shaviyani. The main hubs are the capital Kulhuduffushi and the airport island Hanimaadhoo. See the **MTCC** (p178) website for routes and timetables.

Shaviyani

Totally untouched by tourism until a decade ago, gorgeous and remote Shaviyani Atoll comprises 16 inhabited islands, whose beaches are an important hatching ground for turtles. Now superseded by the island of **Milandhoo**, the atoll's original capital, **Funadhoo**, is a pretty island that houses the ruins of an ancient mosque and 13th-century tombstones. The main mosque on the island of **Kanditheemu** incorporates the oldest known example of Maldives' unique Thaana script.

Sleeping

Sirru Fen Fushi RESORT **$$$**

(☎654 8888; www.sirrufenfushi.com; Gaakoshibi; r US$1132;) Its name translates as 'secret water island' and this is absolutely no understatement – as the only resort in pristine Shaviyani Atoll, Sirru Fen Fushi is truly an escape from the world. Surrounded by stunning azure waters, this gorgeously realised five-star resort is more off the radar than most.

All rooms here have their own plunge pools and direct access to the water, either directly from the beach in front of each beach villa or down the steps of the water villas into the lagoon. Rooms are huge, starting with the 164-sq-metre water villas and topping out at 1155 sq metres for a three-bedroom water villa. Furnishings are Asian and minimalist, with gorgeous carved wooden pieces in otherwise immaculately bare spaces, huge outdoor marble bathtubs, tiled floors and lots of timber.

There are three restaurants and three bars to choose from including Kata (for sushi and izakaya-style dining), Azure (for European fine dining) and Raha Market, where breakfast is served from multiple live-cooking stations. There's the large Arufen Spa for pampering, a dive school,

Northern Atolls

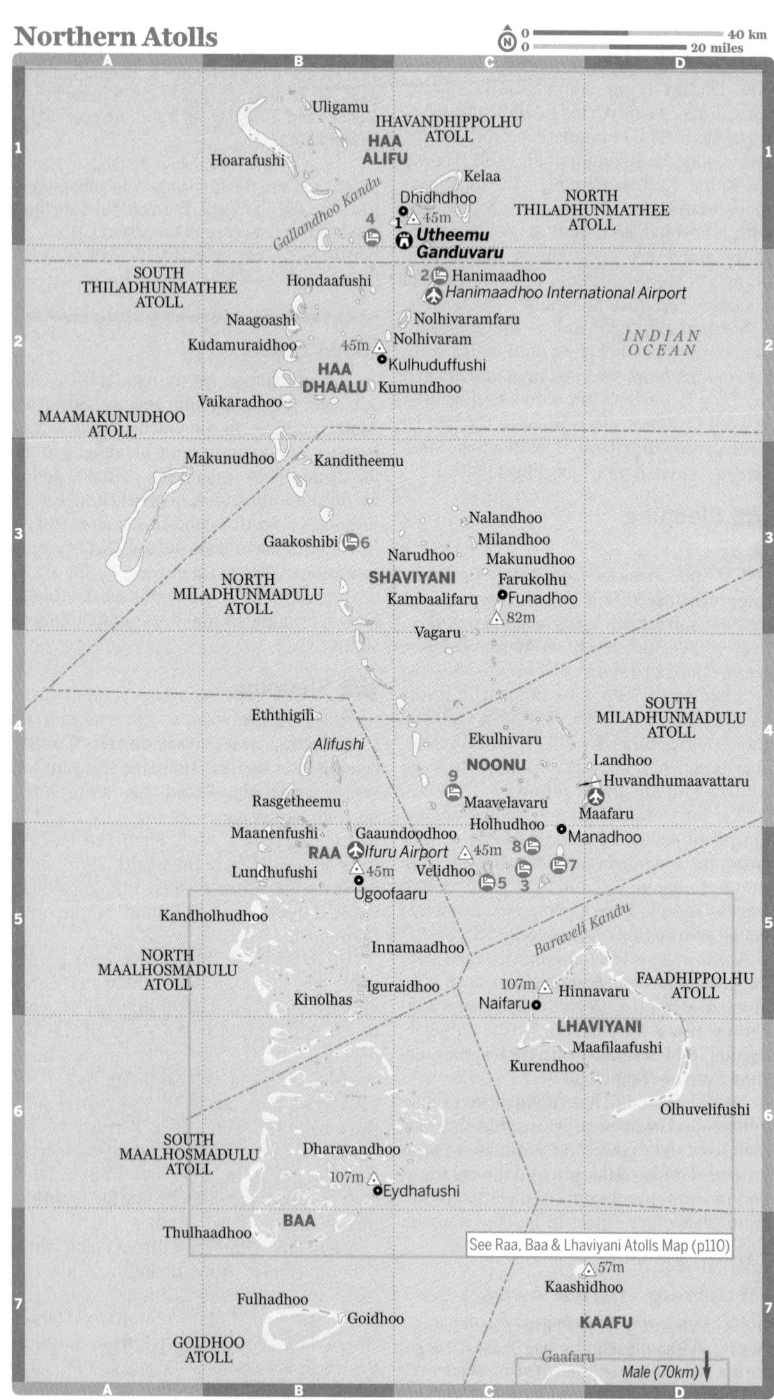

0 40 km
0 20 miles
Uligamu
IHAVANDHIPPOLHU ATOLL
HAA ALIFU
Hoarafushi
Kelaa
Dhidhdhoo
NORTH THILADHUNMATHEE ATOLL
Gallandhoo Kandu
45m
Utheemu Ganduvaru
SOUTH THILADHUNMATHEE ATOLL
Hondaafushi
Hanimaadhoo
Hanimaadhoo International Airport
Naagoashi
Nolhivaramfaru
Kudamuraidhoo
45m
Nolhivaram
INDIAN OCEAN
Kulhuduffushi
HAA DHAALU
Kumundhoo
Vaikaradhoo
MAAMAKUNUDHOO ATOLL
Makunudhoo
Kanditheemu
Nalandhoo
Gaakoshibi
Milandhoo
Narudhoo
Makunudhoo
NORTH MILADHUNMADULU ATOLL
SHAVIYANI
Farukolhu
Kambaalifaru
Funadhoo
82m
Vagaru
Eththigili
SOUTH MILADHUNMADULU ATOLL
Alifushi
Ekulhivaru
NOONU
Landhoo
Huvandhumaavattaru
Rasgetheemu
Maavelavaru
Maafaru
Holhudhoo
Maanenfushi
Gaaundoodhoo
Manadhoo
RAA
Ifuru Airport
45m
45m
Lundhufushi
Velidhoo
Ugoofaaru
Kandholhudhoo
Baraveli Kandu
NORTH MAALHOSMADULU ATOLL
Innamaadhoo
107m
Hinnavaru
FAADHIPPOLHU ATOLL
Iguraidhoo
Kinolhas
Naifaru
LHAVIYANI
Maafilaafushi
Kurendhoo
Olhuvelifushi
SOUTH MAALHOSMADULU ATOLL
Dharavandhoo
107m
Eydhafushi
BAA
Thulhaadhoo
See Raa, Baa & Lhaviyani Atolls Map (p110)
57m
Kaashidhoo
Fulhadhoo
Goidhoo
KAAFU
GOIDHOO ATOLL
Gaafaru
Male (70km)

Northern Atolls

Top Sights

Sights

Sleeping

a water sports centre, Maldivian cooking classes, tennis courts and a kids club. Tourism in Shaviyani Atoll is off to an excellent start.

Getting There & Away

One of Maldives' least accessible atolls, Shaviyani has no airport; the only way to get here is by seaplane charter. Public ferries 111, 112 and 113 each connect the atoll's inhabited islands once or twice a week in a network centred on the island of Funadhoo. See the **Atoll Transfer** (p178) website for routes and timetables.

Noonu

Noonu Atoll contains 13 inhabited islands and a handful of resorts; the capital, **Manadhoo**, has 1400 people. The island of **Landhoo** has the remnants of a *hawitta* (an ancient man-made mound) supposedly left by the fabled Redin, a tall, fair-haired people who may have been the first inhabitants of Maldives. The 2011 decision to create the Edu Faru National Marine Park here, the first of its kind in Maldives, put the atoll on the map. However, the laudable project – which seeks to protect the Edu Faru Archipelago of nine uninhabited islands on the eastern side of the atoll from development and fishing – seems to have derailed somewhat due to a lack of interest from the government, but the diving is still excellent.

Sleeping

Palm Villa Guesthouse GUESTHOUSE $

(990 0067; www.palmvilla-maldives.com; Velidhoo; s/d US$65/85;) This charming place is run by a couple of Danish chefs who were early pioneers of the guesthouse experience in Maldives; it's a great place to relax and enjoy island life. The six spacious, pretty rooms have tiled floors and semi-outdoor bathrooms, and surround a sandy courtyard where guests can relax, socialise and sunbathe without offending locals.

Sun Siam Iru Fushi Maldives RESORT $$

(656 0591; www.thesunsiyam.com; Manadhoo; r from US$615;) This enormous resort is impressive, smart and well run. There is a superb white-sand beach all the way around the long island, making it easy to find a perfect spot in solitude despite the large number of visitors to Manadhoo. There's no superfluous luxury here, but it's a very solid place that is tastefully designed and rigorously staffed.

Especially popular with Chinese and Russian holidaymakers, the resort has 221 rooms, including two enormous sets of water villas. Other accommodation ranges from beach villas with charming thatched roofs to the self-contained three-bedroom 'Celebrity Retreat' with its own private pool. Decor throughout is in a minimalist tropical-Asian style, with lots of black wood and rattan furniture. The list of amenities here is huge: six high-quality restaurants, two pools (one for families, one child-free), free tennis and badminton, dive and water sports centres, a golf simulator, huge spa, good gym and even a karaoke room. The free kids club is superb and has its own pool and infants' nursery room.

Soneva Jani RESORT $$$

(656 6666; www.soneva.com/soneva-jani; Medhufaru; r from US$3055;) The latest creation of the pioneering Soneva group, which kicked off luxury ecotourism in Maldives, this astonishingly ambitious place takes the shopping list of your average millionaire and brings it to life with vast wooden overwater villas that come with huge lap pools, walk-in minibars, retractable roofs, and – in most cases – your own personal water slide.

For now, nearly the entire resort is built on a whimsical winding timber pathway over a huge lagoon. The jetty does eventually meander its way to the island, which is huge and has some good chunks of coral beach, but is otherwise barely used as yet. Future plans for the island include more restaurants, a kids club, a water sports centre and villas, but for now it's all about the water villas; most guests won't even set foot on Medhufaru during their stay.

The centre of the resort is the vast and somewhat sinisterly named The Gathering, one of the largest wooden structures we've seen in Maldives. It's home to four dining experiences; the food is superb. Everything happens here; this is also usually where your Man or Woman Friday will glide magically into view every time you need something. Other facilities include an observatory, the outdoor Cinema Paradiso, a gym and a dive centre.

Soneva Jani is definitely the most talked-about new resort in the country and has lived up to its high expectations, although arguably it will be even more charming once the island is fully developed and it's possible to stay there as well as over the lagoon.

Velaa Private Island RESORT **$$$**
(☎656 5000; www.velaaprivateisland.com; Velaa; r from US$3388; ❄📶🏊) Since opening in 2013, Velaa has become a byword for personal attention and ultimate luxury. Rather than being part of an international hotel chain like many of its ultra-top-end competitors, this impressive place is the personal creation of a Czech couple who turned their private-island fantasy into a business.

The island is a stunner – a perfect circle with beach all the way around, perched above a wide circular reef. There are 43 rooms, which range from the one-bedroom Beach Pool Villa to the four-bedroom Private Residence. All have enormous private pools and are decorated in an exotic pan-Asian style with lots of dark-wood furniture.

The island boasts the white Tavaru Tower, apparently Maldives' highest restaurant at 22m (Everest by local standards), where a teppanyaki restaurant provides the centrepiece to Velaa's interesting design. There's also a Clarins spa, tennis courts, a small golf course and two more fine-dining restaurants.

Cheval Blanc Randheli RESORT **$$$**
(☎656 1515; www.randheli.chevalblanc.com; Randheli; r from US$4065; ❄📶🏊) Want to know where the one per cent really holiday? It's at this ultra-top-end hotel run by the French LVMH group, which has become renowned for its high prices and exclusivity. Indeed, Cheval Blanc Randheli is a dazzling retreat of utter extravagance, extraordinary ambition and see-and-be-seen fabulousness.

The setting is stunning, and it's not at all apparent that the four small islands that make up the resort beyond the main, natural island of Randheli are man-made. The beaches are as excellent as you'd expect them to be, while the public areas are defiantly modern, with little concession to Maldivian tradition. Instead, the Jean-Michel Gathy-designed buildings soar high, contain lots of glass and brushed concrete, and generally conform to the tastes of the resort's demanding clientele.

The rooms are sumptuous, as they should be with the highest rack rates in the country. There are 45 in total – 15 are on the main island, another 15 are expansive water villas built off two of the small islands, and 14 are unique overwater villas on stilts with their own private gardens. The top category room, the four-bedroom Owner's Villa, is on its own private island, and features its own staff detail, a private spa and a private fleet of dhonis. All categories boast a private 12m-long pool and private beach (or terrace with sea access), huge living rooms, outdoor dining pergolas, outdoor showers and every other possible convenience.

Cheval Blanc is famous for its food too, including a US$100 burger. Qualms about money aside, it's also home to French restaurant Le 1947, The Diptyque (for Iberian and Japanese), The Deelani (seafood and Italian) and all-day poolside brasserie The White.

ℹ Getting There & Away

Resorts and inhabited islands in Noonu are served by seaplane charters from Male. With the ultra-high-end clientele the atoll attracts in mind, an **airstrip** (Maafaru) for private jets on the island of Maafaru is currently under construction.

There's a weekly overnight ferry between Male's Fish Market Harbour and Velidhoo (Rf200, 10 hours). The ferry leaves Male on Wednesday night and returns from Velidhoo on Saturday night; there's no seating and passengers sleep on the floor.

Raa

With just a handful of resorts, Raa Atoll is still virtually pristine, making this corner of Maldives popular with divers; most visit on dive safari boats.

The capital island **Ugoofaaru** has one of the largest fishing fleets in the country, while the island of **Alifushi** is famously home to the finest traditional dhoni builders in Maldives. Arab explorer Ibn Battuta, one of the first foreigners known to have visited Maldives, landed on the island of **Kinolhas** in 1343 before moving on to Male.

The channel between Baa and Raa is officially named **Hani Kandu**, though it's also known as Moresby Channel after the Royal Navy officer Robert Moresby, who was responsible for the original marine survey of Maldives made from 1834 to 1836. There's good diving on both sides of Hani Kandu, where mantas abound in October and November.

Sleeping

Adaaran Select Meedhupparu RESORT **$$**
(☎658 7700; www.adaaran.com/selectmeedhupparu; Meedhupparu; all-inclusive r from US$632; ❄📶🏊) Meedhupparu has gorgeous white beaches sloping down to a perfect turquoise lagoon. It's the biggest resort in the Adaaran chain's group of properties in Maldives. The resort is particularly popular with Russian, Chinese and Italian guests who come here for a romantic holiday with plenty of activities and good all-inclusive deals.

The resort is large and features several distinct types of accommodation, including an 'Ayurvedic Village' made up of 24 rooms, and the 'Prestige Water Villas' exclusive area, which offers premium all-inclusive packages and functions as a resort-within-a-resort; it also has its own Balinese spa.

The resort's main restaurant offers high-quality buffet meals where all-inclusive guests eat during their stay. Premium all-inclusive guests can also eat at the Cafe Mass all-day à la carte restaurant and enjoy fine dining at Thavaa in the evenings.

Water sports and diving are big attractions here. The remote location of the resort means that divers never have to share sites – some 30 are regularly visited – with other groups.

Getting There & Away

Ifuru Airport offers three daily flights to Male (US$175, 40 minutes) on **Maldivian** (p104) as well as connections to **Dharavandhoo** (p114) in Baa Atoll. Resort guests travelling to Raa Atoll either use seaplane transfers from Male **airport** (p176) or take domestic flights on Maldivian. Local ferries 203 and 204 connect the atoll's 15 inhabited islands in both directions daily except Fridays. See the **MTCC** (p178) website for timetables and routes.

Baa

Magical Baa Atoll was designated a Unesco World Biosphere Reserve in 2011, mainly because of the extraordinary wealth of marine life at Hanifaru Bay, where both whale sharks and manta rays breed and can be seen in large numbers. Superb snorkelling and diving elsewhere in the atoll is also a major draw.

Baa Atoll's population is spread over 13 inhabited islands as well as in a variety of resorts, some of which are the very best in the country. Within Maldives the atoll – particularly the island of **Thulhaadhoo** – is famous for its colourful traditional lacquerwork boxes and jars. It's also known for the *feyli*, a fine woven-cotton sarong traditionally produced on the atoll capital **Eydhafushi** and still worn today by many locals.

Activities

★**Hanifaru Bay** SNORKELLING
(Rf310) The centrepiece to the Baa Atoll Unesco World Biosphere Reserve, Hanifaru Bay is a vital feeding and breeding ground for manta rays and whale sharks; you have an excellent chance of seeing these incredible sea giants while snorkelling here. The best time to see mantas is from May to November; whale sharks are here year-round. Note that diving is forbidden.

You won't be alone here, though this is one of the few snorkelling sites in the country where access is tightly controlled; the Manta Trust monitors boats coming and going and ensures that there's never more than 80 people snorkelling at a time. Each snorkeller's time in the water is limited to 45 minutes and diving was banned here in 2017. Entry tickets will be provided by your resort and should be handed in to the Manta Trust representatives on arrival. Despite the rules and the crowds, this is one of Maldives' most exciting encounters with the natural world and should not be missed if you're in Baa Atoll.

★**Shark Nursery** DIVING
This is one of the best places in Maldives to see juvenile white-tip and grey-tip reef sharks. Protected from the strong ocean current by its position in a canyon off the main reef, this tranquil spot sees dozens of the sharks resting on the sandy bottom. An absolute must for anyone fascinated by these creatures.

Sleeping

Resorts

Reethi Beach Resort RESORT **$**
(☎660 2626; www.reethibeach.com; Fonimagoodhoo; r from US$299; ❄📶🏊) 🍃 Reethi Beach is a large, long-running resort with plenty of

Raa, Baa & Lhaviyani Atolls

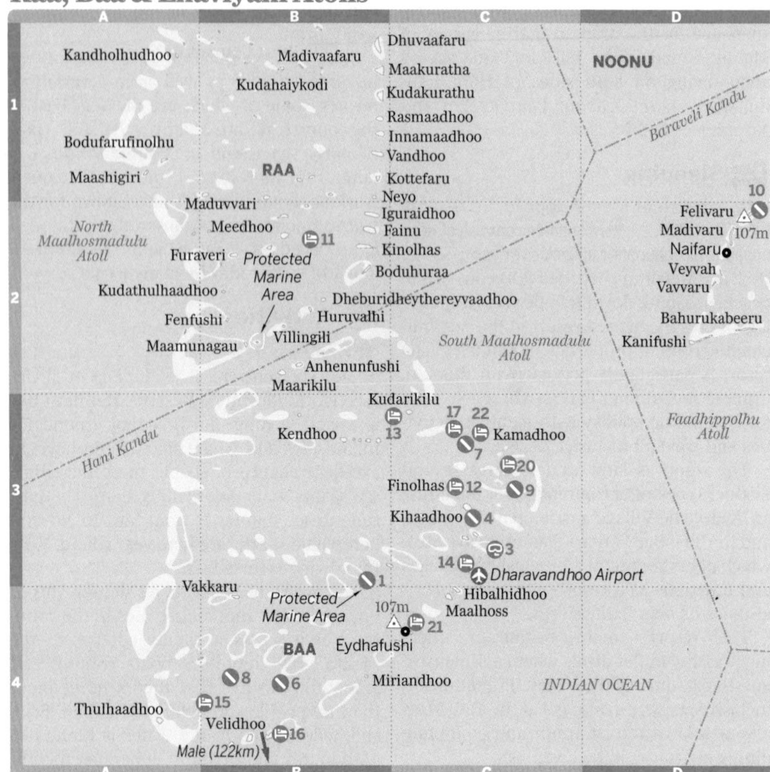

charm. The island has lots of natural vegetation, wide white beaches and an accessible house reef. As one of the few budget options in Baa Atoll, it's a welcome change of pace and a great place to stay for those who want an affordable but still very comfortable Maldivian holiday.

The Deluxe Villas are more spacious and have better beach frontage than the standard Reethi Villas, while the Water Villas are decent given the low prices here, but far from showstopping. Interiors in all are pleasant, if a bit dated, with lots of darkwood furnishings, and each room has its own outside area. The buildings, all with thatched roofs, are designed to blend in with the environment; they also incorporate some Maldivian design elements such as deep horizontal mouldings like those used on the Old Friday Mosque (p60) in Male.

There are five restaurants and five bars on the island; you'll have plenty of choice about where you eat and drink. You'll also find a swimming pool, gym and squash, badminton and tennis courts. Windsurfing, sailing and other water sports are popular because of the wide lagoon. Kitesurfing is also on offer, as are wakeboarding and jet skiing.

The Sea Explorer dive centre is reasonably priced, although qualified divers can also make their own dives off the house reef. The resort has won multiple awards for its sustainable practices including impeccable waste management, excellent water conservation systems and a coral growth program.

Coco Palm Dhuni Kolhu RESORT **$$**

(☎660 0011; www.cocopalm.com; Dhunikolhu; all-inclusive r from US$570; ❄📶🏊) This resort is a favourite with honeymooners and has an enormous number of repeat visitors. The island is a stunner, with a wide beach on one side, thick vegetation and an architecturally interesting space with a tentlike thatched pavilion for reception, restaurant and bar

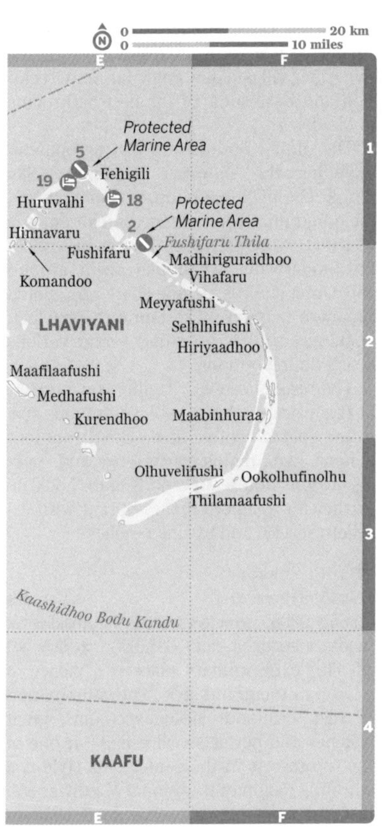

Raa, Baa & Lhaviyani Atolls

Activities, Courses & Tours

1 Dhigali Haa B3
2 Fushifaru Thila E1
3 Hanifaru Bay C3
4 Kakani Thila C3
5 Kuredhoo Express E1
6 Madi Finolhu B4
7 Milaidhoo Reef C3
8 Muthafushi Thila B4
9 Shark Nursery C3
10 Shipyard D2

Sleeping

11 Adaaran Select Meedhupparu B2
12 Amilla Fushi C3
13 Anantara Kihavah Villas C3
14 Aveyla Manta Village C3
15 Coco Palm Dhuni Kolhu B4
16 Finolhu B4
17 Four Seasons Landaa Giraavaru C3
18 Kanuhura E1
19 Kuredu Island Resort & Spa E1
20 Reethi Beach Resort C3
21 Soneva Fushi C4
22 Villa Kamadhoo C3

areas. Erosion means sandbags are evident in some parts, but it's still a gorgeous place.

The beach villa rooms are circular with high, thatched, conical roofs, quality furnishings and open-air bathrooms; deluxe rooms have plunge pools. All meals are buffet in Cowrie, the main restaurant, but they are very good, while the à la carte Cornus has a fabulous menu of pan-Asian dishes. There is also the choice of the Beach Bar and the Conch Bar, both of which offer a food menu. Other nice touches include an outdoor cinema, a green turtle-nesting program, a lovely spa and a dive centre.

★ Amilla Fushi RESORT **$$$**
(660 6444; www.amilla.mv; Finolhoss; r from US$1980;) This stunning new arrival to Baa Atoll has instantly joined the ranks of the finest resorts in the country, having transported the glamour and style of Palm Beach to a gorgeous Indian Ocean island. Amilla Fushi boasts dreamily perfect white-sand beaches, deeply fabulous rooms, an array of superb restaurants, a beautiful infinity pool and a huge marina.

The modernist white water villas here look immediately different from the more typical thatch-timber creations you'll see at most resorts; their cuboid shape is just one thing that this brand new resort has reinvented from scratch.

The rooms here are the thoughtful centrepiece to the island. All feature their own private lap pools and massive bathrooms with double rain showers; they offer total privacy while maintaining direct access to the beach and water. They're huge spaces in brushed concrete and tile with bright tropical accents and a stylishness seen in few other resorts. The most unusual rooms are the 12m-high treehouses, which somehow manage to have their own infinity pools. At the very top end, there are a number of vast residences aimed at families and big groups of friends. While they're absolutely luxurious, completely private and sleekly designed, they're perhaps not as charming as the other rooms.

The public areas are focused on the marina, where there's a stunning infinity pool, several restaurants and – at the end of a long jetty – the raised One of a Kind cocktail bar and the Feeling Koi Japanese restaurant, the island's very best. There's a top-of-the-range spa, dive centre, kids club, tennis courts and water sports facilities. Perhaps best of all, guests are welcome to use the free daily transfers to the resort's sister island Finolhu, allowing them to enjoy the fabulous sandbank and restaurant there once they've tired of the perfect beaches here.

★ **Anantara Kihavah Villas** RESORT **$$$**
(☎660 1020; www.kihavah-maldives.anantara.com; Kihavahuravalhi; r from US$1350; ❄📶🏊) Surrounded by a perfectly circular reef, the thickly vegetated Kihavahuravalhi is ringed by gorgeous white-sand beaches: you couldn't ask for a more idyllic-looking Maldivian island. However, the resort's biggest attraction is its 82 stunning villas, all superbly realised homages to ultimate luxury, crammed full of beautiful Asian furnishings and with highly impressive outdoor bathrooms.

All accommodation here comes with a private pool, whether on land or over water. This is one place, though, where the beach villas are even better than the more expensive water villas – they enjoy far more seclusion and have some of the best bathrooms in Maldives.

The dining options are just as opulent, including the showcase Sea.Fire.Salt.Sky dining complex, made up of four sections, including one (Sea) where you can enjoy a gourmet, wine-paired set menu in a glass box underwater while fish swim around you. Other choices include Fire – a top-notch Japanese teppanyaki restaurant (for which booking ahead is essential) – and various beach dining options.

The resort has every facility you'd expect at this price – a huge pool, sumptuous spa, water sports centre, dive school, outdoor cinema, gym, tennis courts, yoga and cookery lessons and a super kids club. Look no further for a superb luxury option with excellent service and terrific beaches.

★ **Four Seasons Landaa Giraavaru** RESORT **$$$**
(☎660 0888; www.fourseasons.com/maldiveslg; Landaagiraavaru; r from US$1990; ❄@📶🏊) 🌿 This extraordinary place is a palace of a hotel in the grand style. The combination of vast, brilliantly designed rooms, great beaches and perfect service make it one of the top resorts in the country. Its style is a stunning fusion of traditional Maldivian village atmosphere and international designer minimalism; it's also superbly friendly and welcoming.

The rooms here are some of the biggest and best in Maldives. Our favourites are the Beach Villas With Pool: freestanding houses surrounded by coral stone brick walls with a private lap pool in the garden, a mezzanine living room gazebo and direct access to the gorgeous beach. The Sunset and Sunrise Water Villas, which are built from repurposed coral stone, are also huge, beautifully designed and offer ultimate privacy.

The centre of the resort is its large spa, which provides treatments in overwater rooms and offers many different types of yoga (including anti-gravity). There's also a 'night spa' in the jungle where a couple is given romantic treatments together after dark.

With a choice of three vast pools, four great restaurants, an outstanding kids club, a teenagers club, tennis courts, free non-motorised water sports, a dizzying range of motorised water sports and a marine biology

MORE BAA ATOLL DIVES

There are many more fine diving and snorkelling sites in Baa Atoll. Consider the following:

Milaidhoo Reef Strong currents and soft corals on the north side of an uninhabited island, with good snorkelling on the reef top, and dives down to 35m on a cliff overhanging with sea fans and sponges.

Dhigali Haa Well inside the atoll, but still attracts pelagics such as barracuda, grey-tip reef sharks and trevally; also a good place to see nudibranchs, yellow and orange soft corals and anemones.

Muthafushi Thila Overhangs with colourful hard corals in good condition, plus anemones and large schools of blue-striped snapper.

Madi Finolhu A good beginner dive, rarely exceeding 20m, with black coral outcrops, and stingrays and passing mantas over sandy areas.

Kakani Thila Healthy coral formations on the north side, at 25m to 30m, and colourful soft corals tucked into overhangs; also home to Napoleons, jackfish and Oriental sweetlips.

lab with its own turtle rehabilitation centre, it's not a place where you can easily be bored.

A luxurious diving school runs trips in the mornings and afternoons with a maximum of 12 participants in each group. There are 20 dive sites nearby; whale sharks and mantas are very common in September.

This is perhaps the ultimate Maldivian resort: wonderfully conceived, superbly run and home to a glamorous, truly mixed international crowd.

If this isn't enough for you, the resort now runs its own private island, Voavah, an entirely self-contained creation that can sleep up to 14 adults and eight kids, with three pools, a gym and a private island (yes, the private island has its own private island), a yacht and a mere staff of 26.

It retails for around US$45,000 per night in high season.

★Soneva Fushi RESORT **$$$**

(☎660 0304; www.soneva.com/soneva-fushi; Kunfunadhoo; r from US$2440;) Rightly one of the most famous resorts in the country, ecofabulous Soneva Fushi is the place to get back to nature in style. The personal creation of hoteliers Sonu and Eva, it's an incredibly impressive place where rustic private houses are perched on dazzling white-sand beaches behind the thick vegetation of one of Maldives' largest resort islands.

Each villa here is genuinely just that – there are no mere rooms – and they're whimsically and individually designed, built with all-natural materials, fitted with beautiful furnishings and finished in rustic style. Each has its own pool and direct beach access.

All the deluxe and modern features you'd expect of a five-star hotel are included, but most of them are concealed so that no plastic is visible. Bathrooms are vast outdoor creations bigger than most hotel bedrooms. The villas are well-spaced around the edges of the island, affording complete privacy; they're reached by bicycling along sandy tracks that wind through the lush jungle.

With the choice of five superb restaurants (including the wonderful treehouse-style Fresh in the Garden, where you cross a rope bridge to get to your table above the jungle canopy), the food is a real highlight of the resort. A new overwater restaurant complex, Out of the Blue, was under construction in 2018.

Eco-credentials and social responsibility are taken seriously here; you can take a tour of the resort's recycling area and see the ingenious ways many things are reused on the island.

The Soleni Dive Centre has years of experience diving the sites nearby, while the excellent Six Senses Spa, set among the trees, is a place for pure relaxation.

The kids club – which includes a Lego room, offers cooking classes and has its own pool and water slide – is easily one of the best in the country.

More unusual (free) activities include watching an outdoor film at the lovely Cinema Paradiso, and observing the stars in the first resort observatory in Maldives.

Finolhu RESORT **$$$**

(☎660 8800; www.finolhu.com; Kanufushi; r from US$1182;) The second resort in the country from The Small Maldives Island Company (who also manage nearby stunner Amilla Fushi; p111), Finolhu aims itself at a young, wealthy crowd who want to party and enjoy the island's magnificent beaches. While the resort's commitment to 'youth' seems a tad contrived, it's a beautiful resort with fabulous facilities and a dreamy 2km-long sandbank.

Finolhu looks a bit like how a fashionable interior designer imagines a hippy would design a private island: loud music, amusing signs and VW camper vans greet you when you step off the boat. Much of this is just a surface nod to the resort's fairly heavy-handed marketing; at ground level Finolhu is actually little different to most five-star private islands.

The rooms here are divided into the Moorish-style beach villas (which come with retro-looking Marshall bluetooth speakers, Smeg kettles, Nespresso machines and Neal's Yard toiletries) and the vast line of

HANIFARU UNESCO BIOSPHERE RESERVE

The entirety of Baa Atoll was made a Unesco World Biosphere Reserve in 2011, reflecting its rich biodiversity and pristine marine environment, joining the illustrious ranks of places such as the Galapagos Islands, Uluru in Australia and the Pantanal wetlands of Brazil. The centrepiece of the biosphere reserve, the snorkelling site of **Hanifaru Bay** (p109) is legendary for its manta rays; all resorts and guesthouses in Baa Atoll can arrange trips here.

SHIPWRECKED IN PARADISE

Most early visitors to these islands arrived by chance, or rather misfortune, as their ships were wrecked on the treacherous coral atolls. Perhaps the most famous early explorer was French navigator François Pyrard, who found himself stuck on the island of Fulhadhoo in Baa Atoll after his ship, the *Corbin*, was wrecked in 1602. Spending five years on Fulhadhoo and later on Male as an effective prisoner, Pyrard learned Dhivehi (unlike his fellow crew members) and wrote the first extensive account of Maldivian culture: *The Voyage of François Pyrard of Laval to the East Indies, the Maldives, the Moluccas, and Brazil*. Pyrard eventually managed to escape from Male during a Bengali raid in 1611.

water villas, the top category of which comes with plunge pools.

They're big and comfortable but rather gimmicky, including a record player (apparently an object of fascination to its Millennial guests), old ABBA records and a button that says 'press for champagne'.

As well as the main 1 Oak Beach Club, which does food and drink around the vast pool, there is also Kanusan for pan-Asian food, Baa Haa for North African cuisine and the 'retro tuck shop' Milk Bar.

The most striking thing about the entire island is the enormous shimmering white sandbank, one of the longest in the country. Towards its far end there's the charming Fish & Crab Shack, which sits on the gorgeous lagoon and serves up fresh seafood in a relaxed atmosphere.

There's a boat from the main island here every half hour to save you the long, hot walk. Easily one of the best beaches in Maldives, this is where many guests spend much of their time.

Free transfers to sister resort Amilla Fushi run several times a day.

Guesthouses

Three Hearts Guesthouse GUESTHOUSE $
(☎758 1450; www.3heartsmaldives.com; Fulhadhoo; s/d from US$63/75; ❄📶) The island of Fulhadhoo, with a population of just 220 people, is a charming place to experience Maldivian island life, and the Three Hearts Guesthouse is the best place to stay. Rooms include everything you need for a comfortable visit, and the bikini beach is just a short walk through the foliage. Water sports and diving can be arranged.

Aveyla Manta Village GUESTHOUSE $
(☎777 3998; www.mantavillage.com; Dharavandhoo; s/d US$140/152; ❄@📶) Dharavandhoo may be home to Baa Atoll's airport, but it's otherwise a sleepy and very traditional fishing village. This 16-room beachside guesthouse is our top choice here, mainly for its good meals, comfortable and stylish accommodation and very obliging staff. Management is efficient and solar power is used for all electricity.

Villa Kamadhoo GUESTHOUSE $
(☎797 8010; www.kamadhoomaldives.com; Kamadhoo; s/d from US$93/106; ❄📶) This guesthouse on the relatively untouched island of Kamadhoo offers clean and comfortable rooms in one of three locations just a short walk from the bikini beach. Each location has a restaurant, and you'll be looked after very well by the team, who arrange activities including water sports, diving and snorkelling right from the beach.

ℹ Getting There & Away

Baa Atoll is served by **Dharavandhoo Airport** (☎660 0060; Dharavandhoo), a small airstrip with daily scheduled flights to and from Male on both **Maldivian** (p104) and **FlyMe** (p102). Despite this, most resorts in Baa Atoll usually fly their guests in on seaplane charters.

There are two atoll ferry routes – 205 and 206 – that connect the 13 inhabited islands every day except Friday. The network is focused on atoll capital Eydhafushi. See the **MTCC** (p178) website for routes and timetables.

Lhaviyani

Quiet, delightful Lhaviyani Atoll is made up of 50 islands, only five of which are inhabited; a further eight are home to resorts. The capital, **Naifaru**, is well known in Maldives for making handicrafts from mother-of-pearl, a popular souvenir for visitors to the atoll.

Fishing is the main industry here, and the island of **Felivaru** is home to Maldives' first tuna-canning plant, which opened in 1978. Tourism also employs many people, and more resorts continue to be planned and built.

Activities

Lhaviyani is blessed with some fine dive sites, but strong currents mean these are best for intermediate and advanced divers. Top sites include:

Shipyard A demanding dive with two wrecks, just 50m apart, encrusted with hard and soft corals and home to moray eels, sweepers and cruising nurse sharks.

Fushifaru Thila A Protected Marine Area, with good snorkelling atop its soft coral-rich thila, and a broad, fast channel that sees mantas, eagle rays, sharks, grouper, sweetlips, turtles and cleaner wrasse.

Kuredhoo Express Usually done as a long drift dive through the channel next to the Kuredu resort, but with brilliant snorkelling on the eastern side. Come for Napoleon wrasse, grey-tip reef sharks and trevally, soft corals in the overhangs, and plenty of morays, turtles and stingrays.

Sleeping

Kuredu Island Resort & Spa RESORT $$

(☎662 0332; www.kuredu.com; Kuredhoo; all-inclusive r from US$391; ❄📶🏊) Kuredu Island Resort is about as close as you can get to a resort city in Maldives – this mass-market giant packs in the masses and truly is the resort that has everything. Look no further if you want a fun, sociable and action-packed holiday destination as well as the usual gleaming beaches and great diving.

The seven room categories run from the simple but charming Bonthi Garden Bungalows to the Beach Villas, which face the island's best beach.

There are four buffet restaurants around the island, ensuring you'll never have to walk far to get to lunch; these have a fair selection of Asian and international dishes. There are also three à la carte restaurants: choose from fine dining at The Beach, Asian cuisine at Far East and Mediterranean dishes at Franco's.

You can effectively have whatever kind of holiday you're after here, and the sheer number of activities and facilities available is mind-boggling; there's everything from a six-hole golf course to kiteboarding and a football pitch. Other facilities include a gym, tennis courts, a well-used beach volleyball court and a spa, which offers Swedish, Thai and Oriental massages. There are more than 40 dive sites in the atoll; some of the best are accessible from Kuredu.

★ **Kanuhura** RESORT $$$

(☎662 0044; www.kanuhura.com; Kanuhura; r incl half board from US$1250; ❄📶🏊) Kanuhura is a sumptuous, impressive place with magnificent beaches, stunning accommodation and top-notch food. It's classy and stylish without being too formal, romantic without being too quiet, and extremely welcoming to families without allowing kids to run riot. If you want a laid-back, high-end beach holiday with considerable style, this may be for you.

After reopening in 2016 following a full renovation, Kanuhura can now compete with the best resorts in Maldives, having significantly revamped its rooms and upped its culinary offerings. The island itself is big – 1.4km long – with perfect beaches stretching right around it.

The redesigned rooms are breezy and bright with lots of light and stylish furnishings. The beach villas feature Illy espresso machines, curated libraries, separate dressing areas, lovely indoor-outdoor bathrooms, marble fittings and frontage onto the perfect white-powder beach. The more expensive suites and water villas are even bigger and feature several rooms, sun decks and direct access to the water.

The resort's public areas, main restaurants and spa are focused on the pool near the main jetty. Here you'll find A Mano, the very smart main buffet restaurant; a cool little deli that does made-to-order sandwiches; and the Italian restaurant Bottega. At the other end of the island is high-end outdoor dining option Veli Café, which overlooks the resort's own desert island. Called Jehunuhura, this island is perfect for Robinson Crusoe roleplay or a relaxing lunch at its Drift Beach Grill. A complimentary boat shuttles guests back and forth between the two islands.

Elsewhere on Kanuhura there's a superb kids club, games room, full water sports centre, gym, tennis courts, squash court and dive centre that offers visits to more than 40 local dive sites. A club for teenagers is planned, which will complete the picture for this charming family-friendly luxury resort.

Getting There & Away

There's no airport in Lhaviyani Atoll, and all resorts use seaplane charters to bring in their guests. There's a ferry connecting the five inhabited islands every day except Friday, as well as a twice-weekly ferry to and from Male (Rf200, six hours) from Naifaru. See the **Atoll Transfer** (p178) website for routes and timetables.

Southern Atolls

Includes ➡

Best Resorts

- Six Senses Laamu (p124)
- Niyama Private Islands (p122)
- Shangri-La Villingili Resort & Spa (p131)
- COMO Maalifushi (p124)
- Ayada Maldives (p127)

Best Guesthouses

- Reveries Diving Village (p124)
- Veyli Residence (p129)
- Beach Stay Maldives (p123)
- Wave Sound by 3S Maldives (p132)
- Villa Stella (p123)

Why Go?

The Southern Atolls have a justified reputation for independent mindedness. In 1959, the southernmost atolls broke away from Male's rule to form the short-lived United Suvadive Republic before being forcibly taken back under the control of the central government a few years later.

The past few years have seen dozens of new resorts opening here, as well as several new airports, making the entire region very well connected to the capital. Outside the resorts, the Southern Atolls have largely retained a traditional way of life, though guesthouses – now operating on many inhabited islands – have brought new perspectives on the world, foreign visitors and change to the region.

Live-aboards explore the south's pristine dive sites, while surfing boats visit the most remote breaks of the most remote atolls, such as Gaafu Dhaalu and Addu. Welcome to the dreamily perfect world of the southern Maldives.

When to Go

Dec–Apr The best time to see manta rays swimming in the waters of the south.

Feb–Apr & Aug–Oct Surf's up in Gaafu Dhaalu and Addu Atolls.

May–Nov Great visibility makes this an excellent time to snorkel and dive.

Vaavu

Located directly below South Male Atoll – thus easy to reach from both Male and Villa International Airport in South Ari Atoll – Vaavu is nevertheless the least populous region of Maldives, with just 1750 inhabitants spread over five inhabited islands.

The main industries here are fishing and boatbuilding, with tourism a growing – but still minimal – sector.

There are just two resorts in the atoll, though there's a small but growing number of guesthouses.

The capital island is **Felidhoo** (population 500), though visitors are more likely to go to the neighbouring island, Keyodhoo, which has a good anchorage for safari boats. At the northern edge of the atoll, **Fulidhoo** is known for its boatbuilding.

Rakeedhoo, at the southern tip of the atoll, is used as an anchorage by safari boats taking divers to the nearby channel.

Activities

Diving is the big show in town and there are numerous sites to choose from. Favourite dives include:

Vattaru Kandu A remote channel dive on the southern edge of Vattaru Falhu, next to a fine snorkelling area; good for soft corals, sea fans, barracuda, fusilier and white-tip reef sharks.

Devana Kandu A drift dive in a channel divided by a narrow thila, with overhangs, caves, reef sharks and eagle rays, plus soft corals on the southern side.

Fotteyo A brilliant diving and snorkelling site, whose soft coral-covered caves and crannies hide rays, reef sharks, grouper, tuna, jackfish, barracuda, turtles and – rarely – hammerhead sharks.

Rakeedhoo Kandu A challenging dive in a deep channel adorned with sea fans and black corals; turtles, Napoleon wrasse, sharks and schools of trevally are often seen, and there's good snorkelling on the reef top.

Sleeping

Plumeria Maldives BOUTIQUE HOTEL **$**
(332 2822; www.plumeriamaldives.com; Thinadhoo; s/d from US$148/192;) This impressive place has marked the arrival of sophisticated tourism on Thinadhoo. The modern and stylish boutique hotel, which describes itself as offering affordable luxury, boasts a separate beachside restaurant and dive centre. It's a big step up from the standard accommodation offered in guesthouses, and yet its prices are tiny compared to most resorts.

Vaali Beach Lodge Maldives GUESTHOUSE **$**
(790 8421; www.lvmhotels.com; Felidhoo; r US$95;) There are just three rooms at this pleasant and affordable guesthouse on the island of Felidhoo, which, despite being Vaavu's capital, is a very traditional place that's perfect for getting acquainted with the Maldivian way of life. The sand-floored public areas are wonderful for relaxing in, while the spotless modern rooms are comfortable and spacious.

Getting There & Away

Vaavu is easily reached from Male's **New Harbour** (p70), with ferries (Rf50, two hours) leaving Male at 10am on Sunday, Tuesday and Thursday, stopping off at Maafushi in South Male Atoll on the way before calling at Fulidhoo, Thinadhoo, Felidhoo, Keyodhoo and Rakeedhoo.

Boats return from Rakeedhoo at 7am on Saturday, Monday and Wednesday, calling at all the atoll's inhabited islands and then Maafushi before arriving in Male at 2.25pm. See the **MTCC** (p178) website for timetables.

Resorts and guesthouses will arrange private speedboat charters for guests coming from **Villa International Airport** (Map p96; 333 3355; Maamigili) in nearby South Ari Atoll.

Meemu

Meemu Atoll has eight inhabited islands, two resorts and is principally known for its huge coral reefs on the side of the atoll, which make it a popular destination for divers.

The capital is **Muli**, a small and traditional island with little to attract visitors and where guesthouse culture is yet to take off. Nearby **Mulah** and the southerly **Kolhufushi** are more populous than the capital and are important agricultural islands where yams, a local food staple, are grown.

As well as several superb dive sites, Meemu has some excellent surf breaks on its eastern edge, including Veyvah Point, Boahuraa Point and Mulee Point, which are visited – usually on live-aboards – by more adventurous surfers.

Southern Atolls

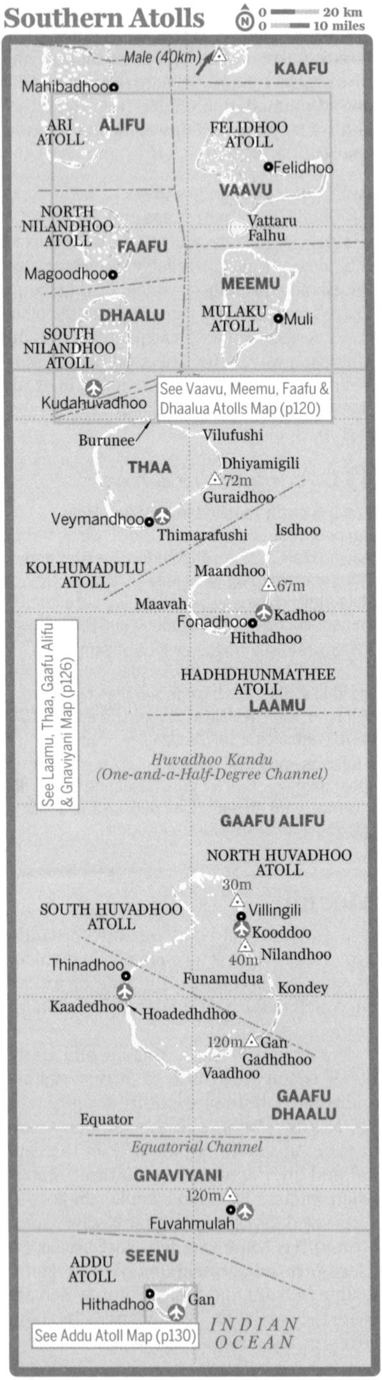

Activities

There are several excellent dive sites in the atoll. Make a beeline for **Shark's Tongue** (Map p120), in the mouth of the Mulah Kandu, where white-tip reef sharks sleep on a sandy plateau, grey-tip reef sharks hang around a cleaning station at 20m, and other shark species cruise between the coral blocks.

An easy shallow dive, **Giant Clam** (Map p120), as its name suggests, has giant clams, lobsters, groupers, and abundant fish, including hard-to-spot stonefish and scorpionfish.

Sleeping

Cinnamon Hakuraa Huraa RESORT $$

(☎672 0014; www.cinnamonhotels.com/en/cinnamonhakuraahuraamaldives/; Hakuraa; r from US$640;) This is a well-designed resort combining romance and water sports. There are some stunning beaches here, friendly staff and plenty of activities. This is a great place to mix activity and indolence, although it's worth noting that you don't get much privacy in the rooms as they're quite closely packed together. Its unusual tented villas are mainly built over water.

The water villas are a solid attraction, and there's an enormous number of them, running along the entire length of one side of the island. Most guests are on all-inclusive packages. There are four restaurants offering quality food.

The dive school is good value and offers what so few centres in Maldives can these days – access to truly pristine and little-visited dive sites. The lagoon is not good for snorkelling, though snorkelling gear and twice-daily trips to nearby snorkelling spots are included in the package.

Getting There & Around

There is no airport in Meemu Atoll; resorts use seaplane charters to deliver their guests. There are interatoll ferry connections to Male from Muli every other day (Rf230, four hours). See the **MTCC** (p178) website for routes and timetables. The Meemu public ferry connects all the inhabited islands in the atoll to each other every day except Friday. See www.atolltransfer.com/meemu-atoll-public-ferry for schedules.

Faafu

Faafu Atoll is perhaps the least visited corner of Maldives and one of the least populated, with just 4200 people living on its five inhabited islands. Its tranquility has attracted interest: in 2017, the Saudi government put forward a proposal to create a Special Economic Zone that would see billions invested in this tiny island. The idea seems to have lost steam, to the relief of atoll residents, who feared they would be relocated if the project went ahead.

For now, the capital island **Nilandhoo** is a small fishing village with a very traditional community. Here you'll find the second-oldest mosque in the country, **Aasaari Miskiiy**, built during the reign of Sultan Mohammed Ibn Abdullah (r 1153–66). It is made of dressed stone and the interior is decorated with carved woodwork. It's possible that the stones were recycled from the ruins of pre-Islamic structures.

There is just one midrange resort and one guesthouse in the atoll, meaning that whoever makes it here will have the place pretty much to themselves.

Activities

There are some highly recommended dive sites in the atoll. South of the resort of the same name, **Filitheyo Reef** descends in big steps, attracting swarms of batfish and Napoleons. Grey-tip reef sharks, rays and trevally are frequent visitors. Off the small island of Feeali, the **Two Brothers** are two thilas in a narrow channel, home to soft corals and sponges, turtles, nudibranchs, pipefish, gobies and other small marine species; it's good for snorkelling as well as diving.

Sleeping

Remora Inn GUESTHOUSE **$**

(986 1621, 775 2229; http://remorainn.com/; Nilandhoo; s/d from US$72/110;) This Polish-Maldivian venture is run by the friendly Magda, who ensures that there's a steady stream of Polish visitors here, although non-Poles won't feel out of place. On the island of Nilandhoo, a place still barely touched by tourism, this carefully designed and thoughtfully decorated place has en-suite rooms with patios or balconies and access to the nearby bikini beach.

Filitheyo Island Resort RESORT **$**

(674 0025; www.aaaresorts.com.mv; Filitheyo; r from US$325;) Filitheyo is a lush, triangular island with superb white-sand beaches and some stellar dive sites within easy reach. The public buildings are spacious open-sided Balinese-style pavilions with palm-thatch roofs and natural touches. The whole place feels chic but laid-back and informal. It's a solid midrange option with many guests on all-inclusive packages who come here to dive and relax.

Most rooms are comfortable timber bungalows that nest among the palm trees and face the beach. They're equipped with amenities including open-air bathrooms and personal sun decks.

Deluxe villas provide extra space and style, while the water villas have sea views, private terraces and an *undholi* (traditional Maldivian swing chair).

Resort facilities include a gym, small spa, infinity pool, reading room and shops. There's an interesting program of excursions and fishing trips in this isolated and little-visited atoll.

Beaches are pretty all around, but the lagoon is shallow on the south side and not suitable for swimming on the east side. The north side has it all – soft sand, good swimming and an accessible house reef that's great for snorkelling. Qualified divers can do unguided dives off the house reef.

Getting There & Away

Getting down to Faafu Atoll is rather tricky; most travellers head directly to **Filitheyo Island Resort** by seaplane, which is organised

SOUTHERN ATOLLS HIGHLIGHTS

Manta Point (p131) Diving with these magnificent creatures at Maa Kandu in Addu Atoll for an unforgettable experience.

Thoondu Beach (Fuvahmulah) Surfing or just catching some rays at one of Maldives' loveliest beaches on the friendly inhabited island of Fuvahmulah.

Tiger Zoo (p128) Descending through the blue to this remarkable diving spot where you're likely to see dozens of large tiger sharks just off the island of Fuvahmulah.

Eedhigali Kilhi & Kottey Protected Area (p130) Discovering Hithadhoo's unusual geography at this excellent nature reserve and birding spot.

Shark's Tongue Seeing both grey-tip and white-tip reef sharks at this superb diving spot in Meemu Atoll.

Vaavu, Meemu, Faafu & Dhaalu Atolls

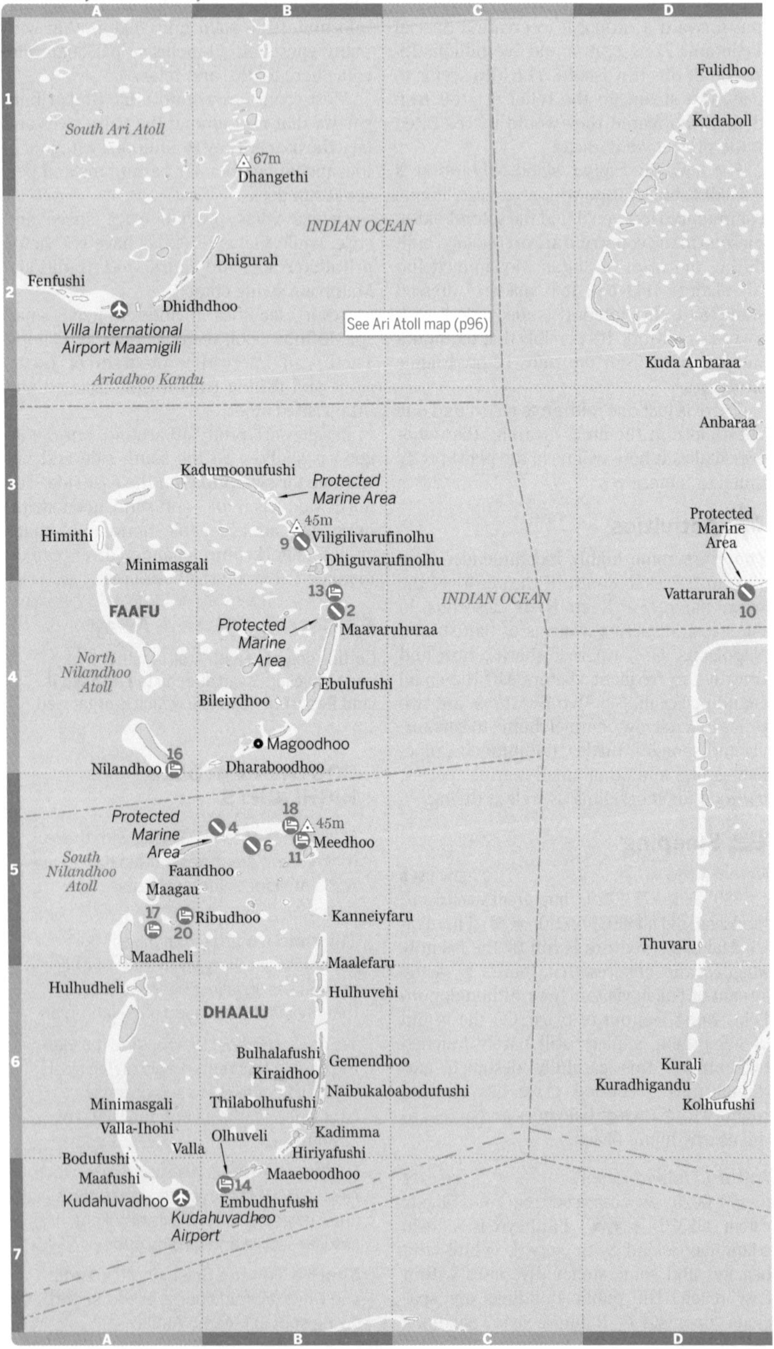

South Ari Atoll
67m
Dhangethi
INDIAN OCEAN
Dhigurah
Fenfushi
Dhidhdhoo
Villa International Airport Maamigili
See Ari Atoll map (p96)
Ariadhoo Kandu
Fulidhoo
Kudaboll
Kuda Anbaraa
Anbaraa
Kadumoonufushi
Protected Marine Area
45m
Viligilivarufinolhu
9
Dhiguvarufinolhu
Himithi
Minimasgali
Protected Marine Area
Vattarurah
10
13
2
INDIAN OCEAN
FAAFU
Protected Marine Area
Maavaruhuraa
North Nilandhoo Atoll
Ebulufushi
Bileiydhoo
Magoodhoo
16
Nilandhoo
Dharaboodhoo
18
Protected Marine Area
4
45m
6
Meedhoo
11
South Nilandhoo Atoll
Faandhoo
Maagau
17
Ribudhoo
20
Kanneiyfaru
Maadheli
Thuvaru
Maalefaru
Hulhudheli
Hulhuvehi
DHAALU
Bulhalafushi
Gemendhoo
Kiraidhoo
Kurali
Kuradhigandu
Naibukaloabodufushi
Minimasgali
Thilabolhufushi
Kolhufushi
Valla-Ihohi
Kadimma
Olhuveli
Valla
Hiriyafushi
Bodufushi
Maaeboodhoo
Maafushi
14
Kudahuvadhoo
Embudhufushi
Kudahuvadhoo Airport

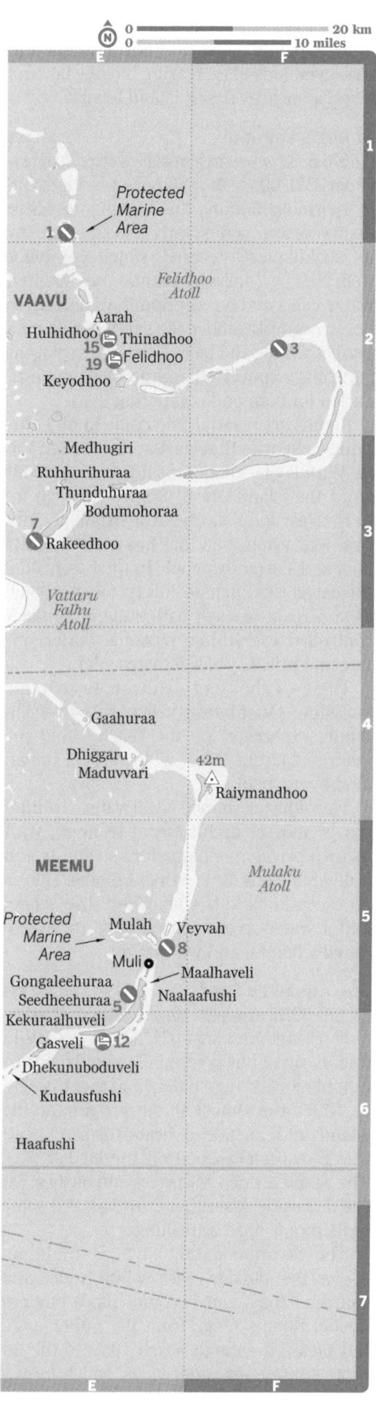

Vaavu, Meemu, Faafu & Dhaalu Atolls

Activities, Courses & Tours

1	Devana Kandu	E1
2	Filitheyo Reef	B4
3	Fotteyo	F2
4	Fushi Kandu	B5
5	Giant Clam	E5
6	Macro Spot	B5
7	Rakeedhoo Kandu	E3
8	Shark's Tongue	E5
9	Two Brothers	B3
10	Vattaru Kandu	D4

Sleeping

11	Beach Stay Maldives	B5
12	Cinnamon Hakuraa Huraa	E6
13	Filitheyo Island Resort	B4
14	Niyama Private Islands	B7
15	Plumeria Maldives	E2
16	Remora Inn	A4
17	St Regis Vommuli	A5
18	Sun Aqua Vilu Reef	B5
19	Vaali Beach Lodge Maldives	E2
20	Villa Stella	A5

by the resort. There are daily speedboats from Male's **New Harbour** (p70) to **Nilandhoo** (p119) (Rf350, three hours); contact **Atoll Transfer** (p178) for timetables and tickets. The Faafu Atoll public ferry (Rf20) connects the atoll's five inhabited islands in both directions daily except Friday.

Dhaalu

Dhaalu Atoll was a latecomer to tourism, with its first resort opening in the late 1990s and just a handful operating today. With a population of around 5000 people spread over seven inhabited islands, it's a quiet corner of the country with excellent diving and snorkelling.

The biggest island is the capital, **Kudahuvadhoo**, a busy fishing centre and home to the atoll's only airport (p123).

In the north of the atoll are the so-called 'Jewellers' Islands', **Ribudhoo** and **Hulhudheli**. Ribudhoo has long been known for its silversmiths and goldsmiths, who are believed to have learnt the craft from a royal jeweller banished here by a sultan centuries ago. Hulhudheli is traditionally a community of silversmiths whose many craftspeople still make jewellery, beads and carvings from mother-of-pearl. There are guesthouses on both islands attracting a small but growing stream of independent travellers.

Activities

There's more good diving in Dhaalu Atoll. **Fushi Kandu** (Map p120) sees eagle rays and white-tip reef sharks on the east side, while thilas inside the channel are frequented by turtles, Napoleon wrasse, yellowmouth morays and schooling snappers. Divers and snorkellers can get closer to small critters at **Macro Spot** (Map p120), a sheltered, shallow giri with lobsters, cowries, glassfish, blennies and gobies.

Sleeping

Resorts

★Niyama Private Islands RESORT **$$$**
(☎676 2828; www.niyama.com; Olhuveli & Embudhufushi; r from US$1120; ❄📶🏊) This gorgeous resort, spread between two lush islands, is an extremely impressive fusion of alluring white beaches, ultra-high-end accommodation and superb service. It features plenty of quirky touches including a tree-house restaurant, an off-shore overwater restaurant and an underground nightclub.

Niyama is flush with awards, and was recently hailed by Conde Nast as one of the world's best resorts.

The two islands are divided into two concepts: chill and play. Olhuveli, the main island, is chill; Embudhufushi is devoted to play. The rooms on both are a highlight: all but one category have their own pools, and all enjoy direct water access. They are lavishly furnished, with huge bathrooms and vast sliding doors leading to spacious gardens; the beach villas are rather more charming than the impressively large but slightly sterile water villas. The upper categories are enormous and are supplied with everything from electric guitars to telescopes to keep itinerant millionaires entertained.

You can get excellent sandwiches to go at the resort's excellent deli. For more substantial fare, there's the poolside all-day restaurant Epicure; Nest, a tree-house restaurant serving pan-Asian food; a very interesting selection of African and South American cuisine at Tribal; and Italian at Blu. There's also fine dining at Edge, an evening-only restaurant built over the reef for which you need to take a bespoke boat; it's undeniably gimmicky, but the food is fabulous. Downstairs from Edge is Subsix, an underwater restaurant where guests can have a gourmet lunch surrounded by colourful fish, and enjoy weekly parties when it turns into a club.

Other attractions include the large, glamorous Lime Spa, dive and water sports centres, gym, kids club, marine biology lab and a perfect nearby desert island to visit.

St Regis Vommuli RESORT **$$$**
(☎676 6333; www.stregismaldives.com; Vommuli; r from US$1200; ❄📶🏊) Opened in late 2016 to enormous fanfare, this highly impressive luxury resort is instantly recognisable by its striking architecture, which combines Gehry-esque curves, manta ray-inspired water villas and a reception that appears to hover magically above the sand. Sitting on a perfect white-sand island, the entire place is gorgeously conceived and an obvious destination for high-end pampering.

Rooms are palatial, and come in nine dizzying categories that start at the Garden Villas With Pool – glamorous little refuges built amid the island's lush jungle – and go up to the vast John Jacob Astor Estate, a giant two-floor water villa that has a vast infinity pool and sleeps six people in total seclusion. All categories include lovely touches such as suncream in each bath suite, fully iPad-controlled everything, personal butler service and private pools for each villa.

There's a choice of six divine restaurants including Orientale – a superb pan-Asian dining experience on the beach – and the main restaurant, Alba, which serves Italian food by the pool.

The lobster-shaped overwater Iridium spa is another architectural triumph, with its own private pool area for spa guests and individual pods for treatment rooms. There's an exceptional kids club, a full dive school and a water sports centre. Staff are exceptionally helpful and welcoming.

Sun Aqua Vilu Reef RESORT **$$$**
(☎676 0011; www.vilureefmaldives.com; Meedhufushi; all-inclusive r from US$768; ❄📶🏊) Vilu Reef is small but perennially popular resort notable for its huge palms and great beaches, which run almost all the way around the island and include a beautiful sand spit; they're especially good on the lagoon side. The island is thick with trees and bushes. On the downside, it's rather crowded, and some of its rooms need refreshing.

The accommodation style is traditional on the outside with white walls and thatched roofs, but becomes more modern inside. Rooms range from the rather worn but pleasant enough beach villas to the far more sumptuous water villas, which form a

HOW TO SPOT A TRULY LUXURIOUS RESORT

In case you have any doubts about where you're staying, this checklist should help to confirm that you're in the very smartest of Maldivian resorts:

- You will not be given a fruit cocktail on arrival, but rather an iced ginger tea, homemade ice cream or fresh melon juice served in dainty earthenware cups.
- The staff (including the general manager) line up on the jetty when you arrive; you have to work the line shaking their hands and feeling like a minor royal.
- You will be assigned a butler – also known in some resorts as Man Friday, *thakuru* or guest entertainment manager – to look after you during your stay.
- You have your own lap pool so you don't have to mix with hoi polloi in the main one.
- You have more towels than you know what to do with in your room, and more brand-name bath products than you can be bothered to swipe.
- Staff members you have never even seen magically glide into view when least expected and address you by your first name.
- Every time you leave your room a fleet of staff will swarm in to clean it, though you will never see them.
- When they bid you farewell, the staff on the jetty will continue waving at your boat or seaplane until you can no longer see them.

huge oval and mirror the shape of the island. On one side, a wide beach faces a lagoon that's perfect for sailing and sheltered swimming; on the other side, a good but more narrow beach runs alongside a house reef that offers good snorkelling.

Divers are well catered for by the reasonably priced diving school, which runs a full range of courses and dives each day. The resort has a buffet main restaurant with limited dining options, and a smarter à la carte place.

Vilu Reef combines friendly informality with some class and style – and it's suited to people looking for well-priced diving without having to go to a budget resort.

Guesthouses

Beach Stay Maldives GUESTHOUSE $
(☎795 7950; www.beachstaymaldives.com; Meedhoo; r from US$55; ❄📶) This six-room guesthouse overlooks the harbour on the charmingly laid-back, predominantly fishing island of Meedhoo. It offers a warm welcome to its guests, who usually visit on great-value all-inclusive seven-night packages (US$1500 per person), which are packed with excursions and activities. The guesthouse has its own bikini beach a short distance away.

Villa Stella GUESTHOUSE $
(☎778 4769; www.housemaldives.com; Ribudhoo; s/d incl full board US$110/150; ❄📶) One of the very first guesthouses in Maldives, Villa Stella is a great place to enjoy life on an inhabited island and to explore local culture. Even though the guesthouse is used to catering to Italians, English is spoken, and the welcome is warm. Meals of fresh fish are excellent and there's also a small bikini beach on Ribudhoo.

ℹ Getting There & Away

A domestic **airport** on the island of Kudahuvadhoo was opened in 2017, making getting to Dhaalu far easier than it was in the past. There are currently three daily flights to and from Male (US$170, one hour), as well as to **Kadhoo Airport** (☎680 0706) in Laamu Atoll and **Gan International Airport** (p176) in Addu Atoll, all on **Maldivian** (p104). Seaplane charters still serve the resorts in Dhaalu, while ferry routes 405 and 406 connect the atoll's seven inhabited islands three times a week; tickets cost Rf25. See the **MTCC** (p178) website for timetables.

Thaa

Thaa Atoll consists of 59 islands; of these, 13 are inhabited and one is a resort. The capital is **Veymandhoo**, with a population of 1100 people. Nearby **Thimarafushi** was expanded recently by reclaiming land to accommodate the atoll's airport (p124), which has daily connections to Male. The atoll is a popular destination for surf safaris and has a number of breaks that can only be reached by boat.

Despite its remote location and small population, there is a surprising number of historical sites here, including the grave of Sultan Osman I, who ruled Maldives for only six months before being banished in 1388 to the island of **Guraidhoo**, where his tomb was discovered in 1922.

On **Dhiyamigili** there are ruins of the palace of Mohammed Imaaduddeen II, a much more successful sultan who ruled from 1704 to 1721 and founded one of Maldives' longest-ruling dynasties.

Sleeping

★ **COMO Maalifushi** RESORT $$$

(☎678 0008; www.comohotels.com/maalifushi; Maalifushi; r US$1580; ❄📶🏊) The first resort in remote Thaa Atoll is this glorious creation of the COMO group. The highlights include superb food, an excellent holistic spa and state-of-the-art rooms, all built from scratch in 2014. The island has great stretches of beach, and enjoys its own atmospheric desert island nearby. Tourism in Thaa Atoll couldn't have gotten off to a better start.

Maalifushi's 59 rooms are as cutting edge as you'd expect them to be, given the resort opened less than five years ago; all but six on the island have their own pools. All are huge, and the palatial water villas are particularly impressive, each with a separate living room/dining area, bedroom, vast terrace and big plunge pools. While the style is rather anonymous, it's thoroughly contemporary and tasteful.

Food is definitely a highlight; the Japanese Tai Restaurant, the all-day Madi and Thila restaurants and in-villa dining are all absolutely top-notch. The overwater Como Shambhala Spa offers a full program of pampering.

Getting There & Away

Thimarafushi Airport (☎791 1775) has one daily flight to and from Male (US$195, 50 minutes) on **Maldivian** (p104). **Resort** (p124) guests can also fly directly to Maalifushi by seaplane charter.

Laamu

Laamu Atoll has about 12,600 people living on its 12 inhabited islands; these include **Gan**, the largest island in the country at a whopping 8km long. Gan is connected to its neighbours **Kadhoo** and **Fonadhoo** by causeways, creating the largest settled area in Maldives outside Male and Addu Atoll. The island of **Kadhoo** houses the atoll's airport (p123), offering regular flights to Male.

Not to be confused with the other two Gans in the south – Gan boasts several guesthouses and a large (by local standards) lake, plus a slew of hard-to-spot Buddhist ruins. As Gan is connected to Kadhoo and Fonadhoo by causeways, it's possible to explore other nearby islands without hiring a boat, so this is a great choice if you'd like to see lots of local life.

At the northeastern tip of the atoll, the island of **Isdhoo** is home to a 300-year-old mosque that was probably built on the site of an earlier temple, because it faces directly west, rather than towards Mecca, which is to the northwest.

Isdhoo also has a *hawitta* (ancient artificial mound) – the 20th-century British archaeologist HCP Bell believed such mounds were the remains of Buddhist stupas, while Norwegian ethnographer Thor Heyerdahl speculated that Buddhists had built these on even earlier mounds left by the legendary Redin people.

Sleeping

★ **Reveries Diving Village** GUESTHOUSE $

(☎680 8877; www.reveriesmaldives.com; Gan; s/d from US$55/71; ❄📶🏊) This smart place, run by a clued-up and passionate team of locals, is one of the best compromises we have found between the luxury of a resort and the cost of a guesthouse. The 20 rooms offer some of the smartest guesthouse accommodation in the country, with stylish furniture, balconies, cable TV and good bathrooms with rain showers.

As its name suggests, the guesthouse is aimed at divers who take advantage of the incredible diving all over the atoll, much of which is still being discovered. There are many other activities on offer too, such as surfing at six nearby breaks, wakeboarding, fishing and kayaking. There's also a small gym and a rooftop spa, plus an enclosed bikini beach in front of the hotel. Meals are taken at one of three good on-site restaurants. Young staff members are keen to help out and ensure you enjoy your stay.

★ **Six Senses Laamu** RESORT $$$

(☎680 0800; www.sixsenses.com/resorts/laamu/destination; Olhuveli; r from US$1300; ❄📶🏊) 🍃 Six Senses Laamu is an amazing place, combining thoughtful luxury, rustic simplicity, outstanding culinary options and plenty of activities. The island truly feels like it's in the middle of nowhere; getting to Olhuveli involves an hour's flight south from Male followed by a 15-minute speedboat ride, but a stay here is certainly worth the extra travel time.

The first impression of the island is created by the giant wooden overwater structure where you dock; here you'll find the reception, several dining and drinking options, a library and even an ice-cream parlour and chocolate bar, where delicious free treats are given to guests all day long. You'll find that the fantastically well-trained staff's efficiency and problem-solving abilities are second to none.

The island itself is ringed by a gorgeous white beach and boasts a fabulous cyan-blue lagoon where dolphins swim in great numbers all year round.

The 97 villas – all either right on the beach or over water – are something truly special; made from ecologically sourced wood, they evoke a grand, classic style with plenty of luxuries such as espresso machines and Bose entertainment systems.

The water villas are particularly impressive, with overwater hammocks, all-glass bathtubs and their own treetop decks. The beach villas – featuring loungers, plunge pools and expansive outdoor bathrooms – are ringed with trees and feel wonderfully private while still offering direct beach access.

The resort houses several superb restaurants. We particularly love Leaf, which overlooks the beach from the treetops; it's reached by crossing a wooden bridge. Sushi at Longitude is absolutely top notch. Elsewhere on the island there's a pool, a yoga and meditation centre, gym, outdoor cinema, wine cellar, gorgeous spa and full diving school and water sports centre.

The resort has a benchmark sustainability program that's almost unrivalled in Maldives; it includes multiple marine-life conservation projects, community-outreach and educational projects, and waste-reduction policies.

Getting There & Around

There are three daily flights with **Maldivian** (p104) between Male and **Kadhoo Airport** (p123) (US$195, 50 minutes), from where it's possible to transfer to **Six Senses Laamu** (p124) and elsewhere in the atoll.

The Laamu public ferry operates two routes. On Monday, Wednesday and Saturday, the 504 connects the inhabited islands along the atoll's eastern edge beginning at Isdhoo and ending at Kadhoo. Route 505 operates on Sunday, Tuesday and Thursday and connects Kadhoo to Maavah, calling at each inhabited island on the way. A ticket costs Rf50. See timetables on the **MTCC** (p178) website.

Gaafu Alifu

The northern half of the giant natural atoll of Huvadhoo – one of the largest coral atolls in the world – Gaafu Alifu has 11 inhabited islands and a population of around 9300. **Villingili**, the capital island, is the most populated, with about 3000 people. Just south, the island of **Kooddoo** has the atoll's airport (p127) and a fish-packing works.

The atoll also has some productive agriculture, much of it on the island of **Kondey**, which is also home to four *hawittas* (Buddhist prayer mounds), evidence of ancient Buddhist settlements. In the centre of the atoll, the island of **Dhevvadhoo** is famous for its traditional textile weaving and coir-rope making. There are also mosques from the 16th and 17th centuries.

Sleeping

Pearl Beach View GUESTHOUSE **$**
(☎791 3623; https://pearlbeach.webflow.io; Nilandhoo; r US$68; ❄📶) A wonderful option on the charming fishing island of Nilandhoo, which has some great beaches and very friendly locals. The small guesthouse, just a short wander from the island's bikini beach, has four simple but spotless rooms that share a small enclosed sand-floored courtyard. The friendly, enthusiastic guesthouse owners can arrange almost any local activity.

BRIDGES OVER TROUBLED WATER

Maldives is famous for having virtually no roads, but there are a few places where you'll find strips of tarmac, and even a few cars using it. Laamu Atoll boasts three road bridges connecting four islands, including **Gan**, the largest island in the country, while nearby Addu Atoll has the longest stretch of road in Maldives – an impressive 14km – connecting five adjacent islands. Needless to say, traffic is limited, and rush hour is nonexistent.

Laamu, Thaa, Gaafu Alifu & Gnaviyani

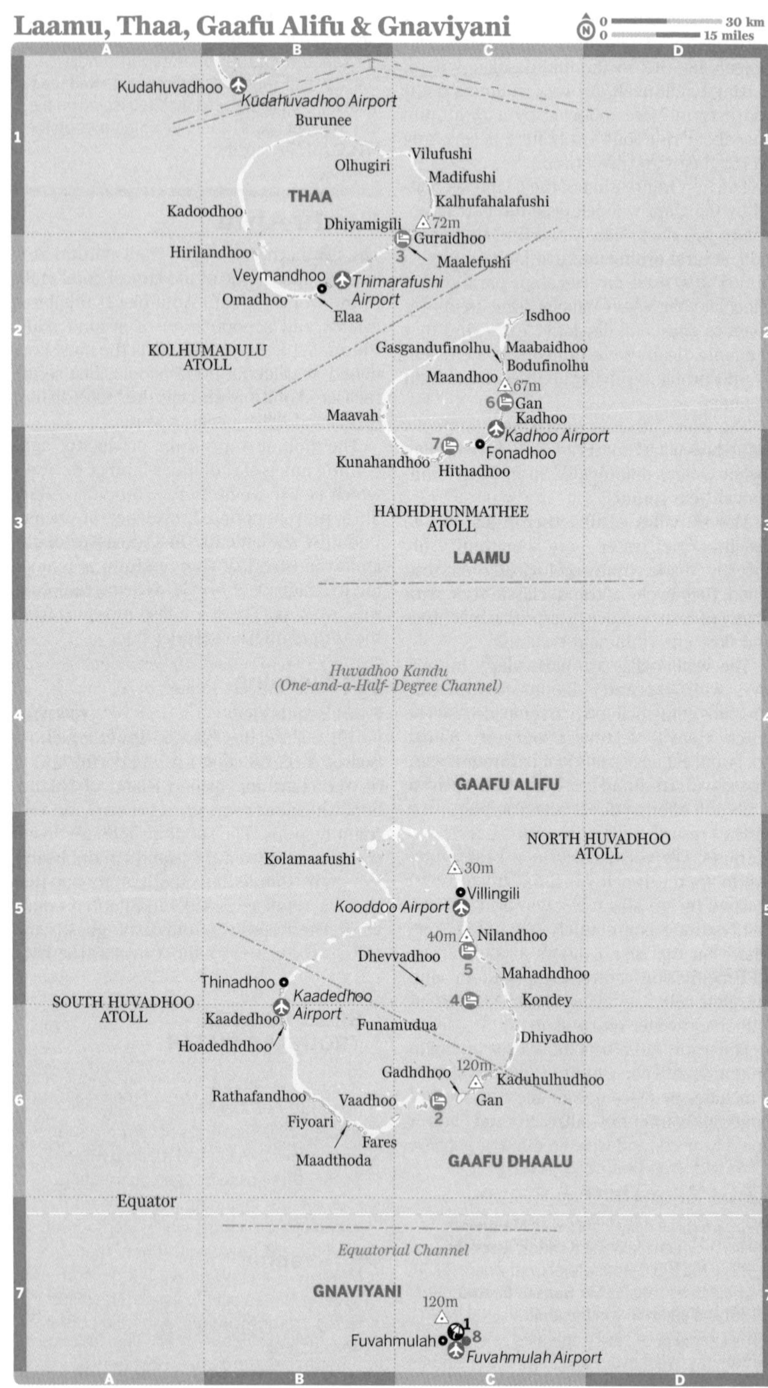

Laamu, Thaa, Gaafu Alifu & Gnaviyani

★ **Park Hyatt Maldives Hadahaa** RESORT **$$$**
(☎682 1234; https://maldiveshadahaa.park.hyatt.com; Hadahaa; r from US$990; ❄ 📶 🏊) Remote, stylish, modern and luxurious: this five-star island's high standards and gorgeous beaches rank it as one of the best hotels in the country. The resort's most striking feature is its thoroughly contemporary architecture, which makes the most of glass, steel and sleek minimalist lines to create some gorgeous structures.

Park Hyatt Maldives Hadahaa is a city hotel that just happens to be on the beach; travellers looking for rustic or traditional will need to head elsewhere. The 50 rooms – 36 on land and a curl of 14 water villas – are spacious, bright and calibrated perfectly to the needs of the urban nomad, with media hubs, flat-screen TVs and remote-control everything.

The beaches are gorgeous and the island is extremely lush, with thick foliage and coconut palms lining the beach. There's a stunning main infinity pool surrounded by a poolside bar, two main restaurants and a number of private dining options. The Vidhun spa, which offers a fantastic array of massages and treatments, is built around its own pool for spa guests to share. There's also an excellent diving centre, water sports centre, a gym and a range of activities and excursions, so nobody will get bored here.

Getting There & Away

Kooddoo Airport (☎682 0001; Kooddoo) has several flights a day to Male (US$212, 70 minutes), most of which stop at **Kadhoo Airport** (p123) in Laamu Atoll en route.

There are six frequent ferries connecting most of the inhabited islands in Gaafu Alifu and its southern neighbour Gaafu Dhaalu, including Kaadedhoo, home to an **airport** (p128). The network is centred on Gaafu Dhaalu's capital island Thinadhoo, and to a lesser extent on Gaafu Alifu's capital Villingili. See the **MTCC** (p178) website for timetables and routes.

Gaafu Dhaalu

Geographically isolated from Male but strategically located on the Indian Ocean trade routes, Gaafu Dhaalu – the southern part of Huvadhoo Atoll – has independent tendencies dating back many years. It had its own direct trade links with Sri Lanka, and a dialect of Dhivehi almost incomprehensible to other Maldivians is spoken here.

The capital island of **Thinadhoo** was a focal point of the so-called 'southern rebellion' against Male rule during the early 1960s, so much so that the army invaded in February 1962 and destroyed all the homes. It now has a population of around 5200; the rest of the atoll's inhabitants are scattered across nine other islands.

While there are several resorts here, Gaafu Dhaalu lies off the main circuit, though surfers gather to surf the uncrowded waves that break around the southeastern edge of the atoll.

On the island of **Gadhdhoo**, women weave soft mats known as *thundu kunaa* from special reeds found on an adjacent island. In the south of Huvadhoo Atoll, only about 20km from the equator, the island of **Vaadhoo** has two *hawittas* (stone prayer mounds) and a 17th-century mosque with ancient tombstones carved with three different kinds of early Maldivian script.

Sleeping

Ayada Maldives RESORT **$$$**
(☎684 4444; www.ayadamaldives.com; Maguhdhuvaa; r from US$990; ❄ 📶 🏊) The first resort built in this pristine corner of Maldives, Ayada

MYSTERIOUS GAN

Just southwest of **Gadhdhoo** (p127), the uninhabited island of Gan – not to be confused with the islands of the same name in Laamu and Addu atolls – has remnants of what was once the most impressive *hawitta* (stone prayer mound) in Maldives. Originally a pyramid with stepped ramps on all four sides – similar to many Mexican pyramids – it was 8.5m high and measured 23 sq metres. Norwegian ethnographer Thor Heyerdahl found stones here decorated with sun motifs, which he believed were proof of a sun-worshipping society even older than the Buddhist and Hindu settlements; this is the subject of Heyerdhahl's book *The Maldive Mystery.* While many of Heyerdhal's theories are now rejected by ethnographers and archaeologists, there is no doubt that his excavations in Maldives in the 1980s were a turning point for the official version of Maldivian history, which had until that time ignored all evidence of pre-Muslim civilisations on the islands.

boasts fantastic accommodation in large and beautifully designed contemporary villas. It's set on a perfect island surrounded by superb and largely undiscovered reefs; there are also some excellent surf breaks nearby. It's a great choice for anyone looking for a luxurious diving and water sports holiday.

There are nine different villa types, sized from around 85 sq metres up to 350 sq metres. They're done out in timber and thatch and enjoy their own pools, sleek and contemporary furnishings with an Asian flavour and lots of luxurious extras such as Nespresso machines, media hubs and full in-room bars.

There are three restaurants on the island, as well as the fabulously indulgent overwater Ile de Joie, where fine wines, cheeses, oysters, caviar and chocolates are all served in a variety of gastronomic combinations. Other facilities include a gorgeously designed AySpa spa, a hammam and steam room, tennis and badminton courts, a full gym, a water sports centre and a top-of-the-range dive school.

This is a great place to escape the crowds and enjoy your own slice of Indian Ocean paradise in sumptuous but laid-back style.

Getting There & Away

Gaafu Dhaalu's **Kaadedhoo Airport** (☎684 2557; Kaadedhoo) has three daily flights (US$212, 70 minutes) to and from Male on **Maldivian** (p104). Resorts in the atoll either fly guests in on seaplane charters or pick them up from Kaadedhoo Airport.

There is a network of six frequent ferries connecting most of the inhabited islands in the atoll, as well as those in Gaafu Alifu. The network is centred on the capital island Thinadhoo. See the **MTCC** (p178) website for routes and timetables.

Gnaviyani

The island of **Fuvahmulah** (also written as Foammulah; both are pronounced like the English word 'formula') makes up Gnaviyani Atoll, a remote place stuck in the middle of the Equatorial Channel with a population of around 8500.

About 5km long and 1km wide, it's the third biggest island in Maldives and one of the most fertile, producing many fruits and vegetables in its neatly tended fields. The natural vegetation is lush, and there are two freshwater lakes – former lagoons – making it geographically about the most varied place in the country.

In recent years the building of a harbour and an airport here have greatly lessened Fuvahmulah's sense of isolation, and the island is slowly welcoming tourism. While there's no bikini beach yet, there is a superb stretch of sand at one end of the island, some great diving, plenty of local colour and a friendly population.

Activities

People flock to Fuvahmulah specifically for the thrill of diving **Tiger Zoo** and taking the plunge with massive tiger sharks, considered the second most dangerous shark in the world after the great white. With this in mind, following safety instructions is important, but the site can be dived without fear of attack, and getting close to these huge creatures is a humbling experience.

Several local dive operators run dedicated trips, including **Fuvahmulah Dive** (☎753 4392; www.fuvahmulahdive.com) and **Farikede Divers** (☎790 0056; www.farikededivers.com; Bahaaru Magu), both on Fuvahmulah; single dives start from US$62.

Sleeping

★Veyli Residence GUESTHOUSE $
(☎777 5226; www.veyli.com; Narugis Magu, Fuvahmulah; r US$80; ❄📶) This homely guesthouse set in a spacious garden is our top choice on the island. The attentive, passionate local owners make it their mission to ensure you have a good time on Fuvahmulah. Rooms have small balconies and are simple but spotlessly clean, with crisp linens on the beds. There are plenty of communal areas and a cafe.

Eating

A relatively large and self-contained island, Fuvahmulah has plenty of cafes and a few restaurants to choose from. The two best restaurants are at opposite ends of the island: **Royal Restaurant** (mains Rf70-175; ⏰9am-midnight Sat-Thu, 2pm-midnight Fri) overlooks the harbour on the southern end, while **Pebbles by Royal** (Genmiskih Magu; mains Rf40-100; ⏰9am-midnight Sat-Thu, 2pm-midnight Fri) is next to the beach on the northern side of the island.

Getting There & Away

There are two daily flights in each direction with **Maldivian** (p104) between Male and **Fuvahmulah Airport** (US$235, 70 minutes). There is also a speedboat to and from **Feydhoo** (☎955 2449, 689 9339; Feydhoo) in Addu Atoll (Rf290, one hour) four days a week. On Monday and Thursday the boat leaves **Fuvahmulah Harbour** at 6am and on Wednesday and Saturday at 9am.

Addu Atoll

Heart-shaped Addu Atoll, just south of the equator, is the most southern point of Maldives. There's a splash of late-colonial flavour here – the island of Gan was used as a British military base until the 1970s – and an independent streak flows through the locals, who speak a different dialect of Dhivehi to that spoken in Male. The atoll enjoyed a brief period of independence as part of the United Suvadive Republic between 1959 and 1963.

The six inhabited islands here are known collectively as Addu City due to the fact that all but one are connected by bridges and causeways, creating at 14km the longest continuous stretch of land in the country.

Addu is the main economic and administrative centre in the southern atolls, and the only place to rival Male in size and importance. There are just three resorts down here, a few guesthouses and some superb diving opportunities.

Sights

Gan

Gan – not to be confused with the islands of the same name in Laamu and Gaafu Dhaalu atolls – has a far more colonial feel than anywhere else in the country. Inhabited since ancient times, Gan was where British archaeologist HCP Bell excavated a large 9m-high mound that he believed to be the ruins of a Buddhist stupa. His expedition made careful measurements of the site, took photos and made precise drawings that were published in his monograph. This was fortunate, as the archaeological sites (and almost everything else on Gan) were levelled to create an air force base in 1956.

The British took over the entire island and constructed airport buildings, barracks, jetties, maintenance sheds, a cinema, a golf course and even Maldives' first and only church. Many of these structures remain (the church emphatically does not); some are picturesquely run down, while others are used for various alternative purposes.

Most of the island's lush native vegetation was cleared, but the British landscaped with new plants – avenues of casuarinas, clumps of bougainvillea, swaths of lawn and rose gardens. It's much more spacious than most resort islands and it has a slightly weird and eerie atmosphere, but it's very peaceful and relaxed – like an old abandoned movie set.

There's a low-key **memorial** to those who served on the base, including Indian regiments. Big guns, which were part of the WWII defences, now guard the memorial.

Feydhoo, Maradhoo & Hithadhoo

Causeways connect Gan to the atoll capital Hithadhoo via Feydhoo and Maradhoo as well as some other tiny islands. You can easily walk from Gan to Feydhoo, which has several mosques. Boats to Fuvahmulah use the modern harbour here.

When the British took over, the villagers from Gan were resettled on Feydhoo, and some of the people from Feydhoo were then moved to the next island, Maradhoo, where they formed a new village. Maradhoo now has a population of 3600 spread over two

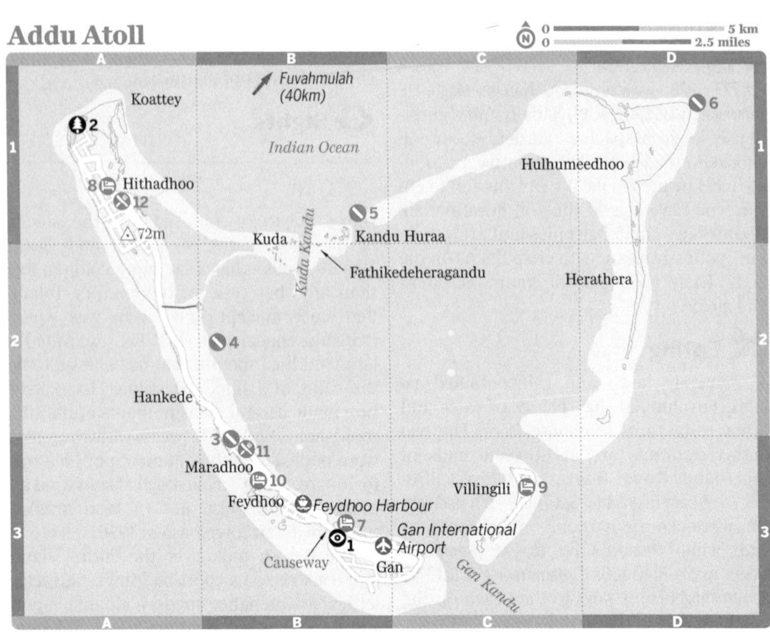

Addu Atoll

Sights
1 British War Memorial ... B3
2 Eedhigali Kilhi & Kottey Protected Area ... A1

Activities, Courses & Tours
3 Aquaventure Maldives ... B3
4 British Loyalty Wreck ... B2
Kuda Kandu ... (see 5)
Maa Kandu ... (see 5)
5 Manta Point ... B1
6 Shark Point ... D1

Sleeping
7 Equator Village ... B3
8 Pebbles Inn ... A1
9 Shangri-La Villingili Resort & Spa ... C3
10 Wave Sound by 3S Maldives ... B3

Eating
11 Palm Village ... B3
12 Suvadive Cafe ... A1

villages that have run together – the southern one is called Maradhoo-Feydhoo.

Further north, the road follows an isthmus that was once three narrow, uninhabited islands before connecting to Hithadhoo (population 10,600), Maldives' largest town outside Male. Hithadhoo's main sight is the **Eedhigali Kilhi & Kottey Protected Area** FREE, a unique natural habitat for birds and other wildlife surrounding Maldives' largest lake.

Hulhumeedhoo

At the northeast corner of the lagoon is the only inhabited island in Addu City not connected to its neighbours by causeways. The island, Hulhumeedhoo, has two adjoining villages, Hulhudhoo and Meedhoo, with a total population of 3500.

Legend says an Arab sailor shipwrecked here in about 872 converted the islanders to Islam 280 years before the people of Male. The island's cemetery is known for its ancient headstones, many of which are beautifully carved with the archaic Dhives Akuru script.

Activities

Despite bleaching inside the lagoon, on the northern edge of the atoll you can dive and snorkel around huge table corals that might be hundreds of years old, plus fields of staghorns that have all but disappeared in most parts of the country.

★Manta Point DIVING

This outstanding dive site is part of **Maa Kandu**, but is often dived specifically to see manta rays who gather at this cleaning station for a few hours in the morning, when the incoming current makes conditions just right for these majestic creatures. The cleaning station is at 20m and there are strong currents, so most divers use a line.

★British Loyalty Wreck DIVING

The *British Loyalty*, an oil tanker used to supply Gan, was torpedoed in 1944 by the German submarine *U-183*. The wreck lies in 33m of water with its port side about 16m below the surface; it has a good covering of soft corals. Turtles, trevally and many reef fish inhabit the encrusted decks, making it a fascinating place to dive.

Aquaventure Maldives DIVING

(☎777 4310; www.aquaventure-maldives.com; Maradhoo) This Maldivian-Dutch venture offers a daily two-tank morning dive and a one-tank afternoon dive. It has excellent equipment and its instructors know the waters of Addu intimately. An open water course can be done here for US$600.

Sleeping

Equator Village RESORT $

(☎689 9000; www.equatorvillage.com; Gan; all-inclusive r US$236; ❄📶🏊) Equator Village is one of the best-value resorts in the country, with low room rates and good all-inclusive packages making this a great deal. Staying here also gives you the opportunity to see something of local life, as Gan is connected to several inhabited islands by a causeway.

It's clear straight away that this was formerly a British RAF base; neat lines of rooms (former barracks!) fan out from the main building and are surrounded by well-tended gardens that overflow with exotic flowers and plants.

The resort has recently had a soft renovation, and though the spruced-up rooms remain functional, they're comfortable and great for divers.

The reception, bar and dining areas have been created from the old mess and look out onto a sizeable swimming pool and through palm trees to the sea beyond. The beach here is nothing special, but there are several lovely stretches of sand an easy boat ride away that can be visited on excursions.

The full-sized billiard table is a handsome inheritance from the Brits, as are the first-class tennis courts. The meals are all buffet with a limited selection. However, most guests are on all-inclusive packages, and can at least wash everything down with plentiful beer or house wine. Free bike use, an island-hopping excursion with a barbecue, and twice-daily snorkelling trips are included in most packages.

The PADI 5-Star Dive Centre is a small but friendly operation that visits the area's stellar dive sites at very reasonable prices.

★Shangri-La Villingili Resort & Spa RESORT $$$

(☎689 7888; www.shangri-la.com/male/villingiliresort; Villingili; r from US$1005; ❄📶🏊) This enormous but beautifully and thoughtfully conceived island ranks among the absolute top resorts in Maldives. It's right in the south of the country, but well worth the extra travel time. The vast water villas, great beaches and selection of super amenities will satisfy even the most demanding travellers.

The island is huge, enough so that the resort has its own nine-hole golf course, which includes Maldives' highest natural point – a dizzying 5m! The island also boasts three freshwater lakes, giving it more topographic variety than most other resorts.

The accommodation is a highlight. Middle Eastern- and Indian-influenced decor, Nespresso machines and vast bathrooms can be found in all rooms. With the exception of the water villas, all seven categories come with their own private pool. Particularly impressive are the palatial water villas, which are at least twice the size of those usually found in luxury resorts, and the treehouse-style villas; raised off the ground, these look and feel like a luxury version of Swiss Family Robinson, complete with a raised infinity pool.

There are three restaurants here. The main restaurant, Dr Ali's, is effectively three restaurants in one, with separate chefs specialising in Indian, Chinese and Arabic flavours. There's also Javvu, which overlooks the beach and serves up Mediterranean cuisine, and the stunning Fashala fine-dining restaurant, which requires advance bookings.

The rest of the resort is just as impressive, with first-rate, white powder-sand beaches, the incredibly lavish CHI spa, a full gym that includes a sauna and steam room, the superb Cool Zone kids club, two tennis courts, dive and water sports centres and a great reef for snorkelling.

MORE ADDU ATOLL DIVES

There are many other exciting dive sites in Addu Atoll. Consider the following:

Shark Point A plateau at about 30m, in the northeast of the atoll, with cruising grey-tip and white-tip reef sharks and bigger sharks further out in deeper water.

Kuda Kandu A superb dive site with strong currents but a huge array of coral between 5m and 15m; scan the reef edge for eagle rays and white-tip reef sharks.

Maa Kandu (p131) Good snorkelling and diving on a wide reef covered with live Acropora corals, big brain corals, long branching staghorns and table corals; good for white-tip reef sharks, eagle rays, turtles and occasional mantas.

★ **Wave Sound by 3S Maldives** GUESTHOUSE $
(☎689 3536; www.3smaldives.com; Maradhoo; r US$90; ❄ 📶) Right on the atoll edge, this bizarrely named seven-room guesthouse is actually a great choice for a beach-focused stay. The vanilla-scented rooms are timber-clad oases of air-con that face out onto a small rocky beach, with views of the sea and a couple of desert islands. There's free snorkelling equipment and bikes for hire (US$5 per day).

Pebbles Inn GUESTHOUSE $
(☎668 0660; www.pebblesinn.com; Hithadhoo; s/d US$79/112; ❄ 📶) This sparkling modern guesthouse has spotless rooms with comfortable beds and gleaming white bedsheets. Each room has a small balcony and those at the front of the building overlook the lagoon. It's the best choice if you want to stay on Hithadhoo, within easy walking distance of shops and restaurants on the island.

Eating

Aside from the comprehensive eating options offered at the atoll's three resorts, you can find several good restaurants on Hithadhoo and Maradhoo, which offer you the chance to have a more local experience.

Palm Village INDIAN $
(Maradhoo; mains Rf45-150; ⏲6am-midnight Sat-Thu, 6am-10.30am & 2pm-midnight Fri) This very pleasant place on the main road is rightly considered one of Addu City's best restaurants. It's popular with a mixed crowd of local families, young people and the occasional tourist. The food is excellent (particularly the dishes on the tandoori menu) and the place is perfect for a long meal, with fan-cooled niches and a roof terrace.

Suvadive Cafe INTERNATIONAL $$
(www.suvadivecafe.com; Hithadhoo; mains Rf75-150; ⏲8.30am-11.45pm Sat-Thu, 2-11.45pm Fri; 📶) This rather stylish place arranged around a large ornamental pond is the best choice for a meal on Hithadhoo. The menu is fairly standard international fare: pizzas, pasta, sandwiches and salads, though it pulls a few surprises including Mongolian rice and nasi goreng. There's good coffee and a selection of breakfasts. Look for the Queen on the photo wall.

Getting There & Away

Maldivian (p104) flies from Male to **Gan International Airport** (p176) and back four to five times a day (US$235, 1½ hours). There are also four direct flights per week from Colombo on SriLankan Airlines, which allow visitors to connect to Addu internationally without flying through Male.

There are speedboats to **Fuvahmulah** (p129) (Rf290, one hour) from **Feydhoo Harbour** (p129) on Monday and Thursday at 10am, and on Wednesday and Saturday at 2pm. There are also several daily connections by both speedboat and dhoni from here to Hulhumeedhoo (Rf55, 15 to 40 minutes).

Getting Around

One good way to get around Addu City is by bicycle, although distances are quite large and there's virtually no shade anywhere along the causeways; you can get hot very quickly. **Equator Village** (p131) includes bike hire in its rates.

Taxis shuttle between the islands and around the villages; from Gan to Hithadhoo should cost Rf150. Taxis wait at the **airport** (p176) or you can order one from Equator Village. There are also hourly buses (Rf20) that run from the airport to Hithadhoo's main road.

Understand Maldives

Maldives Today

Since the contested 2013 election of Abdulla Yameen, Maldives has made the headlines internationally for the wrong reasons. Although tourism continues to thrive, the arrest, detention and subsequent exile of its first democratically elected president, the arrest of two supreme court judges and a state of emergency imposed in early 2018 all serve to reinforce the impression that an almost total state capture has occurred. Despite strong criticism from international bodies, reports of corruption continue, as well as instances of intimidation and arrests of opponents of the government.

Best in Print

Beach Babylon (Imogen Edwards-Jones; 2004) An amusing behind-the-scenes exposé set in a luxurious Maldivian resort.
Dive the Maldives (Sam Harwood & Rob Bryning; 2009) The best guidebook to dive sites and marine life.
Maps of Maldives (Water Solutions Ltd; 2016) Contains maps of each atoll.

Best on Film

The Island President (Jon Shenk; 2011) Fascinating documentary about the rise of former president Nasheed and his quest to make the world care about climate change.
Rogue One: A Star Wars Story (Gareth Edwards; 2016) Laamu Atoll was the setting for the planet of Scarif.

Etiquette

On inhabited islands you must conform to local dress codes. This means shoulders and midriffs need to be covered and, for women, knees too.

During Ramazan it's not acceptable to eat in public during daylight hours, except in resorts.

In the atolls, men don't normally shake hands with women, but it's acceptable for women to shake hands with other women. Likewise, foreign women shaking hands with local men isn't seen as unusual.

Authoritarian Tendencies

Following the coup of 2012, the 2013 presidential election saw the presidency go to Abdulla Yameen, the half-brother of former dictator Maumoon Abdul Gayoom, who ruled unchallenged for 30 years before President Nasheed's short time in office.

Despite the family ties, Yameen and Gayoom quickly fell out and are now political enemies. Indeed, Yameen jailed Gayoom's politician son in 2017 and again in 2018 – for 'attempting to overthrow the government', according to newspaper *Maldives Independent* – and even arrested Gayoom himself during 2018's state of emergency declaration.

President Yameen's controversial rule has been marked by the frequent jailing of political opponents, including former president Mohammed Nasheed, indicted in 2015 for 'terrorism' and sentenced to 13 years imprisonment in a trial that the UN condemned as politically motivated. After seeking medical treatment abroad, Nasheed was granted political asylum in the UK, where he continues to live in exile today.

In 2017, Yameen sent the army to close the People's Majlis (the Maldivian Parliament), where a no-confidence vote against him was about to be held. The following year, two members of the Supreme Court were arrested after signing a ruling releasing many of the regime's political opponents.

At the time of writing it was impossible to make any predictions about the 2018 presidential elections. It's even possible that they won't happen at all, with the state of emergency declared at the start of the year. Widespread concerns remain that the election will not be free and fair and that opposition candidates may not be allowed to stand. Opposition forces are hoping to field a single candidate as a show of unity, but there's as yet no sign of who that might be.

Is It Safe to Go?

Despite the political tension and worryingly authoritarian developments in Male, tourism continues to boom, with 1.2 million tourists arriving in 2017 alone, more than four times the population of the entire country. Hotels at both ends of the spectrum are being built with astonishing speed: new luxury properties at the top end and cheaper guesthouses on inhabited islands are completed almost monthly.

With growing options for travel beyond the established resort islands, this is a fascinating time to visit Maldives, especially the capital and other inhabited islands.

If you do go to Male, do be sure to avoid any large demonstrations of other mass gatherings, however, as there's always the possibility of unrest. The fast pace of change here – despite the current political instability – is all part of the charm of discovering this proud and fiercely independent island nation.

Plots, Scandal and Graft

In September 2015, a small explosion on President Yameen's yacht – an attempt on his life, it was later claimed – occurred as the president and his entourage arrived in Male. A month later the president arrested his vice-president, Ahmed Adeeb, for charges of high treason and terrorism, the fourth high-profile rival of the president to be arrested on terrorism charges since 2013. Adeeb was handed a 10-year jail sentence in 2016, cleansing the executive of potential challengers for the presidency.

Despite this consolidation of power, an even bigger storm was brewing for Yameen: in 2017 an Al Jazeera investigation into corruption in Maldives stunned the nation. In his documentary piece *Stealing Paradise,* journalist Will Jordan identified what he believed was a vast US$1.5 billion graft scheme, in which President Yameen and his associates were allegedly skimming huge sums from the fees paid by foreign companies wanting to lease Maldivian islands to turn into resorts.

While many locals knew that corruption was a problem, nobody had any idea of the scale at which this was apparently operating.

Relations between the government and the press were already fragile following the disappearance in 2014 of Rilwan Abdulla, a journalist for the newspaper *Minivan News,* who received death threats after investigating political corruption and was last seen being abducted at knife-point outside his house.

After the government introduced new laws allowing the state to close media organisations accused of defamation in 2016, the status of the press in Maldives was downgraded from 'Partly Free' to 'Not Free' by democracy organisation Freedom House, a position echoed by organisations such as Reporters Without Borders.

AREA: **90,000 SQ KM (ABOVE WATER 298 SQ KM)**

POPULATION: **392,700**

GDP PER CAPITA: **US$8601**

PERCENTAGE OF POPULATION LIVING IN MALE: **39%**

if Maldives were 100 people

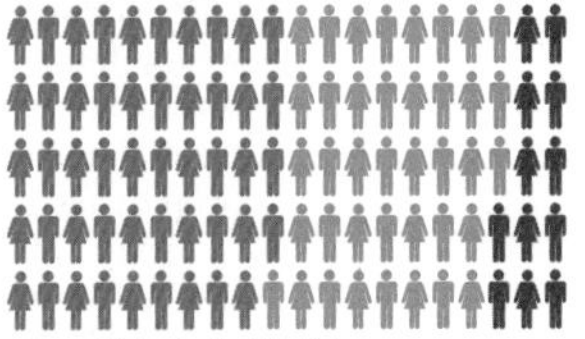

49 would live in the 'Atolls'
39 would live in Male
12 would work in North & South Male Atoll

belief systems

(% of population)

Sunni Muslim

population per sq km

MALDIVES

INDIA

UK

≈ 270 people

History

Maldives is historically a small, isolated and peaceful nation, whose main challenge has been constantly trying to contain the desires of its distant neighbours and would-be colonisers. For the most part, its history is incredibly hazy, with little known of the period before the conversion to Islam in 1153. The pre-Muslim era is full of heroic myths, based on largely inconclusive archaeological discoveries.

Early Days

Some archaeologists, including Thor Heyerdahl, believe that Maldives was well-known from around 2000 BC, and was a trading junction for several ancient maritime civilisations, including Egyptians, Romans, Mesopotamians and Indus Valley traders. The legendary sun-worshipping people called the Redin may have descended from one of these groups.

Around 500 BC the Redin either left or were absorbed by Buddhists, probably from Sri Lanka, and by Hindus from northwest India. HCP Bell, a British commissioner of the Ceylon Civil Service, led archaeological expeditions to Maldives in 1920 and 1922. Among other things, he investigated the ruined, dome-shaped structures *(hawittas)*, mostly in the Southern Atolls, which he believed were Buddhist stupas similar to the *dagobas* found in Sri Lanka.

The Maldive Mystery, by Thor Heyerdahl, the Norwegian explorer of *Kon-Tiki* fame, describes a short expedition in 1982–83 looking for remains of pre-Muslim societies.

Conversion to Islam

For many years Arab traders stopped in Maldives en route to the Far East – their first record of the Maldive islands, which they called Dibajat, is from the 2nd century AD. Known as the 'Money Isles', Maldives provided enormous quantities of cowry shells, an international currency of the early ages. It must have seemed a magical land to discover at the time, a place where money washed up on the shore.

Abul Barakat Yoosuf Al Barbary, a North African, is credited with converting the Maldivians to Islam in 1153. Though little is really known about what happened, Barakat was a *hafiz*, a scholar who knew the entire Quran by heart, and who proselytised in Male for some time before meeting with success.

TIMELINE

1117

The first king of the Theemuge dynasty, and the first king of Maldives, Sri Mahabarana, is crowned, bringing together under one ruler the many fiefdoms that made up the country at the time.

1153

Maldives is converted to Islam by Berber scholar Abul Barakat Yoosuf Al Barbary.

1194

The Isdhoo Loamaafaanu, a copperplate now believed to show the earliest recorded example of Maldivian script, is made. Among other things it details the execution of Buddhist monks in the south of Maldives.

One of the converts was the sultan, followed by the royal family. After conversion the sultan sent missionaries to the atolls to convert them too, and Buddhist temples around the country were destroyed or neglected.

A series of six sultanic dynasties followed, 84 sultans and sultanas in all, although some did not belong to the line of succession. At one stage, when the Portuguese first arrived on the scene, there were actually two ruling dynasties, the Theemuge (or Malei) dynasty and the Hilali.

The Portuguese

Early in the 16th century the Portuguese, who were already well established in Goa in western India, decided they wanted a greater share of the profitable trade routes of the Indian Ocean. They were given permission by the sultan to build a fort and a factory in Male, but it wasn't long before they wanted more from Maldives.

The Story of Mohamed Thakurufaanu, by Hussain Salahuddeen, tells the story of Maldives' greatest hero, who liberated the people from the Portuguese.

In 1558, after a few unsuccessful attempts, Portuguese Captain Andreas Andre led an invasion army and killed Sultan Ali VI. The Maldivians called the captain 'Andiri Andirin' and he ruled Male and much of the country for the next 15 years. According to some Maldivian beliefs, Andre was born in Maldives and went to Goa as a young man, where he came to serve the Portuguese.

Apart from a few months of Malabar domination in Male during the 18th century, this was the only time that another country has occupied Maldives; some argue that the Portuguese never actually ruled Maldives at all, but had merely established a trading post.

According to popular belief, the Portuguese were cruel rulers, and ultimately decreed that Maldivians must convert to Christianity or be killed. There was ongoing resistance, especially from Mohammed Thakurufaanu, son of an influential family on Utheemu Island in the northern atoll of Haa Alifu. Thakurufaanu, with the help of his two brothers and some friends, started a series of guerrilla raids, culminating in an attack on Male in which all the Portuguese were slaughtered.

Travels in Asia & Africa 1325–54, by Ibn Battuta, is the account of a great Moorish globetrotter's travels and includes early testimony of life in Maldives shortly after the arrival of Islam.

This victory is commemorated annually as National Day on the first day of the third month of the lunar year. On the island of Utheemu, there is a memorial centre to Thakurufaanu, Maldives' greatest hero, who went on to found the next sultanic dynasty, the Utheemu, which ruled for 120 years. Many reforms were introduced, including a new judicial system, a defence force and a coinage to replace the cowry currency.

Protected Independence

The Portuguese attacked several more times, and the rajahs of Cannanore in South India (who had helped Thakurufaanu), also attempted to gain control. In the 17th century, Maldives accepted the protection of the Dutch, who ruled Ceylon at the time. They also had a short-lived defence

1333

Ibn Battuta arrives in Maldives for a nine-month stay, during which time he marries twice and apparently leaves disappointed by the moral laxity of the locals.

1337

The Friday Mosque in Male is rebuilt by order of Sultan Ahmed Shihabuddin. The previous Friday Mosque, dating from 1153, had become run-down.

1573

The Portuguese are driven out of Maldives following an attack on the Portuguese garrison led by Mohammed Thakurufaanu. To this day, the event is celebrated as the country's National Day.

1796

The British expel the Dutch from Ceylon and stake their claim to Maldives, declaring it a 'British Protected Area'.

treaty with the French, and maintained good relations with the British, especially after the British took possession of Ceylon in 1796. These relations enabled Maldives to be free from external threats while maintaining internal autonomy. In any case, the remoteness of the islands, along with the prevalence of malaria and the lack of good ports, naval stores or productive land, were probably the main reasons that neither the Dutch nor the British established a colonial administration.

THE LEGEND OF THAKURUFAANU

As the man who led a successful revolution against foreign domination, and then as the leader of the newly liberated nation, Mohammed Thakurufaanu (sultan from 1573 to 1585) is Maldives' national hero. Respectfully referred to as Bodu Thakurufaanu (*bodu* meaning 'big' or 'great'), he is to Maldives what George Washington is to the USA. The story of his raid on the Portuguese headquarters in Male is part of Maldivian folklore, and known to every Maldivian child.

In his home island of Utheemu, Thakurufaanu's family was known and respected as sailors, traders and *kateebs* (island chiefs). The family gained the trust of Viyazoaru, the Portuguese ruler of the four northern atolls, and was given the responsibility of disseminating orders, collecting taxes and carrying tribute to the Portuguese base in Sri Lanka. Unbeknown to Viyazoaru, Thakurufaanu and his brothers used their position to foster anti-Portuguese sentiment, recruit sympathisers and gain intelligence. It also afforded them the opportunity to visit southern India, where Thakurufaanu obtained a pledge from the rajah of Cannanore to assist in overthrowing the Portuguese rulers of Maldives.

Back on Utheemu, Thakurufaanu and his brothers built a boat with which to conduct an attack on Male. This sailing vessel, named *Kalhuoffummi*, has its own legendary status – it was said to be not only fast and beautiful, but to have almost magical qualities that enabled it to elude the Portuguese on guerrilla raids and reconnaissance missions.

For the final assault, they sailed south through the atolls by night, stopping by day to gather provisions and supporters. Approaching Male, they concealed themselves on a nearby island. They stole into the capital at night to make contact with supporters there and to assess the Portuguese defences. They were assisted in this by the local imam, who subtly changed the times of the morning prayer calls, tricking the Portuguese into sleeping late and giving Thakurufaanu extra time to escape after his night-time reconnaissance visits.

In the ensuing battle the Maldivians, with help from a detachment of Cannanore soldiers, defeated and killed some 300 Portuguese. The Thakurufaanu brothers then set about re-establishing a Maldivian administration under Islamic law. Soon after, Bodu Thakurufaanu became the new sultan, with the title of Al Sultan-ul Ghazi Mohammed Thakurufaanu Al Auzam Siree Savahitha Maharadhun, first Sultan of the third dynasty of the Kingdom of Maldives.

1834

Captain Robert Moresby, a British maritime surveyor, begins his celebrated charting of Maldives' waters, the first time the complex atolls, islands and reefs are mapped.

1887

Maldives becomes a self-governing British Protectorate after Borah merchants, British citizens from India, become embroiled in local disagreements. The British step in, but Maldivian sultans continue to rule.

1932

The country writes its first constitution, curbing the sultan's powers.

1953

Maldives declares itself a republic within the British Commonwealth and dissolves the sultanate.

In the 1860s Borah merchants from Bombay were invited to Male to establish warehouses and shops, but it wasn't long before they acquired an almost exclusive monopoly on foreign trade. Maldivians feared the Borahs would soon gain complete control of the islands, so Sultan Mohammed Mueenuddin II signed an agreement with the British in 1887 recognising Maldives' statehood and formalising its status as a crown protectorate.

The Early 20th Century

In 1932 Maldives' first constitution was drawn up under Sultan Shamsuddin, marking the dawn of true Maldivian statehood. The sultan was to be elected by a 'council of advisers' made up of the Maldivian elite, rather than being a hereditary position. In 1934 Shamsuddin was deposed and Hasan Nurudin became sultan.

WWII brought great hardship to Maldives. Maritime trade with Ceylon was severely reduced, leading to shortages of rice and other necessities – many died of illness or malnutrition. A new constitution was introduced in 1942, and Nurudin was persuaded to abdicate the following year. His replacement, the elderly Abdul Majeed Didi, retired to Ceylon, leaving the control of the government in the hands of his prime minister, Mohammed Amin Didi, who nationalised the fish export industry, instituted a broad modernisation program and introduced an unpopular ban on tobacco smoking.

The Maldive Islands: Monograph on the History, Archaeology & Epigraphy is HCP Bell's main work. The Ceylon Government Press published it in 1940, three years after his death. Original copies of the book are rare, though reprints are available from bookshops in Male.

When Ceylon gained independence in 1948, the Maldivians signed a defence pact with the British, which gave the latter control over foreign affairs but not the right to interfere internally. In return, the Maldivians agreed to provide facilities for British defence forces, giving the waning British Empire a vital foothold in the Indian Ocean after the loss of India.

In 1953 the sultanate was abolished and a republic was proclaimed with Amin Didi as its first president, but he was overthrown within a year. The sultanate was returned, with Mohammed Farid Didi elected as the 94th sultan of Maldives.

British Bases & Southern Secession

While Britain did not overtly interfere in the running of the country, it did secure permission to re-establish its wartime airfield on Gan in the southernmost atoll of the country, Addu. In 1956 the Royal Air Force began developing the base, employing hundreds of Maldivians and resettling local people on neighbouring islands. The British were informally granted a 100-year lease of Gan that required them to pay £2000 a year.

When Ibrahim Nasir was elected prime minister in 1957, he immediately called for a review of the agreement with the British on Gan, demanding that the lease be shortened and the annual payment increased. This

1954

The sultanate is restored as debate rages about how best to replace the institution.

1959

The three southernmost atolls of Maldives – Addu, Gnaviyani and Huvadhoo – declare their independence from the rest of the country, founding the United Suvadive Republic.

1962

The United Suvadive Republic is forced to give up its independence bid, fostering wide resentment against the British, who many in the Southern Atolls believe betrayed them.

1965

Maldives finally gains full independence from the UK. The country does not opt to join the British Commonwealth, however, and remains outside the organisation until 1982.

was followed by an insurrection against the Maldivian government by the inhabitants of the southern atolls of Addu, Huvadhoo and Gnaviyani, who objected to Nasir's demand that the British cease employing local labour. They decided to cut ties altogether and form an independent state in 1959, electing Abdulla Afif Didi president and believing that their United Suvadive Republic would be recognised by the British.

In 1960 the Maldivian government officially granted the British the use of Gan and other facilities in Addu Atoll for 30 years (effective from December 1956) in return for the payment of £100,000 a year and a grant of £750,000 to finance specific development projects. Brokering a deal with the British on Gan effectively ruled out the UK recognising the breakaway south, and indeed Nasir eventually sent gunboats from Male to quash the rebellion. Afif fled to the Seychelles, then a British colony, while other leaders were banished to various islands in Maldives.

In 1965 Britain recognised the islands as a sovereign and independent state, and ceased to be responsible for their defence (though it retained the use of Gan and continued to pay rent until 1976). Maldives was granted full independence from Britain on 26 July 1965 and later became a member of the UN.

The Republic

Following a referendum in 1968, the sultanate was again abolished, Sultan Majeed Didi retired to Sri Lanka and a new republic was inaugurated. Nasir was elected president, although as political parties remained illegal, he didn't face much opposition.

In 1972 the Sri Lankan market for dried fish, Maldives' biggest export, collapsed. The first tourist resorts opened that year, but the money generated didn't benefit many ordinary inhabitants of the country. Prices kept going up and there were revolts, plots and banishments, as Nasir attempted to cling to power. In 1978, fearing for his life, Nasir stepped down and skipped across to Singapore, reputedly with US$4 million from the Maldivian national coffers.

A former university lecturer and Maldivian ambassador to the UN, Maumoon Abdul Gayoom, became president in Nasir's place. Hailed as a reformer, Gayoom's style of governance was initially much more open, and he immediately denounced Nasir's regime and banished several of the former president's associates.

A 1980 attempted coup against Gayoom, involving mercenaries, was discovered and prevented, but led to more people being banished. Despite Gayoom's reputation as a reformer, he made no move to institute democracy in Maldives.

Gayoom was re-elected in 1983 and continued to promote education, health and industry, particularly tourism. He gave the tiny country a

1968

Maldives abolishes the sultanate and declares itself a republic again. Ibrahim Nasir becomes the first president of the country.

1972

Just a short distance from Male, Maldives' first holiday resort, Kurumba Island, opens and a small trickle of intrepid travellers begin to arrive in search of the best beaches in the world.

1976

The British Royal Air Force base at Gan in the southern Maldives closes, causing an economic recession.

1978

President Gayoom comes to power, ushering in three decades of massive development and growth in the tourism industry, but simultaneously seeing the stifling of dissent and the banning of political parties.

higher international profile with full membership in the Commonwealth and the South Asian Association for Regional Co-operation (SAARC). The focus of the country's economy remained the development of tourism, which continued throughout the 1980s.

Coconuts are believed to hold magical powers by the more superstitious people in Maldives, and during the 2013 election a coconut found outside a polling station on Guraidhoo was 'arrested' by police on suspicion of performing black magic!

The 1988 Coup

In September 1988, 51-year-old Gayoom began a third term as president, having again won an election where he was the only candidate. Only a month later a group of disaffected Maldivian businessmen attempted a coup, employing about 90 Sri Lankan Tamil mercenaries. Half of these soldiers infiltrated Male as visitors, while the rest landed by boat. The mercenaries took several key installations, but failed to capture the National Security Service (NSS) headquarters.

More than 1600 Indian paratroopers, immediately dispatched by the Indian prime minister, Rajiv Gandhi, ended further gains by the invaders who then fled by boat towards Sri Lanka. They took 27 hostages and left 14 people dead and 40 wounded. No tourists were affected – many didn't even know that a coup had been attempted, isolated as they were in their resorts. The mercenaries were caught by an Indian frigate 100km from the Sri Lankan coast. Most were returned to Maldives for trial: several were sentenced to death, though they were later reprieved and returned to Sri Lanka.

The coup attempt saw the standards of police and NSS behaviour decline. Many people in police captivity reportedly faced an increased use of torture and the NSS became a widely feared entity.

Growth & Development

In 1993 Gayoom was nominated for a fourth five-year term, confirmed with an overwhelming referendum vote (yet again, there were no free elections). While on paper the country continued to grow economically, thanks to the now massive tourism industry and the stable fishing industry, much of this wealth was concentrated in the hands of a small group of people, and almost none of it trickled down to the population of the atolls.

At the same time, Maldives experienced many of the problems of developing countries, notably rapid growth in Male, the negative environmental impact of development, regional disparities, youth unemployment and income inequality.

The 1998 El Niño weather event, which caused coral bleaching throughout the atolls, was detrimental for tourism and signalled that global warming might soon threaten the existence of the country. When Gayoom began a fifth term as president in 1998, the environment and sea-level rises were his priorities.

1988

A coup d'état attempt by Sri Lankan mercenaries in Male is quickly foiled with Indian assistance.

2003

The beating to death of 19-year-old Evan Naseem at Maafushi prison causes public protests in Male and across the country, and the first cracks in the Gayoom regime begin to show.

2004

The Indian Ocean tsunami wreaks havoc on the country, wiping out many towns and villages, leading to the abandonment of several islands and creating thousands of internally displaced people.

2005

The People's Majlis, the Maldivian Parliament, votes to allow multiparty elections after a campaign for democracy that saw many activists beaten, imprisoned and harassed by the authorities.

The 1990s saw rapid development in Maldives – the whole country became linked up with a modern telecommunications system, and mobile phones and the internet became widely available. By the end of the century 90% of Maldivians had electricity and access to basic healthcare, and secondary school centres had been established in the outer atolls.

With Japanese assistance, Male was surrounded by an ingenious sea wall (which was to prove very useful just a few years later when the tsunami struck).

In 1997, to accommodate a growing population, work began on a new island near the capital, Hulhumale, built on reclaimed land an extra metre or so above sea level.

In 2008, the Nasheed government put forward an ambitious plan to buy land in India, Sri Lanka or Australia to create a new homeland for the Maldivian people in case the islands were flooded by climate change.

Uprising & Inundation

When a 19-year-old inmate at Maafushi Prison in South Male Atoll was beaten to death by guards in September 2003, a public outcry quickly followed. Evan Naseem's family put their son's brutally tortured corpse on display in Male and the capital spontaneously erupted in rioting. The People's Majlis (parliament), also known as the Citizens' Council, was stoned and police stations were burned by the mob. The NSS arrested and beat many rioters. In the same month, President Gayoom was renominated as the sole presidential candidate for the referendum by the Majlis, a body made up in no small part of Gayoom family members and people appointed by the president himself.

Realising that something was up, Gayoom made an example of the torturers who killed Evan Naseem, but stopped short of punishing or removing any senior ministers or Adam Zahir, the NSS chief of staff. Meanwhile, seeing that the hour for popular action had come, the Maldivian Democratic Party (MDP) was founded in Colombo, Sri Lanka by young democracy activist and former political prisoner Mohammed Nasheed.

Under pressure from colleagues, and in a move to outflank the growing reform movement, Gayoom launched his own reform program in 2004. His proposals included having multiple candidates in the presidential election, a two-term limit for the president and the legalisation of political parties.

Just as change appeared to be coming to the country, disaster struck. On 26 December 2004 the South Asian tsunami claimed thousands of lives across the continent and caused immense damage. The low-lying Maldives, with no land between them and Indonesia, took a direct hit, over 100 people were killed and dozens of islands and resorts were all but washed away. An estimated 15,000 people were displaced – a huge number in such a tiny country – and some islands were abandoned entirely and remain 'ghost islands' today. The country was exhausted, angry and ready for change.

2007

A bomb in Sultan's Park in Male explodes, injuring 12 tourists. Later the same year three men are sentenced to 15 years in jail for terrorism, admitting they were targeting non-Muslims as part of a jihad.

2008

The first democratic election in Maldives sees Mohammed Nasheed elected to the presidency, beating Maumoon Abdul Gayoom and beginning a new era in Maldivian politics.

2009

President Nasheed holds the world's first ever underwater cabinet meeting to highlight the effects of global warming and rising sea levels on the world's lowest-lying country.

2012

Mohammed Nasheed resigns from the presidency in what is quickly called a coup, following a military mutiny against the government and weeks of protests in Male.

THE UNEXPECTED PRESIDENT

Mohammed Nasheed was born in Male in 1967, and grew up in a middle-class family in the capital. His academic skills allowed him to finish his education in Sri Lanka, and then later at a private school in England, before taking a degree in Maritime Studies at what is now Liverpool John Moores University. He returned to Maldives in 1989 to begin his career as a marine biologist, but instead quickly found himself in trouble with the increasingly authoritarian Gayoom regime, whose police force arrested and imprisoned Nasheed in 1990 for claiming in a newspaper article that the presidential election the year before had been rigged.

Having been named an Amnesty International Prisoner of Conscience in 1991, Nasheed was rarely left alone by Gayoom's government, who considered him a dangerous firebrand and potential threat to their rule in an otherwise largely placid populace that made little demand for democracy. Nasheed spent the 1990s in and out of jail, totalling over 20 stints in prison, including one single period in solitary confinement that lasted 18 months. Despite his virtual outlaw status, he managed to get elected as an MP in 1999, an incredible achievement at the time for someone outside the political establishment. In 2001, however, Nasheed was exiled to a remote island and then – almost comically – expelled from the People's Majlis some time later for non-attendance.

Following his two-and-a-half-year period of internal exile, Nasheed voluntarily left the country for Sri Lanka, where he founded the Maldivian Democratic Party in 2004. Nasheed returned to Maldives in 2005, on the eve of the Gayoom government's decision to allow the formation of political parties. Known then to locals by his nickname 'Anni', Nasheed was given a hero's welcome on his return to Maldives, for the first time giving people unhappy with the long rule of Gayoom an opposition figure around whom to coalesce.

Democracy Arrives

Gayoom surprised many observers by following through with his reform package and a new constitution was ratified in August 2008, which led to the country's first freely contested elections later that year. As no party won an overall majority in the first round, a run-off election was held on 29 October in which the Maldivian Democratic Party's Mohammed Nasheed, with the other candidates throwing their weight behind him, took 53.65% of the vote, becoming the country's first democratically elected leader.

One of Nasheed's first pronouncements as president was that his administration would not seek to prosecute any member of the former government, and in particular former president Gayoom. The government then embarked on a radical reform and liberalisation agenda with the following pledges: to make Maldives a carbon-neutral country within a decade; the creation of a sovereign wealth fund to buy land for the future

2013
Abdulla Yameen, the half-brother of former president Maumoon Abdul Gayoom, is elected to the presidency.

2014
Maldivian journalist Ahmed Rilwan Abdulla, a vocal critic of the government, vanishes after being abducted by armed men, and is presumed murdered.

2014
A fire at Male's water desalination plant leaves the city without drinking water for a week, highlighting the difficulty of life in the middle of the ocean.

2014
A law is passed ending Maldives' 61-year moratorium on capital punishment, to widespread international condemnation.

of Maldives in the event that the country is eventually lost to rising sea levels; a total ban on shark hunting; the privatisation of over 20 cumbersome state-run enterprises; the introduction of a national ferry network; the diversification of the tourism industry by ending the long-term policy of separating locals and travellers; and the creation of tax, pension and health-care systems. In just four years the Nasheed government dragged the country into the 21st century and made a name for Maldives as a progressive Muslim state.

The 2012 Coup & Its Aftermath

All that changed on 7 February 2012, when President Nasheed resigned following a mutiny against his rule by first the police and then the army. As mandated in the constitution, the then vice-president, Dr Mohammed Waheed Hassan, assumed the mantle of the presidency, and the country's new government was quickly recognised by all major powers as legitimate.

Many Maldivians are superstitious and unfortunate events are often blamed on jinnis, invisible spirits with the power to possess people, animals and trees.

Over the next few days, however, it transpired that things weren't as cut and dry as they appeared. The former president claimed that he had been pressured at gunpoint to resign, with various businessmen known to be close to his predecessor, Maumoon Abdul Gayoom, named as ringleaders in what was soon being called a coup d'état by the world's press.

The arrest triggered protests in Male in late January and early February 2012, culminating in the resignation of the president on 8 February, once both the police and the army changed sides and the game was clearly up.

The country then effectively spent 2012 and most of 2013 in limbo, under the rule of Nasheed's former deputy, Mohammed Waheed Hassan, until a fraught presidential election in November 2013 awarded the presidency to Abdulla Yameen, Gayoom's half-brother, who has held the office since then.

Nasheed remained politically active, despite a slow-moving trial against him for exceeding his powers as president in ordering the arrest of Abdulla Mohammed, but in March 2015, he was convicted of rather vague charges of 'terrorism' in a trial that was condemned as constitutionally flawed by observers.

The former president was sentenced to 13 years in jail, but in 2016 he was allowed to travel to the UK for surgery on his back, and during the trip he applied for political asylum, which was granted. Since then, Nasheed has continued to campaign for democratic reform from outside Maldives, while the islands have lurched from constitutional crisis to constitutional crisis under the increasingly autocratic leadership of Abdulla Yameen.

2015

Former president Mohammed Nasheed, is arrested and sentenced to 15 years on charges of terrorism, triggering widespread protests by supporters.

2016

Maldives withdraws from the Commonwealth, accusing the organisation of interfering in its domestic affairs.

2016

Water temperatures rise above 32°C, killing vital algae and causing coral bleaching that destroys vast tracts of coral reefs.

2018

President Yameen declares a state of emergency giving him controversial powers to detain people and curtailing the power of the judiciary and legislature.

Maldivian Way of Life

Away from the tourist resorts, the Maldivian people live and work on their home islands much as they have done for centuries. This traditional and hard-working lifestyle is key to understanding the country. The combination of ancient and modern, Muslim and secular, and conservative and progressive elements in Maldivian society may be contradictory, but getting to know how locals live day-to-day is an enormously rewarding flip side to only meeting Maldivians working in resorts.

National Psyche

Maldivians are devout Muslims. In some countries this might be considered incidental, but the national faith is the cornerstone of Maldivian identity and is defended passionately at all levels of society. Officially 100% of the population are practising Sunni Muslims, and indeed, under the 2008 constitution, it's impossible to be a citizen of Maldives if you are a non-Muslim. There's no scope for religious dissent, which presents some serious human-rights issues, and apostasy for locals is still punishable – in theory at least – by death.

This deep religious faith breeds a generally high level of conservatism, but that does not preclude the arrival of over a million non-Muslim tourists to the islands every year, coming to bathe semi-naked, drink alcohol and eat pork. It's definitely an incongruous situation, and one that has come under some strain since the tourist industry spread to inhabited islands.

Officially only Muslims may become citizens of Maldives. It is possible for foreigners to convert and later become Maldivian nationals, although this is extremely rare.

While the new guesthouses and hotels on inhabited islands enforce local standards of dress and behaviour, just the regular presence of foreigners on islands that have historically been isolated from the outside world has brought great change to traditional atoll villages.

Not quite Asia, not quite Africa and not the Middle East despite the cultural similarities, Maldives has been slow to join the international community (it only joined the Commonwealth and the South Asian Association for Regional Co-operation in the 1980s, and withdrew from the former in 2016). Indeed, a deep island mentality permeates the country, so much so that people's first loyalty is to their own small island before their atoll or even the country as a whole.

The hardship implicit in survival on these remote and relatively barren islands has created a nation of hard workers. The strong work ethic runs throughout the country; historically a lazy Maldivian was a Maldivian who didn't eat.

Another feature of the Maldivian people is their earthy humour and cheerfulness. Joking and laughter is a way of life and you'll notice this without even leaving your resort – take a few minutes to speak to the local staff and you'll see exactly how true this is.

Lifestyle

The most obvious dichotomy in lifestyle in Maldives is between people in the capital Male and those 'in the atolls' – the term used by everyone to denote 'islanders' or anyone who lives outside the immediate area of Male.

In Male, life is considerably easier and more comfortable than in the rest of the country on most fronts, with the obvious exception of space. Life in one of the most densely populated places on earth is very crowded and can feel intensely claustrophobic.

The Maldivian caste system has effectively disappeared today. Traditionally the very lowest caste was that of the palm-toddy tappers *(raa-very)*.

The past two decades of extraordinary growth have created a massive economy in Male, although many residents of the city complain that while there are plenty of opportunities to earn and live well in the commercial and tourism sectors, there's a great lack of challenging, creative jobs if exporting fish and importing tourists are not your idea of fun. With limited education beyond high school and few careers for those who are ambitious but lack good connections, it's no surprise that many young people in Male dream of going abroad, at least to complete their education and training.

On the islands things are far more simple and laid-back, but people's lives aren't always as easy as those in Male. In the atolls most people live on the extended family homestead (it's unusual to live alone or just as a couple in a way that it wouldn't be in Male), and both men and women assume fairly traditional roles. While men go out to work (in general either as fishermen or on jobs that keep them away from home for long stretches at a time in the tourist or shipping industries), women are the homemakers, looking after the children, cooking and maintaining the household. Fish are traded for other necessities at the nearest big island. Attending the mosque is the main religious activity, and on smaller islands it's the main social and cultural activity as well.

You can address Maldivians by their first or last name. Since so many men are called Mohammed, Hassan or Ali, the surname is often more appropriate. In some cases an honorary title like Maniku or Didi is used to show respect.

The most important ritual in a male's life comes when he is circumcised at the age of six or seven. These are big celebrations that last for a week and are far more significant than marriages and birthdays (the latter of which are generally not celebrated). Marriage is important, but it's not the massive celebration it is in most of the rest of Asia.

Rural life for the young can be fairly dull, although, despite appearances, even tiny fishing villages are surprisingly modern and most now have internet access, phones and TV. There are government primary schools on every inhabited island, and many children study the Quran from an even earlier age; but for grades six and seven, children may have to stay away from home to attend a middle school on a larger island. Atoll capitals have an Atoll Education Centre (AEC) with adult education and secondary schooling to grade 10 (16 years old).

Officially, 90% of students finish primary school, and the adult literacy rate is an impressive 98%. English is taught as a second language from grade one and is the usual language of instruction at higher secondary school – most Maldivians with a secondary education will speak decent English, if heavily accented and rather old-fashioned.

The best students can continue to a free-of-charge higher secondary school, which teaches children to the age of 18 – there's one in Male, one in Hithadhoo, in the country's far south, and one in Kulhuduffushi, in

MEDIA IN MALDIVES

The best source of Maldivian news in English can be found online at *Maldives Independent* (www.maldivesindependent.com), a balanced and well-written news site that has supported several major investigations in the past and ruffled feathers across the political spectrum.

Daily newspapers include *Miadhu* (www.miadhu.com) and *Haveeru* (www.haveeru.com.mv), both of which have online English editions. You'll also see *Jazeera* and *Aufathis* on sale, but only in Dhivehi. The state-owned TV channel TVM often hosts talk shows and discussion panels about the political situation, with a pro-government slant.

the far north. Students coming to Male to study generally take live-in domestic jobs, affecting their study time.

Maldives College of Higher Education, also in Male, has faculties of health, education, tourism-hospitality and engineering as well as one for Sharia'a law. Many young Maldivians go abroad for university studies, usually to Sri Lanka, India, Britain, Australia or Fiji, although since 2011 Male's Maldives National University has been offering full degree courses.

Politics

Maldivian politics has undergone a sea change in the past decade. Having spent the second half of the 20th century under a series of strongman authoritarian rulers, the tide finally turned with the democratic election of young progressive Mohammed Nasheed in 2008 before turning abruptly back before he could finish his term in 2012, when a coup forced his resignation.

The country's current constitution, which enacted the separation of powers and provided for a bill of rights for the first time, was created in 2008. The constitution made Maldives a presidential republic, with the president as both head of state and head of government.

The Maldivian president is directly elected by the people and is limited to two five-year terms in office. The People's Majlis (parliament) is in Male, and each of the 20 administrative atolls, plus the island of Male, have two representatives each, elected for five-year terms. The president chooses the remaining eight parliamentary representatives, has the power to appoint or dismiss cabinet ministers, and appoints all judges. All citizens over 21 years of age can vote.

The main political parties operating in Maldives are the ruling Progressive Party of Maldives, former President Nasheed's Maldivian Democratic Party (MDP) and the Republican Party (Jumhooree Party).

Maldives' biggest international ally is China, which in recent years has eclipsed India and donated hundreds of millions of dollars to the country, with an eye to building a submarine base in the country.

Economy

Tourism accounts for 36% of GDP and up to 90% of government tax revenue. The other major field of industry is fishing. Previous policies helped to mechanise the fishing fleet, introduce new packing techniques and develop new markets, which has seen Maldives remain a major fish supplier to markets in Asia and the Middle East. Nevertheless, the fishing industry is vulnerable to international market fluctuations. Most adult males have some experience in fishing, and casual employment on fishing boats is something of an economic backstop. Men are unlikely to take on menial work for low pay when there is a prospect that they can get a few days or weeks of relatively well-paid work on a fishing boat or dhoni.

Trade and shipping (nearly all based in Male) is the third-biggest earner; nearly all food is imported and what little domestic agriculture there is accounts for less than 6% of GDP. Manufacturing and construction make up 15% of GDP: small boat yards, fish packing, clothing and a plastic-pipe plant are modern enterprises, but mostly it's cottage industries producing coconut oil, coir (coconut-husk fibre) and coir products such as rope and matting. Some of the new industrial activities are on islands near Male while others, such as fish-packing plants, are being established in the outer atolls.

Income tax was introduced to Maldives in 2012 – the first time most Maldivians had ever had to pay tax in their life. As well as generating important income for the government, it was also aimed at getting the population to have more of a stake in their society.

Religion

Islam is the religion of Maldives, and officially there are no other religious groups present. All Maldivians are Sunni Muslims. No other religions or sects are permitted, though it's no problem to bring religious items for your own use into the country.

Maldives observes a liberal form of Islam, like that practised in India and Indonesia. Maldivian women do not observe purdah, although the

IDOLATRY

Most countries prohibit the importation of things like narcotics and firearms, and most travellers understand such restrictions, but when you're forbidden to bring 'idols of worship' into Maldives, what exactly does that mean? Maldives is an Islamic nation, and it is sensitive about objects that may offend Muslim sensibilities. A small crucifix, worn as jewellery, is unlikely to be a problem, and many tourists arrive wearing one. A large crucifix with an obvious Christ figure nailed to it may well be prohibited. The same is true of images of Buddha – a small decorative one is probably OK, but a large and ostentatious one may not be.

Maldivian authorities are concerned about evangelists and the objects they might use to spread their beliefs. Inspectors would not really be looking for a Bible in someone's baggage, but if they found two or more Bibles they would almost certainly not allow them to be imported. It would be unwise to test the limits of idolatrous imports – like customs people everywhere, Maldivian authorities take themselves very seriously.

large majority wear a headscarf. Until the election of President Nasheed in 2008, the media was strictly controlled and religious broadcasts were not common. Since the onset of more liberal attitudes towards freedom of speech, religious programming has become extremely popular, and young women throughout the country have reverted to covering their heads in large numbers, making it fashionable and not always just a sign of particular religious devotion.

There have been worrying signs of radicalisation all over the country in recent years; one high-profile case saw a 15-year-old rape victim sentenced to 100 lashes for 'fornication', based on principles of Sharia'a law, a sentence that was eventually quashed by the High Court after a global outcry.

There have been frequent cases of Maldivians being found fighting in Syria for ISIS; indeed, per capita, the islands are said to have sent more fighters to Syria than any other nation.

Prayer Times

The initial prayer session is in the first hour before sunrise, the second around noon, the third in the mid-afternoon around 3.30pm, the fourth at sunset and the final session in the early evening.

Learn more about the amazing development of Hulhumale, the artificial island next to Male that will provide the future base for the government and much of the city's population in the face of rising sea levels, at www.hdc.com.mv

The call to prayer is delivered by the *mudhim* (muezzin). In former days, he climbed to the top of the minaret and shouted it out. Now the call is relayed by loudspeakers on the minaret and the *mudhim* even appears on TV. All TV stations cut out at prayer time, although only TVM (the national channel) cuts out for the entire duration – satellite channels just have their broadcasts interrupted to remind Muslims to go to the mosque.

Shops and offices close for 15 minutes after each call. Some people go to the mosque, some kneel where they are and others do not visibly participate. Mosques are busiest for the sunset prayers and at noon on Fridays.

Ramazan

This month of fasting, which begins at the time of a particular new moon and ends with the sighting of the next new moon, is called Ramazan in Maldives. The Ramazan month starts a little earlier every year because it is based on a lunar calendar of 12 months, each with 28 days. Ramazan begins on 5 May 2019, 23 April 2020 and 12 April 2021.

During Ramazan, Muslims do not eat, drink, smoke or have sex between sunrise and sunset. Exceptions to the eating and drinking rule are granted to young children, pregnant or menstruating women, and those who are travelling. It can be a difficult time for travel outside the resorts, as teashops and cafes are closed during the day, offices have shorter hours and people may be preoccupied with religious observances or the rigours of fasting.

Visitors should avoid eating, drinking or smoking in public, or in the presence of those who are fasting. After a week or so, most Muslims adjust to the Ramazan routine and many say they enjoy it. There are feasts and parties long into the night, big breakfasts before dawn and long rests in the afternoon.

Kuda Eid, the end of Ramazan, is a major celebration that is marked by three days of public holidays. The celebrations begin when the new moon is sighted in Male and a ceremonial cannon is fired to mark the end of Ramazan. There are large feasts in every home for friends and family, and in the atolls men participate in frenzied *bodu beru* (big drum) ceremonies and other dancing, often all night. At this time, it's polite to wish locals 'Eid Mubarak'.

Local Beliefs

On the islands people still fear jinnis, the evil spirits that come from the sea, land and sky. They are blamed for everything that can't be explained by religion or education.

To combat jinnis there are *fandhita,* which are the spells and potions provided by a local hakim (medicine man), who is often called upon when illness strikes, if a woman fails to conceive or if the fishing catch is poor.

The hakim might cast a curing spell by writing phrases from the Quran on strips of paper and sticking or tying them to the patient; or writing the sayings in ink on a plate, filling the plate with water to dissolve the ink, and making the patient drink the potion. Other concoctions include *isitri,* a love potion used in matchmaking, and its antidote *varitoli,* which is used to break up marriages.

Sport

Soccer is the most popular sport and is played all year round. On most islands, the late-afternoon match among the young men is a daily ritual, although volleyball and cricket are also common. There's a soccer league in Male, played between club teams with names such as Valencia and Victory, and annual tournaments against teams from neighbouring countries. Matches are also held at the National Stadium in Male.

Maldives has participated in the Olympics since 1988, but has yet to win any medals. Unsurprisingly, the team has never taken part in the winter Olympics.

Cricket is played in Male for a few months each year, beginning in March. Volleyball is played indoors, on the beach and in the waterfront parks. The two venues for indoor sport are the Centre for Social Education, on the west side of Male, and a newer facility just east of the New Harbour, used for basketball (men and women), netball, volleyball and badminton.

Traditional games include *bai bala,* where one team attempts to tag members of the other team inside a circle, and a tug-of-war, known as *wadhemun. Bashi* is a women's game, played on something like a tennis court, where a woman stands facing away from the net and serves a tennis ball backwards, over her head. There is a team of women on the other side who then try to catch it.

Thin mugoali (meaning 'three circles') is a game similar to baseball and has been played in the atolls for more than 400 years. The *mugoali* (bases) are made by rotating on one foot in the sand through 360 degrees, leaving a circle behind. You'll sometimes see *bashi* in Male parks or on village islands in the late afternoon, but traditional games are becoming less popular as young people are opting for international sports.

THE ALL-PURPOSE MALDIVIAN DHONI

The truck and bus of Maldives is the sturdy dhoni, a vessel so ubiquitous that the word will become part of your vocabulary just hours after landing. Built in numerous shapes and sizes, the dhoni has been adapted for use in many different ways. The traditional dhoni is thought to derive from the Arab dhow, but the design has been used and refined for so long in Maldives that it is truly a local product.

Traditionally, dhonis have a tall, curved prow that stands up like a scimitar cutting through the sea breezes. Most Maldivians say this distinctive prow is purely decorative, but in shallow water a man will stand at the front, spotting the reefs and channels, signalling to the skipper and holding the prow for balance.

The flat stern is purely functional – it's where the skipper stands and steers, casually holding the tiller with his foot or between his legs. The stern platform is also used for fishing, and for one other thing – when a small dhoni makes a long trip, the 'head' is at the back. If nature calls, go right to the stern of the boat, face forward or backwards as your needs and gender dictate, and rely on the skipper, passengers and crew to keep facing the front. Longer distance dhonis that are part of the national ferry system now tend to come with built-in toilets.

The details on a dhoni are a mix of modern and traditional. The rudder is attached with neat rope lashing, but nowadays the rope is always plastic, not coir (coconut fibre). The propeller is protected so it won't snag on mooring lines or get damaged on a shallow reef. The rooftop of the dhoni often functions as a sundeck and a place to relax, though most sun-wary Maldivians prefer to stay in the shade downstairs.

The best dhoni builders are said to come from Raa Atoll, and teams of them can be contracted to come to an island to make a new boat. Twelve workers, six on each side of the boat, can make a 14m hull in about 45 days. The keel is made from imported hardwood, while the hull planks are traditionally from coconut trees. A lot of the work is now done with power tools, but no plans are used.

Women in Maldives

Traditional gender roles, especially in the atolls, have generally been the norm in Maldivian society, with women tending to their children, cooking and doing other household duties and men spending the day fishing before socialising at the mosque.

Modernisation and development may have changed the traditional way of life somewhat, but in many cases has conferred a double burden on many women – income generation plus domestic responsibilities. More opportunities and better education mean that more women are ready to join the workforce or take up income-generating activities at home. This has become a necessity rather than a choice for most women living in Male, as rising expenses and changing lifestyles demand a dual income to meet basic family expenses.

Life expectancy for a Maldivian is about 77 years for men and 80 years for women.

Traditionally, a woman could choose a suitor and name a bride-price *(rhan)*. The bride-price is paid by the husband to the wife, at the time of marriage or in instalments as mutually agreed, but must be repaid in full if there's a divorce. The wedding itself is a low-key affair, but is often followed by a large banquet for all family and friends, who can easily number in the hundreds.

Women in Maldives can, and do, own land and property but in general women have a fraction of the property that men have. While inheritance generally follows Islamic Sharia'a law in Maldives, land is divided according to civil law, whereby a daughter and son inherit equal shares of land.

There is little overt discrimination between the sexes, and although it's a fully Muslim society, women and men mingle freely and women enjoy personal liberty not experienced by women in most Muslim societies.

Wildlife in Maldives

The world beneath the water is one of the most compelling reasons to visit Maldives. Whether you're diving on a reef thriving with life or walking across your resort's lagoon on a wooden walkway, you'll find yourself seeing many of the spectacular and unusual creatures for which Maldives is famous. Maldives' combination of amazingly clear and warm water, rich marine life and good environmental protection ensures that anyone with an interest in the underwater world won't go home disappointed. There are even a few interesting critters on land to watch out for.

Marine Life in Maldives

Unsurprisingly, the vast majority of Maldives' natural riches can be found below the surface of the ocean.

Life on the Reef

Reefs are often referred to as the rainforests of the sea, and rightly so – even though they take up just 0.1% of the ocean's surface, they are home to around a quarter of all underwater species. Reefs are created by the calcium carbonate secreted by corals, and are most commonly found in shallow, warm waters, making Maldives a perfect environment for these complex and delicate ecosystems.

As well as the many types of coral, there are various shells, starfish, crustaceans and worms living directly on the reef. Then there are the 700 species of fish that directly or indirectly live off the reef, which can be divided into two types: reef fish, which live inside the atoll lagoons, on and around coral-reef structures; and pelagics, which live in the open sea, but come close to the reefs for food.

Despite its total size of 90,000 sq km, Maldives is 99% water and has just 298 sq km of land, effectively making it smaller than Andorra.

Coral

These are coelenterates, a class of animal that also includes sea anemones and jellyfish. A coral growth is made up of individual polyps – tiny tube-like fleshy cylinders. The top of the cylinder is open and ringed by waving tentacles (nematocysts), which sting and draw any passing prey inside. Coral polyps secrete a calcium-carbonate deposit around their base, and this cup-shaped skeletal structure is what forms a coral reef – new coral grows on old dead coral and the reef gradually builds up.

Most reef building is done by hermatypic corals, whose outer tissues are infused with zooxanthellae algae, which photosynthesises to make food from carbon dioxide and sunlight. The zooxanthellae is the main food source for the coral, while the coral surface provides a safe home for the zooxanthellae – they live in a symbiotic relationship, each dependent on the other.

The zooxanthellae give coral its colour, so when a piece of coral is removed from the water, the zooxanthellae soon die and the coral becomes white. If the water temperature rises, the coral expels the algae and loses its colour in a process called 'coral bleaching', something that happened in 2016, and the legacy of which is sadly evident on coral reefs across the country today.

Polyps reproduce by splitting to form a colony of genetically identical organisms – each colony starts life as just a single polyp. Although each polyp catches and digests its own food, the nutrition then passes between the polyps to the whole colony. Most coral polyps only feed at night; during the day they withdraw into their hard limestone skeleton, so it is only after dark that a coral reef can be seen in its full, colourful glory, which is the reason so many divers like to do night dives.

The whale shark is an evolutionary oddity, skipping almost the whole food chain to ensure its survival: despite being the biggest fish in the water, it feeds solely on plankton.

Hard Corals

These *Acropora* species take many forms. One of the most common and easiest to recognise is the staghorn coral, which grows by budding off new branches from the tips. Brain corals are huge and round with a surface looking very much like a human brain. They grow by adding new base levels of skeletal matter, then expanding outwards. Flat or sheet corals, like plate coral or table coral, expand at their outer edges.

Soft Corals

These are made up of individual polyps, but do not form a hard limestone skeleton. Lacking the skeleton that protects hard coral, it would seem likely that soft coral would fall prey to fish, but they seem to remain relatively immune either due to toxic substances in their tissues or to the presence of sharp limestone needles. Soft corals can move around and will sometimes engulf and kill off a hard coral. Attractive varieties include fan corals and whips. Soft corals thrive on reef edges washed by strong currents.

Megafauna

As on an African wildlife safari, it is the big animals that divers most hope to see in Maldives. Alongside vast shoals of reef fish, Maldives is home to a huge variety of megafauna, from turtles, dolphins and manta rays to the mighty whale shark, the largest fish in the ocean.

Sharks

Juvenile reef sharks can be seen without getting into the water: they love to swim about in the warm water of the shallow lagoon right next to the beach and eat small fish all day long. They're tiny – most are around 50cm long – but are fully formed sharks, so can scare some people! They don't bite, although feeding or provoking them still isn't a good idea.

Get out into the deeper water and adult sharks are visible, but you'll have to go looking for them. The most commonly seen shark in Maldives are white-tip and grey-tip reef sharks. The white-tip reef shark is a small, non-aggressive, territorial shark, rarely more than 1.5m long and often seen over areas of coral or off reef edges. Grey-tip reef sharks are also timid, shallow-water dwellers and often grow to over 2m in length.

Male sharks show their interest in females by biting them on the sides, often causing wounds, even though the female shark skin has evolved to be thicker than the male equivalent.

Other species are more open-sea dwellers, but do come into atolls and especially to channel entrances where food is plentiful. These include the strange-looking hammerhead shark, tiger sharks, lemon sharks, nurse sharks and the whale shark, the world's largest fish species, a harmless plankton eater. Sharks pose little danger to divers in Maldives – there's simply too much else for them to eat.

Stingrays & Manta Rays

Among the most dramatic creatures in the ocean, rays are cartilaginous fish – like flattened sharks. Stingrays are sea-bottom feeders, and are equipped with crushing teeth to grind the molluscs and crustaceans they sift out of the sand. They are occasionally found in the shallows, often lying motionless on the sandy bottom of lagoons. A barbed and poisonous spine on top of the tail can swing up and forward, and will deliver a very painful injury to anyone who stands on one, but you're unlikely to get close to it as the sound of you approaching will probably frighten it away first.

Manta rays are among the largest fish found in Maldives and a firm favourite of divers. They tend to swim along near the surface and pass overhead as a large shadow. They are quite harmless and, in some places, seem quite relaxed about divers approaching them closely. Manta rays are sometimes seen to leap completely out of the water, landing back with a tremendous splash. The eagle ray is closely related to the manta, and is often spotted by divers.

Hammerhead sharks are among the most spectacular underwater creatures in Maldives. Your best chance of seeing them is early in the morning in Northern Ari and Rasdhoo Atolls.

Whales & Dolphins

Whales dwell in the open sea, and so are not found in the atolls, but may be spotted on dive safaris or boat trips. Species seen in Maldives include beaked, blue, Bryde's dwarf, false killer, melon-headed, sperm and pilot whales. Sightings are not common, however.

By contrast, dolphins are extremely common throughout Maldives and you're very likely to see them, albeit fleetingly. These fun-loving, curious creatures often swim alongside boats, and also swim off the side of reefs looking for food. Most resorts offer dolphin cruises, which allow you to see large schools up close. Species known to swim in Maldivian waters include bottlenose, Fraser's, Risso's, spotted, striped and spinner dolphins.

Turtles

Most turtle species are endangered worldwide. Four species nest in Maldives: green, olive ridley, hawksbill and loggerhead. Leatherback turtles visit Maldivian waters, but are not known to nest. Turtle numbers have declined in Maldives, as elsewhere, but they can still be seen by divers at many sites. The catching of turtles and the sale or export of turtle-shell products is now totally prohibited, and you should report it if you come across it.

Turtles are migratory and the population can be depleted by events many miles from their home beach, such as accidental capture in fishing nets, depletion of sea-grass areas and toxic pollutants. Widespread collection of eggs and the loss of nesting sites are both problems in Maldives today, although both the government and various environmental foundations have done a lot to educate locals about the importance of turtle protection. Nevertheless, turtle eggs are a traditional food and are used in *velaa folhi,* a special Maldivian dish, which is still legally made today.

Resort development has reduced the availability of nesting sites, while artificial lights confuse hatchling turtles, which are instinctively guided into the water by the position of the moon. Beach chairs and boats can also interfere with egg laying and with hatchlings. Some attempts are being made to artificially improve the survival chances of hatchlings by protecting them in hatching ponds and cages in some resorts with professional marine biologists in residence.

Maldivian turtles are protected, but they are still caught illegally. The charity Ecocare Maldives has campaigned to raise awareness of the turtles' plight. See www.ecocare.mv.

Reef Fish

Hundreds of fish species can be spotted by anyone with a mask and snorkel. On almost any dive or snorkelling trip in Maldives you're pretty certain to see several types of butterflyfish, angelfish, parrotfish, rock cod, unicornfish, trumpetfish, bluestripe snapper, Moorish idol and Oriental sweetlips, as well as far less common species.

Fish-spotting Guide

You don't have to be a hardcore diver to enjoy the rich marine life of Maldives. Hundreds of fish species can be spotted by anyone with a mask and snorkel. On almost any dive or snorkelling trip in Maldives you're pretty certain to see several types of butterflyfish, angelfish, parrotfish, rock cod, unicornfish, trumpetfish, bluestripe snapper, Moorish idol and Oriental sweetlips. You'll also inevitably see far less common ones.

For a comprehensive online guide to the fish of Maldives, visit www.popweb.com/maldive. For more information, try *Photo Guide to Fishes of the Maldives* by Rudie H Kuiter (Atoll Editions).

Male and female shark populations live in same-sex groups and rarely meet, save for mating.

Anemonefish

Maldives anemonefish are around 11cm long, orange, dusky orange or yellow, with differences in face colour and the shape and thickness of the head bar marking. Their mucous coating protects them from the venomous tips of sea anemone tentacles, allowing them to hide from predators among the anemones' tentacles. In return for this protection, they warn the anemones of the approach of fish such as butterflyfish, which feed on the tentacle tips. Juveniles are lighter in colour than adults, and have greyish or blackish pelvic fins.

Angelfish

Of the many species, 14 are found in Maldives, mostly found in shallow water, though some inhabit reef slopes down to 20m. They can be seen individually or in small groups. Small species are around 10cm, the largest around 35cm. They feed on sponges and algae. Regal (or empress) angelfish have bright yellow bodies with vertical dark blue and white stripes. The emperor, or imperial, angelfish are larger (to 35cm) and live in deeper water, with almost horizontal blue-and-yellow lines and a dark blue mask and gill markings; juveniles are quite different in shape and markings.

Boxfish

These unusual looking and highly poisonous fish are sometimes encountered by divers in Maldives. They usually grow up to half a metre in length and feed on worms and other invertebrates on the reef and ocean floor. Boxfish are literally boxed in by a thick external skin, with holes for moving parts such as the eyes, gills and fins. That, coupled with their poisonous flesh, makes them formidable creatures. It's a joy to see them swimming, their tiny fins moving their large bodies effortlessly across the reef.

The whale shark is the largest fish in the world – they regularly reach up to 12m in length and are one of the biggest diving attractions when they cruise the kandus in May.

Butterfly Fish

There are over 30 species in Maldives; they are common in shallow waters and along reef slopes, singly, in pairs or in small schools. Species vary in size from 12cm to 30cm when mature, with a flattened body shape and elaborate markings. Various species of this carnivorous fish have specialised food sources, including anemones, coral polyps, algae and assorted invertebrate prey. Bennett's butterflyfish, bright yellow and 18cm long, is one of several species with a 'false eye' near the tail to make predators think it's a larger fish facing the other way. Spotted butterflyfish, which grow to 10cm long, are camouflaged with dark polka dots and a dark band across its real eye.

Flutemouth

The smooth flutemouth is very common in shallow waters in Maldives, often occurring in small schools. They are very slender, elongated fish, usually around 60cm in length, but deep-sea specimens grow up to 1.5m. Flutemouths (cornetfish) eat small fish, often stalking prey by swimming behind a harmless herbivore. The silver colouring seems almost transparent in the water, and it can be hard to spot flutemouths even in shallow sandy lagoons.

Flying Gurnard

These beautiful fish feature wing-like fins that make them look like small rays from afar, something they use to their advantage when trying to catch prey, as well as to defend themselves by frightening off would-be attackers. Juveniles even have a pattern on their fins that looks like an eye, a good defence tactic. Flying Gurnards usually don't grow to more than 30cm and feed on bottom fish.

Groupers

This large reef fish is commonly seen on the reef, normally alone, and it can be very skittish when approached by divers. Most commonly spotted are black groupers with blue spots or red groupers with green or blue spots; they tend to be around 40cm to 60cm in length. Groupers feed on mobile invertebrates and small fish, generally hunting in the evening when other species on the reef are looking for a place to sleep for the night. Groupers are cunning hunters and juveniles often mimic wrasses to get close to prey.

Young male anemonefish living within the anemone are under the control of a single dominant female. When she dies, the largest male fish changes sex and replaces her as the dominant female.

Jacks & Trevallies

These fast silver fish are formidable hunters. While they spend much of their time in the open ocean, they feed on reefs, preying on confused fish that stray too far from safety. With 20 different kinds of jacks and trevallies in Maldives, it's common to see them hunting on the reef. The giant trevally truly lives up to its name and can measure up to 1.7m in length.

Lionfish

These attractive fish are firm favourites with divers and are easily recognised by their long and thin fanlike fins, which deliver a very painful sting and are used to trap prey. Raised fins can be a sign of alarm – in such a case stay clear and don't corner the fish, as it may attack. Usually reddish brown in colour and growing only to 20cm, lionfish are commonly seen on the reef, although they are experts at camouflage, so are often missed even by experienced divers.

Moray Eels

A common sight on the reefs of Maldives, these large, usually spotted eels are routinely seen with their heads poking out of holes on the reef edge. Those on reefs visited by divers tend to be extremely easy to approach, but will withdraw entirely into their holes (or swim away altogether) if humans come too close. They can also deliver an extremely strong bite, so do not feed or provoke them. Growing up to 2m long, they are one of the most easily spotted large creatures on the reef.

Moray eels' bodies are almost entirely made up of muscle, which they employ when hunting to twist and crush their prey, much like a constrictor.

Moorish Idol

The Moorish idol is commonly seen on reef flats and reef slopes in Maldives, often in pairs. Usually 15cm to 20cm long, it is herbivorous, feeding primarily on algae. They are attractive, with broad vertical yellow-and-black bands, pointed snouts, and long, streamer-like extensions to the upper dorsal fin.

Parrotfish

More than 20 of the many parrotfish species are found in Maldives – they include some of the most conspicuous and commonly seen reef fish. The largest species grow to more than a metre, but those around 50cm long are more typical. Most parrotfish feed on algae and other organisms growing on and around a hard-coral structure. With strong, beak-like mouths, they scrape and bite the coral surface, then grind up the coral chunks, swallowing and filtering to extract nutrients. Snorkellers often hear the scraping, grinding sound of parrotfish eating coral, and notice the clouds of coral-sand faeces that parrotfish regularly discharge. Colour, pattern and even sex can change as parrotfish mature – juveniles and females are often drab, while mature males can have brilliant blue-green designs.

Pilot fish can often be seen swimming alongside sharks or other large pelagic fish, eating scraps of whatever the larger fish kills. In return the pilot fish eats parasites on the larger fish.

Pufferfish

There are 18 species of the aptly named pufferfish in Maldives. These incredible creatures have poisonous flesh (which can kill a human if eaten without the correct preparation) and the amazing power to inflate themselves like a balloon when attacked or feeling threatened. Pufferfish vary enormously in colour and size, though Bennett's pufferfish, with its green, orange and blue pattern, is the most beautiful. The scribbled pufferfish, one of the largest seen in Maldivian waters, is the most commonly seen.

Rock Cod

Hundreds of species are currently classified as *Serranidae,* including rock cod and grouper, which are common around reefs. Smaller species reach 20cm; many larger species grow to 50cm and some to over a metre. Rock cod are carnivorous, feeding on smaller fish and invertebrates. Vermillion rock cod (or coral grouper) are often seen in shallow waters and near the coral formations in which they hide; they are a brilliant crimson colour covered with blue spots and are up to 40cm long.

Snapper

There are 28 species of snapper that have been documented in Maldives, mostly in deep water. Small species are around 20cm and the largest grow to 1m (snapper, themselves carnivorous, are popular with anglers as a fighting fish and are excellent to eat). Blue-striped snapper, commonly seen in schools near inshore reefs, are an attractive yellow with blue-white horizontal stripes. Red snapper (or red bass) are often seen in lagoons.

Surgeonfish

The surgeonfish are so named for the tiny scalpel-sharp blades that are found on the sides of their bodies, near their tails. When they are threatened they will swim beside the intruder swinging their tails to inflict cuts, and can cause nasty injuries. Over 20 species of surgeon, including the powder-blue surgeonfish, are found in Maldives, often in large schools. The adults range from 20cm to 60cm. All species graze for algae on the sea bottom or on coral surfaces.

Pipefish have a very unusual mating system. The female deposits the egg into the sperm on the underside of the male's body, where fertilisation occurs and the pregnant male then incubates the eggs for a month before hatching.

Sweetlips

Only a few of the many species are found in Maldives, where they inhabit outer-reef slopes. Some species grow up to 1m, but most are between 50cm and 75cm; juveniles are largely herbivorous, feeding on algae, plankton and other small organisms; older fish hunt and eat smaller fish. Oriental sweetlips, which grow to 50cm, are superb-looking, with horizontal dark and light stripes, dark spots on fins and tail, and large, lugubrious lips. Brown sweetlips are generally bigger, duller and more active at night.

Triggerfish

There are over a dozen species in Maldives, on outer-reef slopes and also in shallower reef environments. Small species grow to around 25cm and the largest species to over 75cm. Triggerfish are carnivorous. Orange-striped triggerfish (30cm) are common in shallow reef waters.

Titan triggerfish have yellow and dark-brown crisscross patterning and grow up to 75cm; they can be aggressive, especially when defending eggs, and will charge at divers. The clown triggerfish (up to 40cm) is easily recognised by its conspicuous colour pattern, with large, round, white blotches on the lower half of its body.

The sea snake is an air-breathing reptile with venom 20 times stronger than any snake on land. Basically, don't touch them if you're lucky enough to see any!

Unicornfish

From the same family as the surgeonfish, unicornfish grow from 40cm to 75cm long (only males of some species have the horn for which the species is named), and are herbivores. Spotted unicornfish are very common blue-grey or olive-brown fish with narrow dotted vertical markings (males can change their colours for display, and exhibit a broad white vertical band); their prominent horns get longer with age. Bignose unicornfish (or Vlaming's unicorn) have only a nose bump for a horn.

RISE & RISE OF THE ATOLLS

A coral reef is not, as many people believe, formed of multicoloured marine plants. It is a living colony of coral polyps – tiny, tentacled creatures that feed on plankton. Coral polyps are invertebrates with sac-like bodies and calcareous or horny skeletons. After extracting calcium deposits from the water around them, the polyps excrete tiny, cup-shaped, limestone skeletons. These little guys can make mountains.

A coral reef is the rock-like aggregation of millions of these polyp skeletons. Only the outer layer of coral is alive. As polyps reproduce and die, the new polyps attach themselves in successive layers to the skeletons already in place. Coral grows best in clear, shallow water, and especially where waves and currents from the open sea bring extra oxygen and nutrients.

Charles Darwin put forward the first scientific theory of atoll formation based on observations of atolls and islands in the Pacific. He envisaged a process where coral builds up around the shores of a volcanic island to produce a fringing reef. Then the island sinks slowly into the sea while the coral grows upwards at about the same rate. This forms a barrier reef, separated from the shore of the sinking island by a ring-shaped lagoon. By the time the island is completely submerged, the coral growth has become the base for an atoll, circling the place where the volcanic peak used to be.

This theory doesn't quite fit Maldives, though. Unlike the isolated Pacific atolls, Maldivian atolls all sit on top of the same long, underwater plateau, around 300m to 500m under the surface of the sea. This plateau is a layer of accumulated coral stone over 2000m thick. Under this is the 'volcanic basement', a 2000km-long ridge of basalt that was formed over 50 million years ago.

The build-up of coral over this ridge is as much to do with sea-level changes as it is with the plateau subsiding. When sea levels rise the coral grows upwards to stay near the sea surface, as in the Darwin model, but there were at least two periods when the sea level actually dropped significantly – by as much as 120m. At these times much of the accumulated coral plateau would have been exposed, subjected to weathering, and 'karstified' – eroded into steep-sided, flat-topped columns. When sea levels rose again, new coral grew on the tops of the karst mountains and formed the bases of the individual Maldivian atolls.

Coral grows best on the edges of an atoll, where it is well supplied with nutrients from the open sea. A fringing reef forms around an enclosed lagoon, growing higher as the sea level rises. Rubble from broken coral accumulates in the lagoon, so the level of the lagoon floor also rises, and smaller reefs can rise within it. Sand and debris accumulate on the higher parts of the reef, creating sandbars on which vegetation can eventually take root. The classic atoll shape is oval, with the widest reefs and most of the islands around the outer edges.

Geological research has revealed the complex layers of coral growth that underlie Maldives, and has shown that coral growth can match the fastest sea-level rises on record, some 125m in only 10,000 years – about 1.25cm per year. In geological terms, that's fast.

Wrasse

Some 60 species of this large and very diverse family can be found on reefs, sandy lagoon floors or in open water. The smallest wrasse species are only 10cm; the largest over 2m. Most wrasse are carnivores; larger wrasse will hunt and eat small fish. Napoleonfish (also called Napoleon wrasse) are the largest wrasse species, often seen around wrecks and outer-reef slopes; they are generally green with fine vertical patterning. Large males have a humped head.

The hump on the head of a Napoleon wrasse becomes larger and more pronounced as the fish ages.

Wildlife on Land

Stand still on a Maldivian beach for a minute or two and you'll see a surprising amount of wildlife: the ubiquitous hermit crabs scurrying across the warm sands; cawing crows in the palm trees, their call instantly recognisable; majestic flying foxes swooping over the islands during the late afternoon; and you will rapidly realise that Maldives is a fun place for nature lovers. And that's before you get to the amazing variety of life down on the reef. The best thing about wildlife in Maldives is that it's almost universally safe. Who said this wasn't paradise?

Land Animals

One of the most unforgettable sights in Maldives is giant fruit bats flying over the islands to roost in trees at dusk. Their size and numbers can make it quite a spectacle. Colourful lizards and geckos are very common and there is the occasional rat, usually euphemistically dismissed as a 'palm squirrel' or a 'Maldivian hamster' by resort staff.

The mosquito population varies from island to island, but it's generally not a big problem except after heavy rains. Nearly all the resorts spray pesticides daily to get rid of those that are about. There are ants, centipedes, scorpions and cockroaches, but they're no threat to anyone.

Local land birds include crows (many of which are shot by resorts on regular culls), the white-breasted water hen and the Indian mynah. There are migratory birds, such as harriers and falcons, but waders like plover, snipe, curlew and sandpiper are more common. Thirteen species of heron can be seen in the shallows (nearly every resort has one or two in residence) and there are terns, seagulls and two species of noddy.

In 2009 the Maldivian government set aside large areas of Baa and Ari Atolls as marine protected areas for the breeding of endangered whale sharks, manta rays and reef sharks.

National Parks in Maldives

There are 25 Protected Marine Areas in Maldives, usually popular diving sites where fishing of any kind is banned. These are excellent as they have created enclaves of marine life that's guaranteed a safe future. There's also the Hanifaru Bay (p109), a Unesco World Biosphere Reserve in Baa Atoll, one of the country's most important and fully protected feeding grounds for manta rays and whale sharks.

Maldives' first marine national park was officially formed in 2012, but its boundaries remained undetermined in 2015, and progress has been decidedly slow after the change of government following the 2012 coup. However, in theory the park will cover the Edu Faru archipelago, nine uninhabited islands in Noonu Atoll, and will be by far the biggest reserve in the country, enjoying full national park status.

Aside from the new marine national park, there are no specially designated island reserves in Maldives. However, the vast majority of the islands in Maldives are uninhabited and permission from the government is needed to develop or live there. With some of the tightest development restrictions in the world, Maldives' future as pristine wilderness in many parts is assured.

Environmental Issues & Responsible Travel

Adrift in the middle of the Indian Ocean and almost totally reliant on the marine environment for its food, Maldives is a country where environmental issues play a larger than normal role in everyday life. Moreover, lying at such a low level above the sea makes Maldives one of the most vulnerable places on earth to rising sea levels, and its fragile and unusual ecology means that responsible and thoughtful travel is important for anyone who cares about the impact of their holiday on locals.

However you spend your time in the country, you will never be far removed from the environmental issues. Resorts use enormous amounts of electricity and water, their imported food (not to mention guests) have significant environmental consequences, and in some cases they are not particularly responsible about their sewage disposal or energy use.

We take into account resorts' environmental policies and highlight resorts that have implemented particularly sustainable and ecologically sound practices.

Environmental Issues

As a small island nation in a big ocean, Maldives had a way of life that was ecologically sustainable for centuries, but certainly not self-sufficient. The comparatively small population survived by harvesting the vast resources of the sea and obtaining the other necessities of life through trade with the Middle East and Asia.

In the modern age, Maldives' interrelationship with the rest of the world is greater than ever, and it has a high rate of growth supported by two main industries: fishing and tourism. Both industries depend on the preservation of the environment, and there are strict regulations to ensure sustainability.

To a great extent, Maldives avoids environmental problems by importing so many of its needs. This is, of course, less a case of being environmentally friendly than of just moving the environmental problems elsewhere.

Bluepeace (www.bluepeacemaldives.org) is an organisation campaigning to protect Maldives' unique environment. Its comprehensive website and blog is a great place to start for anyone interested in the ecology of Maldives and the most pressing environmental issues of the day.

One of the biggest problems facing Maldives today is its waste disposal processes, or lack thereof. The issue gets worse every year as tourism numbers grow exponentially, with more waste produced. At present there is a 'rubbish island' near Male, which is overflowing and where trash cannot be burned quickly enough.

There are no landfills in Maldives due to a lack of land, and the current government does not seem interested in finding a solution. Sadly, floating rubbish in the sea is a common sight and can blight the most pristine of beaches.

Beach erosion is a constant problem facing most islands in Maldives. Changing currents and rising sea levels mean that beaches shrink and grow, often unpredictably, with the resulting sandbags holding the beach in place often marring that perfect white sand beach photo.

Global Warming

The depletion of freshwater aquifers is one of Maldives' biggest environmental problems. As all freshwater comes from rainwater collected below ground and from desalination, water conservation is extremely important.

Along with Tuvalu, Bangladesh and parts of the Netherlands, Maldives has the misfortune to be one of the lowest-lying countries in the world at a time in history when sea levels are rising. Indeed, its highest natural point – said to be Mount Villingili, at a whopping 2.4m – is the lowest in any country in the world.

Thanks in part to its crusading former president, Maldives has become a byword around the world for the human consequences of global warming and rising sea levels, as an entire nation seems set to lose its way of life and may even be forced to leave for good the islands it calls home.

While the political will to get an international agreement on how best to combat climate change may finally be within sight, Maldives has long been making contingency plans in the likely event that whatever the international community does will be too little, too late.

These contingency plans range from an already well-established project to reclaim land on a reef near Male to create a new island 2m above sea level, to a plan to set aside a portion of the country's annual billion-dollar tourism revenue for a sovereign wealth fund to purchase a new homeland for the Maldivians if rising sea levels engulf the country in decades to come.

Both options are fairly bleak ones – the prospect of moving to the new residential island of Hulhumale is not one relished by most Maldivians, who are attached to their home islands and traditional way of life, but the prospect of the entire country moving to India, Sri Lanka or even Australia (as has been suggested) is an even more sobering one.

Perhaps because of its perilous situation, Maldives has become one of the most environmentally progressive countries in the world. Before its dramatic collapse in 2012, the Nasheed government pledged to make the country carbon neutral within a decade, managed to impose the first total ban on shark hunting anywhere in the world and made ecotourism a cornerstone of its tourism strategy.

Bodu raalhu (big wave) is a relatively regular event in Maldives, when the sea sweeps over the islands, causing damage and sometimes even loss of life.

The successive governments of Presidents Waheed and Yameen have focused far less on a progressive environmental agenda, but it's certain that environmental issues will continue to play a prominent role in Maldivian politics.

In the long term it's simply not an option to protect low-lying islands with breakwaters, and if the sea continues to rise as predicted then there is no long-term future for much of the country.

There have been bold efforts made to ensure the survival of the human population of Maldives in the future in the worst-case scenario that waters wash over many of the lower-lying islands. Most obviously this includes the land reclamation project that has created 2m-high

AN ALTERNATIVE GEOGRAPHY

While Maldives has appeared in the *Guinness Book of Records* as the world's flattest country, with no natural land higher than 2.4m above sea level, it's also one of the most mountainous countries in the world. Its people live on peaks above a plateau that extends 2000km from the Lakshadweep Islands near India to the Chagos Islands, well south of the equator. The plateau is over 5000m high and rises steeply between the Arabian Basin in the northwest and the Cocos-Keeling Basin in the southeast. Mountain ranges rise above the plateau, and the upper slopes and valleys are incredibly fertile, beautiful and rich with plant and animal life. The entire plateau is submerged beneath the Indian Ocean and only scattered, flat-topped peaks are visible at the surface. These peaks are capped not with snow, but with coconut palms.

MALDIVES' VOLCANIC PAST

The geological formation of Maldives is fascinating and unique. The country is perched on the top of the enormous Laccadives-Chagos Ridge, which cuts a swath across the Indian Ocean from India to Madagascar. The ridge, a meeting point of two giant tectonic plates, is where basalt magma spews up through the earth's crust, creating new rock. These magma eruptions created the Deccan Plateau, on which Maldives sits. Originally the magma production created huge volcanoes that towered above the sea. While these have subsequently sunk back into the water as the ocean floor settled, the coral formations that grew up around these vast volcanoes became Maldives, and this explains their idiosyncratic formation into vast round atolls.

Hulhumale island next to the airport, which one day will house around half the country's population and all of the government. At present, over 40,000 people have now moved to the island and the island continues to grow at an impressive pace.

If the day does indeed come when waters engulf the entire country, then in theory the government's sovereign wealth fund may be used to buy land elsewhere in the world for at least some, if not all, of the Maldivian population. India and Sri Lanka are the most likely destinations due to proximity and similarities in culture, climate and cuisine, but Australia is also frequently mooted given its large amount of free space.

The 2011 film *The Island President* is a fascinating documentary that followed the progress (or frankly, lack of progress) of former president Nasheed as he lobbied internationally for an agreement to curtail global warming and prevent Maldives from being one of the first victims of the world's rising sea levels. It's well worth watching to see just what an enormous challenge it is for such a tiny country to be heard on the international stage, regardless of the urgency of its message.

Fisheries

Net fishing and trawling is prohibited in Maldivian waters, which include an 'exclusive economic zone' extending 320km beyond all the atolls, meaning foreign craft cannot fish using these methods in the country's waters either. All fishing is by pole and line, with over 75% of the catch being skipjack or yellowfin tuna. The no-nets policy helps to prevent over-fishing and protects other marine species, such as dolphins and sharks, from being inadvertently caught in nets – something that has catastrophic implications for marine biodiversity elsewhere around the world.

The small but active shark-meat trade was still claiming thousands of sharks a year until a nationwide ban was introduced in 2009. Shark numbers have been recovering ever since.

The local tuna population appears to be holding up despite increased catches, and Maldivian fisheries are patrolled to prevent poaching. But the tuna are migratory, and can be caught without limit in international waters using drift nets and long-line techniques.

The Nasheed government banned the hunting of reef sharks in 2009, extending the ban to all sharks a year later. The ban was intended to arrest the plummeting number of sharks, whose fins were sold by local fishermen to Asian markets. This move has been widely celebrated by environmentalists, and while shark numbers are rising, there's a long way still to go before shark populations rebuild fully.

Tourism

Tourism development is strictly regulated and resorts are established only on uninhabited islands that the government makes available. Overwhelmingly, the regulations have been effective in minimising the impact on the environment – the World Tourism Organisation has cited Maldives as a model for sustainable tourism development.

Maldives has a very small proportion of arable land – just 13% – meaning that fish and imported foods make up the bulk of most people's diets.

Construction and operation of the resorts does use resources, but the vast majority of these are imported. Large amounts of diesel fuel are used to generate electricity and desalinate water, and the demand for hot running water and air-conditioning has raised the overall energy cost per guest.

Extraordinarily, most resorts simply pump sewage directly out into the sea. While an increasing number of resorts do treat their own sewage and dispose of it responsibly, the majority still do not. New resorts are now required to do so by law, but the older resorts can still get away with this negligent behaviour.

WATER, WATER, EVERYWHERE

Ensuring a supply of freshwater has always been imperative for small island communities. Rainwater quickly soaks into the sandy island soil and usually forms an underground reservoir of freshwater, held in place by a circle of saltwater from the surrounding sea. Wells can be dug to extract the fresh groundwater, but if water is pumped out faster than rainfall replenishes the supply, then salty water infiltrates from around the island and the well water becomes brackish.

One way to increase the freshwater supply is to catch and store rainwater from rooftops. This wasn't feasible on islands that had only small buildings with roofs of palm thatch, but economic development and the use of corrugated iron has changed all that. Nearly every inhabited island now has a government-supported primary school, which is often the biggest, newest building on the island. The other sizable building is likely to be the mosque, which is a focus of community pride and the social centre of every island. Along with education and spiritual sustenance, many Maldivians now also get their drinking water from the local school or the mosque.

Expanding tourist resorts required more water than was available from wells or rooftops, and as resorts grew larger, tourists' showers became saltier. Also, the groundwater became too salty to irrigate the exotic gardens that every tourist expects on a tropical island. The solution was the desalination of seawater using 'reverse osmosis' – a combination of membrane technology and brute force.

Now every resort has a desalination plant, with racks of metal cylinders, each containing an inner cylinder made of a polymer membrane. Seawater is pumped into the inner cylinder at high pressure and the membrane allows pure water to pass through into the outer cylinder from which it is piped away. Normally, when a membrane separates freshwater from saltwater, both salt and water will pass through the membrane in opposite directions to equalise the saltiness on either side – this process is called osmosis. Under pressure, the special polymer membrane allows the natural process of osmosis to be reversed.

Small, reliable desalination plants have been a boon for the resorts, providing abundant freshwater for bathrooms, kitchens, gardens and, increasingly, for swimming pools. Of course, it's expensive, as the plants use lots of diesel fuel for their powerful pumps and the polymer membranes need to be replaced regularly. Many resorts ask their guests to be moderate in their water use, while a few are finding ways to recycle bath and laundry water onto garden beds. Most have dual water supplies, so that brackish groundwater is used to flush the toilet while desalinated seawater is provided in the shower and the hand basin.

Is desalinated water good enough to drink? If a desalination plant is working properly, it should produce, in effect, 100% pure distilled water. The island of Thulusdhoo, in North Male Atoll, has the only factory in the world where Coca-Cola is made out of seawater. In most resorts, the water from the bathroom tap tastes just fine, but management advises guests not to drink it. The precariousness of Maldives' water supply was highlighted in late 2014, when a fire at Male's only desalination plant left the city without running water for an entire week.

Efficient incinerators must be installed to get rid of garbage that can't be composted, but many resorts request that visitors take home plastic bottles, used batteries and other items that may present a disposal problem.

When the first resorts were developed, jetties and breakwaters were built and boat channels cut through reefs without much understanding of the immediate environmental consequences. In some cases natural erosion and deposition patterns were disrupted, with unexpected results. More structures were built to limit damage and sand pumped up to restore beaches. This was expensive and it marred the natural appearance of islands. Developers are now more careful about altering coasts and reefs. Environmental studies are required before major works can be undertaken.

Responsible Travel

Given the strictures of travelling to Maldives, in most cases your chances to be a truly responsible tourist are limited. First, you're almost certain to arrive in the country by long-haul flight, with all the emissions that entails. Second, you'll be using electricity-thirsty air-conditioning wherever you go, eating imported food and drinking expensively desalinated water (or even more costly imported water). Nevertheless, there are a few things you can do to lessen your carbon footprint and take care of the local environment.

First of all, choose your resort carefully. We have given resorts with excellent sustainability credentials a sustainable icon in the reviews – these are resorts with the best environmental records in the country. This can mean anything from having a comprehensive recycling program; using home-grown food; not using plastic bottles; using ecologically sound wood for their buildings; serving only sustainably sourced food in their restaurants; running environmental education programs for the local community; stimulating coral growth on the reef; and donating money to offset the carbon footprint of its guests.

If in doubt, contact your resort directly before you book with them and ask them for some information on their environmental record – any good resort will very happily provide this, and if they don't, then don't book with them.

Other things you can do to be a responsible visitor to Maldives: taking home any plastic bottles or batteries you bring with you; respecting rules about not touching coral when diving or snorkelling; picking up any litter you may see on the beach; using water and air-conditioning judiciously; avoiding imported mineral water and drinking desalinated water instead; not replacing your towels daily; and not buying souvenirs made from turtle-shell or coral, which can still be found in many places.

An excellent organisation to look out for is the nonprofit environmental protection NGO Ecocare (www.ecocare.mv), whose comprehensive website gives interesting accounts of environmental problems and current campaigns.

Arts, Crafts & Architecture

Despite Maldives being a small country with a widely dispersed population, Dhivehi culture has thrived in isolation from the rest of the world, finding expression in Maldivian arts and crafts, and retaining a strong national identity even in the modern age. Islamic beliefs, Western and Indian fashions, pop music and videos have all shaped local culture, but on public occasions and festivals the celebrations always have a recognisably local, Maldivian style. *Bodu beru* (traditional drum and dance performance) remains vibrant, rock bands sing Dhivehi lyrics and traditional crafts are surviving in the face of modernity. It's actually remarkable that such a tiny population maintains such a distinctive culture in a globalised world.

Arts

Song & Dance

Bodu beru means 'big drum' in Dhivehi and gives its name to the best-known form of traditional music and dance in the country. It tends to be what resorts put on once a week as an exponent of local culture, but despite this sanitised framing, a performance can be very sophisticated and compelling.

Dancers begin with a slow, nonchalant swaying and swinging of the arms, becoming more animated as the tempo increases and finishing in a rhythmic frenzy. In some versions the dancers even enter a trance-like state. There are four to six drummers in an ensemble and the sound has strong African influences.

Drums are the foundation stone of traditional music in Maldives, but some musicians also use the *bulbul tarang*, a harmonium-like stringed instrument invented on the Indian subcontinent.

Thankfully, these performances are not just to be found in resorts. If you're staying on an inhabited island, you'll often hear the *bodu beru* being played as groups of young men hang out and dance together after sundown. Witnessing it can be a fantastic experience, as the dancing becomes more and more frenetic as the night goes on, and there's no chance that this performance is for tourists.

Apart from *bodu beru,* the music most visitors will experience at resorts will rarely be a highlight. Local rock bands often perform in the bars in the evening, where they usually do fairly naff covers of old favourites as well as performing their own material. They may incorporate elements of *bodu beru* in their music, with lots of percussion and extended drum solos when they're in front of a local audience. Some popular contemporary bands are Seventh Floor, Mezzo and Zero Degree Atoll.

Literature

Despite the unique Maldivian script that dates from the 1600s, most Maldivian myths and stories come from an oral tradition and have only recently appeared in print. Many are stories of witchcraft and sorcery, while others are cautionary tales about the evils of vanity, lust and greed, and the sticky fates of those who transgressed.

Some are decidedly weird and depressing, and don't make good bedtime reading for young children. Male bookshops sell quite a range of local stories in English. Again, most of these are legends of the past, many overlaid with Islamic meaning. Novelty Press published a small book called *Mysticism in the Maldives,* which is still available in some shops.

Alternatively, if you're looking for thematic beach reading, you could always try the Hammond Innes thriller *The Strode Venturer,* which is set in Maldives, or for some real escapist fun and a great behind-the-scenes look at one of the country's top resorts, Imogen Edwards-Jones' *Beach Babylon* is a good pick.

In 2012 an Islamist mob attacked Male's National Museum and destroyed around 30 priceless carvings depicting Buddha, effectively wiping out all significant pre-Islamic relics in Maldives.

Visual Arts

There is no historical tradition of painting in Maldives, but demand for local art (however fabricated) from the tourist industry has created a supply in the ultra-savvy Maldivian market, with more than a few locals selling paintings to visitors or creating beach scenes for hotel rooms.

The National Art Gallery in Male puts on an exhibition of Maldivian art every few years. It combines photography, painting and some conceptual art, and is well worth a visit if it happens to coincide with your time in Male. Some local names to look out for are Eagan Badeeu, Ahmed Naseer and Hassan Shameem.

Some islands were once famous for wood and stone carving – elaborate calligraphy and intricate intertwining patterns are a feature of many old mosques and gravestones.

A little of this woodcarving is still done, mainly to decorate mosques. The facade of the Majlis building in Male is decorated with intertwined carvings, for example.

Crafts

Mats

Natural-fibre mats are woven on many islands, but the most famous are the ones known as *thundu kunaa,* made on the island of Gadhdhoo in Gaafu Dhaalu Atoll. This was once an endangered art form, but renewed interest thanks to the increase in tourism has arguably saved it from disappearing.

A Danish researcher in the 1970s documented the weaving techniques and the plants used for fibre and dyes, and noted that a number of traditional designs had not been woven for 20 years. Collecting the materials and weaving a mat can take weeks, and the money that can be made selling the work is not much by modern Maldivian standards. Some fine examples now decorate the reception areas of tourist resorts, and there's a growing appreciation of the work among local people and foreign collectors.

Coconut palm oil is a traditional product that has been widely used in Maldives, most commonly as a fuel for lamps before electricity. Today many islanders make shampoo, soap and lotions from the oil; they sell these items to tourists.

Lacquer Work

Traditionally, lacquer work *(laajehun)* was for containers, bowls and trays used for gifts to the sultan – some fine examples can be seen in the

SITTING IN MALDIVES

Maldives has two unique pieces of furniture. One is the *undholi,* a wooden platform or netting seat that's hung from a tree or triangular frame. Sometimes called a bed-boat, the *undholi* is a sofa, hammock and fan combination – swinging gently creates a cooling movement of air across the indolent occupant.

The *joli* is a static version – net seats on a rectangular frame, usually made in sociable sets of three or four. Once made of coir rope and wooden sticks, these days steel pipes and plastic mesh are now almost universal – it's like sitting in a string shopping bag, but cool; you'll see these curious and ingenious inventions all over inhabited islands.

National Museum in Male. Different wood is used to make boxes, bowls, vases and other turned objects.

Traditionally the lathe is hand-powered by a cord pulled round a spindle. Several layers of lacquer are applied in different colours. They then harden, and the design is incised with sharp tools, exposing the bright colours of the underlying layers. Designs are usually floral motifs in yellow with red trim on a black background (most likely based on designs of Chinese ceramics). Production of lacquer work is a viable cottage industry in Baa Atoll, particularly on the islands of Eydhafushi and Thulhaadhoo.

The crown jewel of Maldivian arts and crafts is the unique dhoni boat, which anyone travelling in Maldives will have the chance to see and, normally, travel on as well. Made entirely from wood, and having evolved from the Arab dhow, the dhoni is a most uniquely Maldivian creation and something that all locals are proud of.

Jewellery

Ribudhoo Island in Dhaalu Atoll is famous for making gold jewellery, and Hulhudheli, in the same atoll, for silver jewellery. According to local belief, a royal jeweller brought the goldsmithing skills to the island centuries ago, having been banished to Ribudhoo by a sultan. It's also said that the islanders plundered a shipwreck in the 1700s, and reworked the gold jewellery they found to disguise its origins.

Architecture

A traditional Maldivian village is notable for its neat and orderly layout, with wide sandy streets in a regular, rectangular grid. Houses are made of concrete blocks or coral stone joined with mortar, and the walls line the sides of the streets. Many houses will have a shaded courtyard in front, enclosed by a chest-high wall fronting the street. This courtyard is an outdoor room, with *joli* (netted) and *undholi* (swing) seats, where families sit in the heat of the day or the cool of the evening. A more private courtyard behind, the *gifili,* has a well and serves as an open-air bathroom.

Mosques tend to be the most interesting and attractive buildings you'll see on inhabited islands. Some date back to the 16th century and are extremely impressive examples of craftsmanship both for their coral-carved exteriors and their teak and lacquer-work interiors, although in most cases you'll have to view the insides from the doorway, as non-Muslims are not normally allowed to enter mosques in Maldives.

The government plans to properly excavate the country's large number of pre-Islamic Buddhist sites in a bid to attract travellers interested in more than just beaches and diving.

Male has several very beautiful 16th- and 17th-century mosques, as well as its impressive, modern Grand Friday Mosque, the city's most striking and, arguably, iconic building – its large golden dome is visible for miles around.

One island that is particularly worth visiting to see traditional Maldivian architecture is Utheemu, in the very far northern atoll of Haa Alifu. Here you'll find the best example of a 16th-century Maldivian nobleman's house. Although rather hyperbolically called Utheemu Palace, the building is nevertheless fascinating to tour for its interiors and interesting outer design.

Survival Guide

Directory A–Z

Accommodation

Ouch. That's most people's reaction to Maldivian resort prices, and it's fair to say this is not and will never be a cheap place to stay.

There are almost no single rooms in resorts, so singles are nearly always doubles for single occupation, with a similar price tag to a double room. Therefore we just list the standard room price (r) in the cheapest accommodation category, which is for two people unless otherwise stated.

Prices include a service charge (normally 10–12%), GST (12%) and the green tax (US$6 per person per night in resorts, US$3 per person per night in guesthouses).

Resorts

The majority of travellers will stay at one of the roughly 120 self-contained island resorts throughout Maldives.

Each is on its own island and provides accommodation, meals, and activities for its guests, ranging from the most basic beach huts, with a buffet three times a day and a simple diving school, to vast water villas with every conceivable luxury, multiple à la carte dining options and all kinds of activities, from kiteboarding to big-game fishing.

Most resorts have a range of room categories, so for simplicity we generally give the rate for the cheapest room. However, be warned, these prices are nothing more than a guideline. They are based on the best rates available in high season online, and so booking through a travel agent may well get you access to far better deals.

Budget resorts (up to US$350 per room per night) tend to be busier and more basic in their facilities and level of sophistication than more expensive resorts.

Few budget resorts are being built these days – their thunder rather stolen by the advent of independent tourism in Maldives – so those that do exist tend to date from the 1980s or '90s and are often in need of a lick of paint.

Midrange resorts (from US$350 to US$750 per night) are noticeably slicker and have a better standard of facilities and accommodation, all carried off with some style, and are truly luxurious at the top end of the bracket.

Top-end resorts (more than US$750 per night) are currently what Maldives is all about.

The standards in this category range from the very good to the mind-bogglingly luxurious, and high-end resorts are exceptionally ambitious and competitive with one another.

These days most are backed by international hotel chains and are huge financial undertakings that sometimes take years to build. Many more top-end resorts are currently under construction in Maldives.

Booking resorts through travel agents is nearly always cheaper than doing so directly, with some amazing deals to be had compared with the eye-watering rack rates.

However, increasingly some resorts offer great deals via their websites and on hotel booking sites such as www.booking.com or www.tripadvisor.com, so it's always worth checking online.

Last-minute deals can also bring big savings; simply call the resort you want to visit a day or two beforehand on the off chance that they'll offer you a competitive rate to up their occupancy.

BOOK YOUR STAY ONLINE

For more accommodation reviews by Lonely Planet authors, check out http://lonelyplanet.com/hotels/. You'll find independent reviews, as well as recommendations on the best places to stay. Best of all, you can book online.

Guesthouses

Until 2009, laws prohibited the construction of guesthouses on islands inhabited by locals. Since the change in the law under former president Mohammed Nasheed, guesthouses have sprung up all over the country and are continuing to affect massive social change in this traditional and conservative nation.

'Guesthouse' is a catch-all term used for any type of accommodation on an inhabited island, be it a hotel, boutique hotel or the closest thing to a resort.

Staying at a guesthouse offers a totally different experience to staying in a resort, and so your first important decision once you've decided to come to Maldives is whether you want a resort- or a guesthouse-based holiday. It's quite possible to combine the two, of course. If you choose a guesthouse holiday, you'll have far more contact with local life and far cheaper accommodation, but staying in one also entails certain restrictions, particularly with regards to alcohol and attire.

Hotels in Male

As hotels in Male are far cheaper than those of island resorts, we've used a separate price breakdown for the capital's hotels: budget (under US$80), midrange (US$80 to US$150) and top end (over US$150). These apply also to hotels on Hulhumale, the man-made extension island of the capital, 2km away.

Safari Boats

Live-aboard safari boats allow you to travel extensively throughout the country, visiting great dive sites, desert islands and small local settlements usually too remote to see many travellers.

They have an enjoyable, social atmosphere. Live-aboards range from simple to luxurious, and you generally get what you pay for. Prices range from bargain basement to exorbitant, depending on the facilities available.

Children

Part of the appeal of staying on a desert island is the fact that there isn't much to do apart from relax, which can be limiting for children. Younger kids will enjoy playing in the water and on the beach, but older children and teenagers may find resort life a little confining after a few days, and they may get bored.

- Families should look for resorts that offer lots of activities.
- Kayaking and fishing trips are always popular, and many places also offer courses in sailing, windsurfing and other water sports.
- The minimum age for scuba diving is 10 years, but most resorts offer a 'bubble blowers' introduction for younger kids, which is very popular, and supervised snorkelling is always possible.
- Kids clubs – for those aged 12 and under – and clubs for teenagers are very common in bigger, smarter resorts. These are free and the kids clubs run activities all day long, while teenagers are generally able to do what they want – even if it means playing computer games in a darkened air-conditioned room. Where resorts have good kids clubs or a generally welcoming child-friendly policy, we've included the child-friendly icon.
- Although exotic cuisine is sometimes on the menu, you'll always find some standard Western-style dishes that kids will find appealing.
- Young children are more susceptible to sunburn than adults, so bring sun hats and plenty of sunblock. Lycra swim shirts are an excellent idea – they can be worn on the beach and in the water and block out most UV radiation.

Practicalities

Note that some resorts do not encourage young children – check with the resort before you book. Children under five are often banned from honeymoon resorts and there is normally a minimum age requirement of 10 or 12 for water villas, given the obvious safety issues. Where kids are welcome, it's no problem booking cots and organising high chairs in restaurants, and there's often a kids club and babysitting services as well.

SLEEPING PRICE RANGES

For each option a room rate is quoted for the high season (December to March, outside Christmas and New Year), with the normal meal plan with which rooms are sold.

CATEGORY	RESORTS	HOTELS IN MALE
$ budget	<US$350	<US$80
$$ midrange	US$350-750	US$80-150
$$$ top end	>US$750	>US$150

Climate

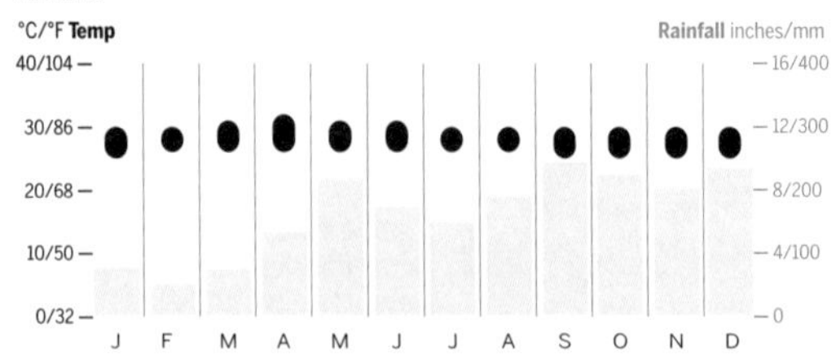

Baby supplies are available in Male, but usually not in resorts, so bring all the nappies and formula you'll need for the duration of the holiday. Outside resorts, breast-feeding should only be done in private given the conservative nature of Maldivian society.

Customs Regulations

The immigration cards issued to you on your flight to Male include a great list of items that are banned from the republic.

Alcohol, pornography, pork, narcotics, dogs, firearms, spear guns and 'idols of worship' cannot be brought into the country and you're advised to comply.

Baggage is usually X-rayed and may be searched carefully, and if you have any liquor it will be taken and held for you till you're about to leave the country.

This service will not extend to other prohibited items, and the importation of multiple bibles (one for personal use is fine), pornography and, in particular, drugs, will be treated very seriously.

The export of turtle shell, or any turtle-shell products, is forbidden.

Electricity

Electricity supply is 220V to 240V, 50Hz AC. The standard socket is the UK-style three-pin, although there are some variations, so an international adaptor can be useful; most resorts supply adaptors for non-UK travellers.

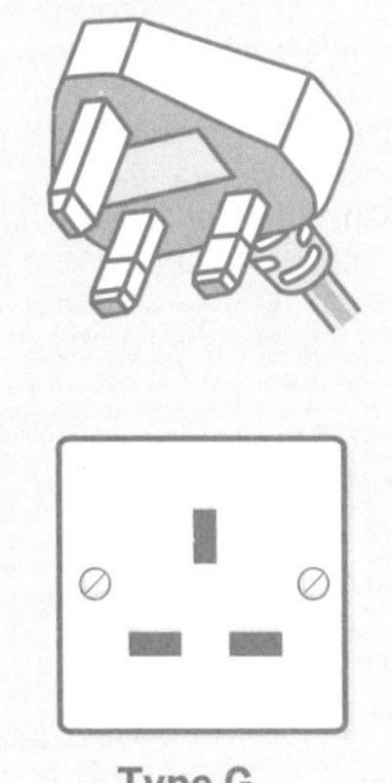

Type G
230V/50Hz

Embassies & Consulates

The few existing foreign representatives in Male are mostly honorary consuls with limited powers; most countries have no diplomats in Maldives at all. In an emergency, contact your country's embassy or high commission in Colombo, Sri Lanka.

If you lose your passport in Maldives, you'll generally need to be deported to Sri Lanka or India in order to receive a replacement.

Etiquette

Maldivians are very polite people and can often be quite shy if you meet them outside resorts.

While used to foreigners and their behaviour, there are a few things that they'll appreciate.

Greetings Shake hands with men when you meet them. Local women do not generally shake hands.

Eating Eat with your right hand only when dining on an inhabited island. The left hand is considered unclean, and while it can be used to cut food, it should not be used to move food to the mouth.

Dress Remember how conservative the islands are outside resorts. Men should not walk around bare chested and women should wear long skirts and avoid low-cut tops.

Religion Non-Muslims are generally not allowed to enter mosques anywhere in Maldives, except by specific invite.

Food

The following price ranges refer to a main course in Male.

$ less than Rf100

$$ Rf100–250

$$$ more than Rf250

Gay & Lesbian Travellers

By Maldivian law all extramarital sex is illegal, but there is no specific mention of homosexuality in the country's legal index. This grey area means that while gay life does certainly exist in Maldives, it's all generally conducted with great discretion, often online.

Of course in the country's resorts, things are very different. Same-sex couples will be able to book a double room without issues (from budget to luxury).

Maldivian hotel staff are the model of discretion), and it's common to see same sex-couples enjoying Maldivian holidays together. Public displays of affection may embarrass Maldivian resort staff, but won't result in anything but blushes on their part.

In Male and on inhabited islands discretion is key and public displays of affection should not be indulged in by anyone, gay or straight – Maldives remains an extremely conservative place.

Insurance

A travel-insurance policy to cover theft, loss and medical problems is highly recommended.

Some policies offer lower and higher medical-expense options; the higher ones are chiefly for countries that have high medical costs, and this would be a good idea for a Maldives trip.

Some policies specifically exclude 'dangerous activities', which can include diving, so check your policy carefully if you plan to dive; though anyone diving in Maldives is automatically obliged to buy Maldivian diving insurance as part of the package.

Worldwide travel insurance is available at www.lonelyplanet.com/bookings. You can buy, extend and claim online anytime – even if you're already on the road.

Internet Access

All resorts, hotels and guesthouses have free wi-fi for guests. While a few resorts limit data per user, it's otherwise entirely free across the board and generally a decent speed.

Do be aware, however, that on some resort islands you won't have total coverage by the resort wi-fi, and on inhabited islands you won't be able to use it outside the guesthouse itself.

Most independent travellers purchase a SIM card at the airport on arrival. These are valid for a maximum of two weeks and come pre-loaded with data, depending on the plan you buy. This is a far cheaper option than roaming on your home number.

Legal Matters

- Alcohol is illegal outside resorts – you're theoretically not even allowed to take a can of beer out on a boat trip. Some foreign residents in the capital have a liquor permit, which entitles them to a limited amount per month, strictly for personal consumption at home.
- Illicit drugs are around, but are not widespread. Penalties are heavy. 'Brown sugar', a semirefined form of heroin, has become a problem among some young people in the capital and even in some outer islands.
- Apart from the police and the military, there is a chief on every atoll and island who must keep an eye on what is happening, report to the central government and be responsible for the actions of local people.
- Resorts are responsible for their guests and for what happens on their island. If a guest sunbathes or goes swimming in the nude, the resort can be fined, as well as the visitor.

Maps

Put simply, Maldives is a nightmare to map. The islands are so small and scattered that you're forever trying to distinguish between the tiny islands and the reefs that surround them.

Another problem is scale – the country is over 800km from north to south, but the largest island is only about 8km long, and most are just a few hundred metres across.

For anyone doing a serious amount of travel, especially diving, *Maps of Maldives* (Water Solutions Ltd, 2016) is indispensable and in a very practical book form, alleviating the need to fold out a vast map. It includes everything from shipwreck sites to protected marine areas. It can be found at some bookshops in Male, or ordered online.

Money

The currency of Maldives is the rufiyaa (Rf), which is divided into 100 larees. Notes come in denominations of 500, 100, 50, 20, 10, five and two rufiyaa, but the last two are uncommon. Coins are in denominations of two and one rufiyaa, and 50, 25 and 10 larees.

Most resort and travel expenses will be billed in dollars, and most visitors never even see rufiyaa, as resort bills are settled by credit card and you'll never need to pay for things in cash.

If you're staying in a resort, all extras (including diving costs) will be billed to your room, and you pay the day before departure.

For people staying in guesthouses it's another situation entirely, and while you'll be able to pay for most things by credit card, you'll need cash for meals outside the guesthouse, souvenirs and any other sundry expenses.

ATMs

ATMs can be found easily in Male and at the airport, and nearly all allow you to withdraw funds from international accounts. They're also now commonly found on inhabited islands, particularly the bigger ones. That said, in many cases there is only one ATM on each island, so it's never ideal to be reliant on them.

Bargaining

Bargaining is not part of Maldivian culture and should not be attempted in most situations. However, it's perfectly acceptable to haggle somewhat at a shop selling tourist souvenirs on an inhabited island.

Cash

It's perfectly possible to have a holiday in Maldives without ever touching cash of any sort, as in resorts everything will be chalked up to your room number and paid by credit card on departure. You won't need Maldivian rufiyaa unless you're using local shops and services on inhabited islands.

In Male, it's possible to pay for everything using US dollars, though you'll be given change in rufiyaa and you'll need to pay for things with small notes.

Be aware that there are restrictions on changing rufiyaa into foreign currency. If you take out cash in rufiyaa from an ATM, you won't be able to change the remainder back into US dollars or any other foreign currency.

Therefore if you need lots of local currency, exchange foreign cash for rufiyaa at a bank and keep the receipt to be allowed to change the remainder back at the airport.

Credit Cards

Every resort takes major credit cards including Visa, Amex and MasterCard. A week of diving and drinking could easily run up a tab of over US$2000, so ensure your credit limit can stand it.

Guesthouses also accept major credit cards, but do double-check this with yours before you travel.

Taxes & Refunds

➡ Visitors are not able to reclaim Maldives GST, which is added to most items at 12%.

➡ All visitors are also subject to a green tax, charged at US$6 per person per night in resorts, or US$3 per person per night in guesthouses.

➡ Service charges between 10% and 12.5% are added to all resort, guesthouse and restaurant bills automatically.

Tipping

General Tipping is something of a grey area in Maldives, where a 10% to 12.5% service tax is added to nearly everything.

Hotels It's good form to leave a tip for your room staff and in smarter resorts your *thakuru* (butler). Give any tips to the staff personally, not to the hotel cashier – US dollars, euros and local currency are equally acceptable.

Restaurants Tipping is not customary at independent restaurants or on local islands.

Travellers Cheques

Banks in Male will change travellers cheques and cash in US dollars, but other currencies are trickier. Most will change US-dollar travellers cheques into US dollars cash with a commission of US$5.

Changing travellers cheques to Maldivian rufiyaa should not attract a commission. Some of the authorised moneychangers around town will exchange US-dollar or euro travellers cheques at times when the banks are closed.

Opening Hours

The Maldivian working week runs from Sunday to Thursday; Friday and Saturday are the weekend. Friday sees many businesses closed.

Most shops close for between 15 and 30 minutes at prayer time, which can be unusual to Western shoppers. Typical business hours outside resorts are as follows:

Banks 8am–1.30pm Sunday to Thursday

Businesses 8am–6pm Sunday to Thursday

Government offices 7.30am–2pm Sunday to Thursday

Restaurants noon–10pm Saturday to Thursday, 4–11pm Friday

Photography

➡ On inhabited islands in the atolls, exercise caution about photographing locals. Always ask for permission before you take a picture, and remember that the islands are conservative places, so be polite and not too intrusive.

➡ Do be aware that photographing the National Security Services Headquarters in Male is not allowed and that you could be quickly arrested for breaking this rule.

➡ There are no restrictions on photography in the resorts or much of the rest of the country, so snap away – photography is very popular among visitors.

Post

Postal services are quite efficient, with mail to overseas destinations delivered promptly. A high-speed Express Mail Service (EMS) is available to many countries from Male's **main post office** (Map p62; ☎331 5555; Boduthakurufaanu Magu; ⏰9am-7.30pm Sun-Thu, 10am-3.30pm Sat).

Parcel rates can be quite expensive and will have to clear customs at the main post office. At the resorts you can buy stamps and postcards at the shop or the reception desk.

Generally there is a mailbox near reception, and there's a full post office at Male Airport too.

Public Holidays

If you're in a resort, Maldivian holidays will not affect you – service will be as normal. Christmas, New Year, Easter and European school holidays will affect you more – they're the busiest times for tourists and bring the highest resort prices.

Elsewhere, holidays are mainly religious. If a holiday falls on a Friday or Saturday, the next working day will be declared a holiday.

Most Maldivian holidays are based on the Islamic lunar calendar and thus dates vary greatly from year to year.

Ramazan Known as Ramazan or *roarda mas* in Maldives, the Islamic month of fasting is an important religious occasion that starts on a new moon and continues for 28 days. Expected starting dates for the next few years are: 15 May 2018, 5 May 2019, and 23 April 2020. The exact date depends on the sighting of the new moon in Mecca and can vary by a day or so either way.

Kuda Eid Also called Id-ul-Fitr or Fith'r Eid, this occurs at the end of Ramazan, with the sighting of the new moon, and is celebrated with a feast.

Bodu Eid Also called Eid-ul Al'h'aa (Festival of the Sacrifice), 66 days after the end of Ramazan, this is the time when many Muslims begin the pilgrimage (haj) to Mecca.

National Day A commemoration of the day Mohammed Thakurufaanu and his men overthrew the Portuguese on Male in 1578. It's on the first day of the third month of the lunar calendar.

Prophet's Birthday The birthday of the Prophet Mohammed is celebrated with three days of eating and merriment. The approximate start dates for the next few years are 21 November 2018, 9 November 2019 and 28 October 2020.

Huravee Day The day the Malabars of India were kicked out by Sultan Hassan Izzuddeen after their brief occupation in 1752.

Martyr's Day Commemorates the death of Sultan Ali VI at the hands of the Portuguese in 1558.

The following are fixed holiday dates:

New Year's Day 1 January

Independence Day Celebrates the ending of the British protectorate (in 1965) on 26 and 27 July.

Victory Day Celebrates the victory over the Sri Lankan mercenaries who tried to overthrow the Maldivian government in 1988. A military march is followed by lots of schoolchildren doing drills and traditional dances, and more entertaining floats and costumed processions on 3 November.

Republic Day Commemorates the second (current) republic, founded in 1968 on 11 November. Celebrated in Male with lots of pomp, brass bands and parades. Sometimes the following day is also a holiday.

Safe Travel

Maldives is an exceptionally safe destination, where you will barely even have to think about danger.

- If you do have important valuables in your room, it's a good idea to use the safe that is supplied in most places. If there's not one in your room, you can leave items at reception.
- Be careful of mopeds in Male.
- Take care when diving or snorkelling and follow all rules.

Smoking

A smoking ban prohibits smoking from most public buildings and from the inside of restaurants and cafes. Resorts are a lot more permissive, but will generally only allow smoking in designated areas outside.

Telephone

- There are two telephone providers operating in Maldives: Dhiraagu and Ooredoo.
- Both providers offer good coverage, although given the unique geography of the country there are still lots of areas without coverage in the atolls.
- You can buy a local SIM card for around US$10 and use it in your own phone if it's unlocked (check with your provider before you leave) – this becomes worth the price almost immediately if you're using your phone locally. There are offices of both providers at the airport, so it's easy to pick up a local SIM on your way to your resort.
- All resorts have telephones, either in the

PRACTICALITIES

Newspapers & Magazines The best source of news in Maldives is the excellent *Maldives Independent* (www.maldivesindependent.com), an online English-language newspaper with sharp and well-researched local reporting. Of the main Maldivian dailies, *Miadhu* (www.miadhu.mv) has an English edition online.

TV Television Maldives, the national TV station, is broadcast from Male during the day, with regular breaks for prayer. The rest of the schedule is made up of political programs, variety shows and Al Jazeera re-broadcasts in English. There's news in English at 9pm. Other local TV channels include DhiTV and VillaTV. Nearly all resorts and most Male hotels have satellite TV, including BBC World News, CNN, Al Jazeera, Star Movies and HBO alongside Sri Lankan, Indian and European channels.

Weights & Measures Maldives uses the metric system.

rooms or available at reception. Charges vary from high to astronomical, starting around US$15 for three minutes; avoid them totally and use web-based phone services.

➡ The international country code for Maldives is 960. All Maldives numbers have seven digits and there are no area codes.

➡ To make an international call, dial 00.

Time

Maldives is five hours ahead of GMT, in the same time zone as Pakistan. When it's noon in Maldives, it's 7am in London, 8am in Berlin and Rome, 12.30pm in India and Sri Lanka, 3pm in Singapore and 4pm in Tokyo.

Around half of Maldivian resorts operate one hour ahead of Male time to give their guests the illusion of extra daylight in the evening and a longer sleep in the morning. This can make it tricky when arranging pick-up times and transfers, so always check whether you're being quoted Male time or so-called resort time.

Toilets

In Male, public toilets charge Rf2. On local islands, you may have to ask where the *fahana* is. In general you're better off using toilets in cafes and restaurants in Male – they're usually cleaner and free.

Tourist Information

The official tourist office is the **Maldives Tourism Promotion Board** (MTPB; Map p62; ☎332 3228; www.visitmaldives.com; 4th Fl, Veelanaage Bldg, Ameeru Ahmed Magu, Male; ⏰9am-5pm Sun-Thu), which has a somewhat informative website and a desk at the airport in Male. However, most tourism promotion is done by private travel agents, tour operators and resorts.

Travellers with Disabilities

At Male's Velana International Airport, passengers must use steps to get on and off planes, but it should be no problem to get assistance for mobility-challenged passengers.

Transfers to nearby resorts are by dhoni, speedboat or seaplane and a person in a wheelchair or with limited mobility will need assistance, which the crews will always be happy to provide.

All resorts have ground-level rooms, few steps, and reasonably smooth paths to beaches, boat jetties and all public areas, but some of the more rustic and 'ecofriendly' resorts have a lot of sand floors. Staff – something there's never a shortage of in Maldives – will be on hand to assist disabled guests. When you decide on a resort, call them directly and ask about the layout.

Many resort activities are potentially suitable for disabled guests. Fishing trips and excursions to inhabited islands should be easy, but uninhabited islands may be more difficult to disembark on.

Catamaran sailing and canoeing are possibilities, especially if you've had experience in these activities.

Anyone who can swim will be able to enjoy snorkelling. The **International Association for Handicapped Divers** (www.iahd.org) provides advice and assistance for anyone with a physical disability who wishes to scuba dive.

As no dogs are permitted in Maldives, it's not a destination for anyone dependent on a guide dog.

Download Lonely Planet's free Accessible Travel guides from http://lptravel.to/AccessibleTravel.

Visas

Maldives issues a 30-day stamp on arrival to holders of all passports. Citizens of India, Pakistan, Bangladesh or Nepal are given a 90-day stamp.

If you want to stay longer you'll either need to apply for an extension to the 30-day stamp or leave the country when your 30 days is up, then return.

You should know the name of your resort or hotel and be able to show a return air ticket out of the country if asked by immigration officials.

Visa Extensions

To apply for an extension, go to the **Department of Immigration & Emigration** (Map p62; ☎333 0401; www.immigration.gov.mv; 1st Fl, Veelanaage Bldg, Ameer Ahmed Magu, Male; ⏰9am-3pm Sun-Thu), near Jumhooree Maidan in Male. Fill in the Application for Permit Extension form, which will need to be co-signed by a local sponsor. The main requirement is evidence that you have accommodation, so it's best to have your resort, travel agent or guesthouse manager act as a sponsor and apply on your behalf.

Have your sponsor sign the form, and bring it back to the office, along with your passport, a passport photo and your air ticket out of the country. You have to have a confirmed booking for the new departure date before you can get the extension – fortunately, the airlines don't ask to see a visa extension before they'll change the date of your flight.

You'll be asked to leave the documents at the office and return in a couple of days to pick up the passport with its extended visa (get a receipt for your passport). Extensions are for a maximum of 30 days.

Volunteering

There are few volunteering opportunities in Maldives, but those that do exist tend to be focused on sustainable development, wildlife protection and teaching. Bear in mind that for the most part, volunteers will be living on small, remote islands without many creature comforts, and will also be expected to raise money to fund their trip.

The **Maldivian High Commission** (☎+44 207 224 2135; www.maldivesembassy.uk; 22 Nottingham Pl, London W1U 5NJ, UK) can help with some placements and its webpage is useful for those considering volunteer work.

Some organisations that offer volunteering opportunities include the following:

➡ www.maldiveswhalesharkresearch.org

➡ www.volunteermaldives.com

➡ www.atollvolunteers.com

Women Travellers

Culturally, resorts are European enclaves and visiting women will not have to make too many adjustments. Topless bathing and nudity are strictly forbidden, but bikinis are perfectly acceptable on resort beaches, and Maldivian staff are used to seeing women in states of undress and will not react badly.

In Male, reasonably modest dress is appropriate – shorts should cover the thighs and shirts should cover the shoulders and not be very low cut. Local women don't go into teashops in Male, but a foreign woman with a male companion will not cause any excitement.

Feminine hygiene products are widely available in resorts, on local islands and in Male. In more out-of-the-way parts of the country, quite conservative dress is in order. It is very unlikely that a foreign woman would be harassed or feel threatened on a local island, as Maldivian men are conservative and extremely respectful.

Work

There is an enormous work market for foreigners in Maldives, as almost 50% of resort staff generally come from abroad (a Maldivian law stipulates that 50% of all resort staff must be Maldivian).

Resorts are keen to hire people with a background in the hospitality industry, including managers, administrators, divemasters, masseurs, biologists, chefs, sommeliers and yoga instructors, and the positions tend to be well compensated and provide for plenty of 'off-island' time.

Contact resorts directly for opportunities or take a look at any international employment website to find out what's available.

Transport

GETTING THERE & AWAY

For such a tiny country, Maldives is easily reached from almost anywhere in the world and enjoys multiple daily flights from most major air hubs in Asia, Europe and the Middle East. Flights, cars and tours can be booked online at lonelyplanet.com/bookings.

Air

Almost every visitor to Maldives arrives at **Velana International Airport** (Map p42; ☎332 3506; www.maleairport.com), on the island of Hulhule, 2km across the water from the capital island, Male. It's an aged terminal awaiting an upgrade to a world-class airport terminal that has been on the cards for years; progress has been agonisingly slow, though it is now finally being built.

Two further airports in the country receive international flights: **Hanimaadhoo International Airport** (Map p106; ☎652 0095), which has a weekly flight to Trivandrum in India and **Gan International Airport** (Map p130; ☎689 8010; www.ganairport.com), which has two flights a week to Colombo in Sri Lanka.

The national airline is **Maldivian** (Map p62; ☎333 5544; www.maldivian.aero; Boduthakurufaanu Magu), which connects Maldives internationally to various cities in China, India and Bangladesh, as well as throughout the country domestically.

A second domestic airline, **FlyMe** (Map p62; ☎301 3000; www.flyme.mv; Maajeedhee Magu), operates flights that are often cheaper than those on Maldivian, though at present it only flies to two routes within the country.

A third airline, **Mega Maldives Airlines** (Map p62; ☎300 6672; www.megamaldivesair.com; H.Sakeena Manzil, Medhuziyaarai Magu, Male), connects Male to Beijing and Shanghai only.

The international carriers serving Male are a mixture of scheduled and charter airlines. Some airlines only fly in certain seasons and many change services frequently in line with traveller demand. These include:

Aeroflot (www.aeroflot.com)

Air Asia (www.airasia.com)

Air France (www.airfrance.com)

Air India (www.airindia.com)

Alitalia (www.alitalia.com)

Austrian Airlines (www.aua.com)

British Airways (www.ba.com)

Cathay Pacific (www.cathaypacific.com)

China Eastern (www.ceair.com)

China Southern (www.csair.com)

Emirates (www.emirates.com)

Etihad (www.etihad.com)

Finnair (www.finnair.com)

Iberia (www.iberia.com)

Korean Air (www.koreanair.com)

Japan Airlines (www.jal.com)

CLIMATE CHANGE & TRAVEL

Every form of transport that relies on carbon-based fuel generates CO_2, the main cause of human-induced climate change. Modern travel is dependent on aeroplanes, which might use less fuel per kilometre per person than most cars but travel much greater distances. The altitude at which aircraft emit gases (including CO_2) and particles also contributes to their climate change impact. Many websites offer 'carbon calculators' that allow people to estimate the carbon emissions generated by their journey and, for those who wish to do so, to offset the impact of the greenhouse gases emitted with contributions to portfolios of climate-friendly initiatives throughout the world. Lonely Planet offsets the carbon footprint of all staff and author travel.

DEPARTURE TAX

Departure tax is included in air ticket prices.

Lufthansa (www.lufthansa.com)

Malaysia Airlines (www.malaysiaairlines.com)

Oman Air (www.omanair.com)

Qatar Airways (www.qatarairways.com)

Singapore Airlines (www.singaporeairlines.com)

SriLankan Airlines (www.srilankan.aero)

Spicejet (www.spicejet.com)

Thai Airways (www.thaiairways.com)

Turkish Airlines (www.turkishairlines.com)

Sea

While it may look like an obvious transport route, there are no scheduled boat connections between either India or Sri Lanka and Maldives; nor do cargo ships generally take paying passengers. You might be lucky if you ask around in Colombo or Trivandrum, but it's unlikely.

Yacht

Yachts and super-yachts cruise Maldivian waters throughout the year, but this is not a standard port of call, and most people fly here to meet their craft.

The negatives for yacht captains include the maze of reefs that can make Maldives a hazardous place to cruise, the high fees for cruising permits, the bureaucracy that attends any journey, the restrictions on where yachts can go and the absence of lively little ports with great eating options and waterfront bars: the Caribbean this is not.

A large marina has been built at **Hideaway Beach Resort & Spa** (Map p106; ☎650 1515; www.hideawaybeachmaldives.com; Dhonakulhi; r from US$840;) in the far north of the country, and this is the only place currently set up for servicing yachts in a professional way. Addu Atoll (p129), in the far south, also has a sheltered anchorage, a luxury resort and refuelling and resupply facilities.

The three points where a yacht can get an initial 'clear in' are Uligamu (Haa Alifu) in the north, Hithadhoo/Gan (Addu Atoll) in the south, and Male. Call in on VHF channel 16 to the National Security Service (NSS) Coastguard and follow instructions.

If you're just passing through and want to stop only briefly, a 72-hour permit is usually easy to arrange. If you want to stay longer in Maldivian waters, or stop for provisions, you'll have to do immigration, customs, port authority and quarantine checks, and get a cruising permit. This can be done at any of the three clear-in facilities.

If you want to stop at Male, ensure you arrive well before dark, go to the east side of Villingili island, between Villingili and Male, and call the coastguard on channel 16. Officially, all boats require a pilot, but this isn't usually insisted upon for boats under 30m.

Carefully follow the coastguard's instructions on where to anchor, or you may find yourself in water that's very deep or too shallow. Then contact one of the port agents, such as **Island Sailors** (Map p59; ☎333 2536; www.islandsailors.com; Janavary Hingun) or **Real Sea Hawks Maldives** (Map p62; ☎330 5922; www.realseahawksmaldives.com; G.Reynis, Rahdhebai Magu, Male).

Port agents can arrange for port authority, immigration, customs and quarantine checks, and can arrange repairs, refuelling and restocking.

Before you leave Maldivian waters, don't forget to 'clear out' at Uligamu, Hithadhoo or Male.

GETTING AROUND

Air

There are 12 regional airports in the country, all of which are linked to the capital by regular flights.

Domestic flights are run by two domestic airlines, **Maldivian** (Map p62) and **FlyMe** (Map p62). Flights fill up fast, so reserve in advance to ensure you get the flight you want.

Guesthouses get access to discounted flights, so it's best to ask your accommodation to book your flights if possible.

Seaplane

The use of seaplanes means that almost every corner of the country can be reached by air, given that they don't require a runway.

Travellers mainly use the services of **Trans Maldivian Airways** (TMA; Map p73; ☎334 8447, 334 8454; www.transmaldivian.com; Velana International Airport) and **Maldivian** (Map p62). Both fly tourists from the seaplane port next to **Velana International Airport** (Map p42) out to resorts on 18-seater DeHavilland Twin Otter seaplanes.

Normally each resort has a contract with just one of the carriers, though some resorts have their own seaplane, which they operate independently.

All seaplane transfers are made during daylight hours and offer staggering views of the atolls, islands, reefs and lagoons.

The cost is normally between US$350 and US$600 return, depending on the distance and the deal between the resorts.

Charter flights for sightseeing, photography and emergency evacuation can also be arranged.

Call either company for rates and availability.

ENTERING THE COUNTRY

Visas are not needed for visits of 30 days or less. However, you must know the name of your resort, hotel or guesthouse, so if you haven't got accommodation pre-arranged for your first night, pick a place at random to write on the immigration form.

Note that cargo capacity on the seaplanes is limited to 20kg in most cases, with extra weight charged at a premium, and some heavy items may have to wait for a later flight.

Boat

For short hops, boat is nearly the only option for getting around, given Maldivian geography and its almost 1200 islands, only a few of which are connected to each other by causeways.

Dhoni Charters

Most resorts or guesthouses will be able to help you arrange a dhoni charter. The price depends on where you want to go, for how long and on your negotiating skills – somewhere between Rf1000 and Rf2000 for a day is a typical rate on an inhabited island, but if you want to start at 6am and go nonstop for 12 hours, it could be quite a bit more.

From a resort, charter will cost more (from US$400 to US$800 per day) and you'll only get one if they're not all being used for excursions or diving trips.

Ferry

The national public ferry network, established in 2010, means that all the inhabited islands in the country are connected by ferry to at least somewhere else, even if it is just a couple of times a week to another island in the atoll. This means that if you have plenty of time, independent travel to even the most remote inhabited islands is possible.

These ferries will not, however, help you travel between resorts, as they only stop at inhabited islands. To reach resorts you'll still need to do so by far pricier speedboat or seaplane transfers.

For specific timings you'll need to check with the guesthouse you're heading to, as they will have the most reliable and up-to-date transport information.

Timetables can be found on the websites of **Maldives Transport and Contracting Company** (MTCC; Map p62; ☎332 6822, 799 8821; www.mtcc.com.mv; 7th Floor, MTCC Tower, Boduthakurufaanu Magu, Male) – go to www.mtcc.com.mv/content/comprehensive-transport-network – or **Atoll Transfer** (Map p62; ☎797 3501; www.atolltransfer.com; 2nd Fl, G. Noomaraage, Lily Magu, Male), but services are often cancelled or timings changed at short notice, so never rely on online information alone.

Speedboat

Resorts in North and South Male Atoll, as well as some in North and South Ari, Vaavu and Faafu atolls, transfer their guests from Male airport by speedboat, which costs anything from US$80 to US$450 return depending on the distance.

One relatively new trend that has massively changed things for independent travellers is the growth of regular private speedboat services between **Velana International Airport** (Map p42) or Male to inhabited islands.

These services, aimed primarily at tourists and wealthy locals looking to travel between atolls fast and relatively affordably, have cut journey times to many islands by two thirds or more.

There are at least daily services between both Male and Velana International Airport and over a dozen inhabited islands in North and South Male Atoll, North and South Ari Atoll, Vaavu Atoll and Faafu Atoll.

These are offered by private companies and timetables can be found online at www.atolltransfer.com.

The best way to find out the full list of services you want to visit is to ask the guesthouse you intend to stay at, as they will have all the up-to-date transport information you need. Guesthouses will also be able to book you a place on the speedboat, which is important as some services won't run without a certain number of bookings.

Some Male-based travel agencies offer speedboat charter from Male, which, if you can afford it, is absolutely the best way to get around. **Inner Maldives** (Map p62; ☎300 6886; www.innermaldives.com; Ameer Ahmed Magu) has good-value launches for charter at around US$600 per day, excluding the (substantial) fuel prices.

For the price you'll get the services of the captain and a couple of crew members for a 10-hour day.

If chartering a boat for the day, standard practice is for the client to pay for the tank to be refuelled on arrival back at Male.

Car & Motorcycle

The only places where visitors will need to travel by road are in the island cities of Male, Fuvahmulah and Hulhumale, and between a few islands in Laamu and Addu Atoll that are connected by causeways.

Taxis are available in all these places, and driving is on the left, UK style. There are no local car-hire firms.

Health

Maldives is not a dangerous destination, with few poisonous animals and – by regional standards – excellent health care and hygiene awareness. Staying healthy here is mainly about being sensible and careful.

BEFORE YOU GO

There are a few sensible steps to take before you leave for Maldives. If you have a pre-existing medical condition, speak to your doctor before you travel to discuss any issues and make sure you have a supply of any medication not available locally in Maldives.

Insurance

Make sure that you have adequate health insurance and that it covers you for expensive evacuations by seaplane or speedboat.

However, as diving insurance is mandatory in Maldives, dive outfits always include this with a dive price, so there is no reason to pay extra for diving insurance on your travel policy.

Medical Checklist

Be aware that in resorts all medical care will be available only through the resort doctor or, when the resort doesn't have a doctor in residence, from a nurse or a member of staff with access to simple medical supplies. Bringing a few basics such as plasters for small cuts is a good idea, as is mosquito repellent for the evenings on most islands.

Mosquito nets are often provided by resorts where there is a mosquito problem, but bringing your own is a good idea if they're not included and you tend to get bitten.

IN MALDIVES

Maldives' health-care system is excellent by Indian Ocean standards, but with the islands' dispersed geography, it may be necessary to travel to another island for treatment in the event of a medical emergency.

Availability & Cost of Health Care

Most resorts have a resident doctor, or share one with another nearby resort. However, if you are seriously unwell it will be necessary to go to Male, or to the nearest atoll capital with a hospital if you're in a far-flung resort.

The Maldivian health service relies heavily on doctors, nurses and dentists from overseas, and facilities outside the capital are very limited. The country's main hospital is the **Indira Gandhi Memorial Hospital** (Map p59; ☎333 5211; www.mhsc.com.mv; Buruzu Magu) in Male. Male also has the **ADK Private Hospital** (Map p62; ☎331 3553; www.adkhospital.mv; Sosun Magu), which offers high-quality care at high prices, but as it's important to travel with medical insurance to Maldives, the cost shouldn't be too much of a worry.

The capital island of each atoll has a government hospital or at least a health centre – these are being improved, but for any serious problem you'll still have to go to Male. Costs in Male and on inhabited islands are generally very low, but even the issuing of basic medicines in a resort can be very expensive.

You will normally need to pay for treatment upfront – keep receipts to claim later from your health insurance.

RECOMMENDED VACCINATIONS

The only vaccination officially required by Maldives is one for yellow fever if you're coming from an area where yellow fever is endemic. Malaria prophylaxis is not necessary. Basic traveller vaccinations such as jabs against hepatitis, tetanus, typhoid and cholera are always a good idea, however.

Health Issues

Mosquitoes

Mosquitoes vary from non-existent to very troublesome depending on which island you're on and what time of year it is. In general, mosquitoes aren't a huge problem because there are few areas of open freshwater where they can breed and most resorts spray their islands to eradicate mosquitoes anyway.

However, they can be a problem at certain times of the year (usually after heavy rainfall), so if they do tend to annoy you, use repellent or burn mosquito coils, available from resort shops at vast expense (bring your own just in case).

Wearing long sleeves and trousers in the evenings is another good way to protect yourself.

Malaria is not present in Maldives. Dengue fever, a viral disease transmitted by mosquitoes, occurs in Maldivian villages but is not a significant risk on resort islands or in the capital.

Traveller's Diarrhoea

A change of water, food or climate can all cause a mild bout of diarrhoea, but a few rushed toilet trips with no other symptoms is not indicative of a serious problem. Dehydration is the main danger with any diarrhoea. Fluid replacement and rehydration salts remain the mainstay in managing this condition.

TAP WATER

Tap water in Maldives is all treated rainwater and it's not advisable to drink it, not least as it has generally got an unpleasant taste. Nearly all resorts supply purified drinking water to their guests for free – some cheaper resorts make you pay for it, though. Either way, it's a far better option.

Heat Exhaustion

Dehydration and salt deficiency can cause heat exhaustion. Take the time to acclimatise to high temperatures, drink sufficient liquids and don't do anything too physically demanding.

Salt deficiency is characterised by fatigue, lethargy, headaches, giddiness and muscle cramps; salt tablets may help, but adding extra salt to your food is better.

Heatstroke

This serious condition can occur if the body's heat-regulating mechanism breaks down and the body temperature rises to dangerous levels. Long, continuous periods of exposure to high temperatures and insufficient fluids can leave you vulnerable to heatstroke.

The symptoms are feeling unwell, not sweating very much (or at all) and a high body temperature (39°C to 41°C, or 102°F to 106°F). Where sweating has ceased, the skin becomes flushed and red. Severe, throbbing headaches and lack of coordination will also occur, and the sufferer may be confused or aggressive.

Hospitalisation is essential, but in the interim get victims out of the sun, remove their clothing, cover them with a wet sheet or towel and then fan continuously. Give them fluids if they are conscious.

Environmental Hazards

Most of the potential danger (you have to be extremely unlucky or very foolhardy to actually get hurt) lies under the sea.

Anemones

These colourful creatures are poisonous, and putting your hand into one can give you a painful sting. If stung, consult a doctor as quickly as possible; the usual procedure is to soak the sting in vinegar.

Coral Cuts & Stings

Coral is sharp stuff and brushing up against it is likely to cause a cut or abrasion. Most corals contain poisons and you're likely to get some in any wound, along with tiny grains of broken coral.

The result is that a small cut can take a long time to heal. Wash any coral cuts very thoroughly with freshwater and then treat them liberally with antiseptic. Brushing against fire coral or the feathery hydroid can give you a painful sting and a persistent itchy rash.

Sea Urchins

Sea urchins generally grow on reefs, and most resorts remove them if they're a danger to casual waders in the shallows, though the waters are generally so clear that it's easy to spot them. Watch out, as the spines are long and sharp, break off easily and once embedded in your flesh are very difficult to remove.

Stingrays

These rays lie on sandy seabeds, and if you step on one, its barbed tail can whip up into your leg and cause a nasty, poisoned wound. Sand can drift over stingrays, so they can become all but invisible. Fortunately, they will usually glide away as you approach. If you're wading in sandy shallows, try to shuffle along and make noise. If stung, bathing the affected area in hot water is the best treatment; medical attention should be sought to ensure the wound is properly cleaned.

Stonefish

These fish lie on reefs and the seabed, and are well camouflaged. When stepped on, their sharp dorsal spines pop up and inject a venom that causes intense pain and sometimes death. Stonefish are usually found in shallow, muddy water, but also on rock and coral seabeds.

Bathing the wound in very hot water reduces the pain and effects of the venom. An antivenene is available, and medical attention should be sought, as the after-effects can be long-lasting.

Diving Health & Safety

There are some additional considerations if you are planning to scuba-dive in Maldives.

Health Requirements

Officially, a doctor should check you over before you do a course, and fill out a form full of diving health questions. In practice, most dive schools will let you dive or do a course if you're under 50 years old and complete a medical questionnaire yourself, but the check-up is still a good idea – especially if you have any problem with your breathing, ears or sinuses.

If you are an asthmatic, have any other chronic breathing difficulties or any inner-ear problems, you should not do any scuba-diving. Be aware that most dive centres will not let you dive if you are taking any regular medicine for other ailments.

Diving Safely

The following laws apply to recreational diving in Maldives, and divemasters should enforce them:

- Maximum depth is 30m – this is the law in Maldives.
- Maximum time is 60 minutes.
- No decompression dives.
- Each diver must carry a dive computer.
- Obligatory three-minute safety stop at 5m.
- Last dive no later than 24 hours before a flight, including seaplanes.

Decompression Sickness

This is a very serious condition – usually, though not always, associated with diver error. The most common symptoms are unusual fatigue or weakness; skin itch; pain in the arms, legs (joints or mid-limb) or torso; dizziness and vertigo; local numbness, tingling or paralysis; and shortness of breath.

Signs may also include a blotchy skin rash, a tendency to favour an arm or a leg, staggering, coughing spasms, collapse or unconsciousness. These symptoms and signs can occur individually, or a number of them can appear at one time.

The most common causes of decompression sickness (or 'the bends' as it is commonly known) are diving too deep, staying at depth for too long or ascending too quickly. This results in nitrogen coming out of solution in the blood and forming bubbles, most commonly in the bones and particularly in the joints or in weak spots such as healed fracture sites.

Avoid flying after diving, as it causes nitrogen to come out of the blood even faster than it would at sea level. Low-altitude flights, like a seaplane transfer to the airport, can be just as dangerous because the aircraft are not pressurised.

The only treatment for decompression sickness is to put the patient into a recompression chamber. That puts a person back under pressure similar to that of the depth at which they were diving so nitrogen bubbles can be reabsorbed.

The time required in the chamber is usually three to eight hours. There are decompression chambers at both **Baros** (Map p73; ☎664 2672; www.baros.com; Baros; r from US$1112; ❄📶🏊) and **Kuramathi Island** (Map p96; ☎666 0527; www.kuramathi.com; Kuramathi; r incl full board from US$642; ❄📶🏊) resorts. Tragically, a British tourist died in Maldives in 2015 from the bends, so precautions should be taken very seriously.

Insurance for Diving

All divers must purchase compulsory Maldivian diving insurance before their first dive in Maldives. This will automatically be done at the dive school where you do your first dive, and is not expensive. This remains valid for 30 days, no matter where in the country you dive.

In addition to normal travel insurance, it's a very good idea to take out specific diving cover, which will pay for evacuation to a recompression facility and the cost of hyperbaric treatment in a chamber. Evacuation is normally by chartered speedboat or seaplane, both of which are very expensive. **Divers Alert Network** (DAN; www.diversalertnetwork.org) is a nonprofit diving-safety organisation. It can be contacted through most dive shops and clubs, and it offers a DAN TravelAssist policy that provides evacuation and recompression coverage.

Travelling with Children

Maldives is an exceptionally safe destination for children, with almost no medical dangers from the environment.

The biggest worry, as with all travellers, will be the strength of the sun. Ensure that kids are well covered with waterproof sunscreen (it's best to bring this with you as the mark-up in the resorts can be huge) and that they take it easy during the first few days.

A sun-proof rash top or all-body swimsuit will keep away harmful rays and meet local approval on grounds of modesty.

Language

The language of the Maldives is Dhivehi (also commonly written as 'Divehi'). It is related to an ancient form of Sinhala, a Sri Lankan language, but also contains some Arabic, Hindi and English words. There are several dialects throughout the country.

English is widely spoken in Male, in the resorts, and by educated people throughout the country. English is also spoken on Addu, the southernmost atoll. On other islands, especially outside the tourism zone, generally only Dhivehi is spoken.

The Romanisation of Dhivehi is not standardised, and words can be spelt in a variety of ways. This is most obvious in Maldivian place names, eg Majeedi is also spelt Majidi, Majeedhee and Majeedee; Hithadhoo also becomes Hithadhu and Hitadhu; and Fuamulak can be Fua Mulaku, Foahmmulah or Phoowa Moloku.

DHIVEHI SCRIPT

Dhivehi has its own script, Thaana. It was introduced by the Maldivian hero Thakurufaanu during the Islamic revival of the late 16th century. Dhivehi shares Arabic's right-to-left appearance for words (and left-to-right for numbers). The list below shows the letters of the Thaana alphabet and their closest English equivalents, and a few words to show the way the letters combine.

ހ (h) ށ (sh) ނ (n) ރ (r) ބ (b)
ޅ (lh) ކ (k) އ (a) ވ (v) މ (m)
ފ (f) ތ (t) ދ (dh) ތ (th) ލ (l)
ގ (g) ޏ (gn) ސ (s) ޑ (d) ޒ (z)
ޓ (t) ޔ (y) ޕ (p) ޖ (j) ޗ (ch)

palm tree	ruh	ރުއް
cat	bulhaa	ބުޅާ
egg	bis	ބިސް

BASICS

Hello.	a-salam alekum
Hi.	kihine
Goodbye.	vale kumu salam
See you later.	fahung badaluvang
Peace.	salam
How are you?	haalu kihine?
Very well. (reply)	vara gada
Fine./Good./Great.	barabah
OK.	enge
Yes.	aa
No.	noo
Thank you.	shukuria
I/me	aharen/ma
you	kale
she/he	mina/ena
What did you say?	kike tha buni?
What is that?	mi korche?
How much is this?	mi kihavaraka?
I'm leaving.	aharen dani
Where are you going?	kong taka dani?
How much is the fare?	fi kihavare?
bathroom	gifili
cheap	agu heyo
dance	nashani
eat	kani
enough	heo
(very) expensive	(vara) agu bodu
go	dani
inside	etere
little (people/places)	kuda
mosquito (net)	madiri (ge)
name	nang/nama
now	mihaaru

outside	berufarai
sail	duvani
sleep	nidani
stay	hunani
swim	fatani
toilet	fahana
walk	hingani
wash	donani
water (rain/well)	vaare/valu feng

EATING & DRINKING

I'm a vegetarian.	aharen ehves baavatheh ge maheh nukan
What is the local speciality?	dhivehi aanmu keumakee kobaa?
What is this?	mee ko-on cheh?
The meal was delicious.	keun varah meeru
Thank you for your hospitality.	be-heh-ti gaai kamah shukuriyya

PEOPLE & PLACES

atoll chief	atolu verin
evil spirit	jinni
father	bapa
fisherman	mas veri
foreigner (tourist/expat)	don miha
friend	ratehi
island chief	kateeb
mother	mama
prayer caller	mudeem
religious leader	gazi
toddy man	ra veri
VIP, upper-class person	befalu

atoll	atolu
house	ge
island	fushi/rah
lane, small street	golhi/higun
mosque	miskiiy
reef/lagoon	faru
sandbank	finolhu
street	magu

TIME, DAYS & NUMBERS

day	duvas
night	reggadu
today	miadu
tomorrow	madamma
tonight	mire
yesterday	iye

Monday	horma
Tuesday	angaara
Wednesday	buda
Thursday	brassfati
Friday	hukuru
Saturday	honihira
Sunday	aadita

1	eke
2	de
3	tine
4	hatare
5	fahe
6	haie
7	hate
8	ashe
9	nue
10	diha
11	egaara
12	baara
13	tera
14	saada
15	fanara
16	sorla
17	satara
18	ashara
19	onavihi
20	vihi
30	tiris
40	saalis
50	fansaas
60	fasdolaas
70	hai-diha
80	a-diha
90	nua-diha
100	sateka

GLOSSARY

bai bala – traditional game where one team tries to tag another inside a circle

bashi – traditional women's team game played with a tennis ball, racket and net

BCD – buoyancy control device; a vest that holds air tanks on the back and can be inflated or deflated to control a diver's buoyancy and act as a life preserver; also called a buoyancy control vest (BCV)

bodu beru – literally 'big drum'; made from a hollow coconut log and covered with stingray skin; *bodu beru* is also Maldivian drum music, often used to accompany dancers

chew – wad of areca nut wrapped in an areca leaf, often with lime, cloves and other spices; commonly chewed after a meal

Dhiraagu – the Maldives telecommunications provider, it is jointly owned by the government and the British company Cable & Wireless

Dhivehi Raajje – 'Island Kingdom'; what Maldivians call the Maldives

dhoni – Maldivian boat, probably derived from an Arabian dhow; formerly sail-powered, many dhonis are now equipped with a diesel engine

divemaster – male or female diver qualified to supervise and lead dives, but not necessarily a qualified instructor

faru – also called *faro*; ring-shaped reef within an atoll, often with an island in the middle

feyli – traditional sarong, usually dark with light-coloured horizontal bands near the hem

finolhu – sparsely vegetated sand bank

fushi – island

garudia – a soup made from dried and smoked fish, often eaten with rice, lime and chilli.

giri – coral formation that rises steeply from the atoll floor and almost reaches the surface; see also *thila*

hawitta – ancient mound found in the southern atolls; archaeologists believe these mounds were the foundations of Buddhist temples

hedhikaa – finger food; also called 'short eats'

hingun – wide lane

house reef – coral reef adjacent to a resort island, used by guests for snorkelling and diving

inner-reef slope – where a reef slopes down inside an atoll; see also *outer-reef slope*

joli – also called *jorli*; net seat suspended from a rectangular frame; typically there are four or five seats together outside a house

kandu – sea channel connecting the waters of an atoll to the open sea; feeding grounds for pelagics, such as sharks, stingrays, manta rays and turtles; good dive sites, but subject to strong currents

kateeb – chief of an island

long eats – a substantial meal with rice and *roshi*

magu – wide street

mas – fish

miskiiy – mosque

mudhim – muezzin; the person who calls Muslims to prayer

munnaaru – minaret, a mosque's tower

NSS – National Security Service; the Maldivian army, navy, coastguard and police force

outer-reef slope – outer edge of an atoll facing open sea, where reefs slope down towards the ocean floor; see also *inner-reef slope*

PADI – Professional Association of Diving Instructors; commercial organisation that sets diving standards and training requirements and accredits instructors

pelagic – open-sea species such as sharks, manta rays, tuna, barracuda and whales

raa veri – toddy seller

Ramazan – Maldivian spelling of Ramadan, the Muslim month of fasting

Redin – legendary race of people believed by modern Maldivians to have been the first settlers in the archipelago and the builders of the pre-Islamic *hawittas*

reef flat – shallow area of reef top that stretches out from a lagoon to where the reef slopes down into the deeper surrounding water

roshi – unleavened bread

short eats – finger food; also called *hedhikaa*

STO – State Trading Organisation

Thaana – Dhivehi script; the written language unique to the Maldives

thila – coral formation that rises steeply from the atoll floor to within 5m to 15m of the surface; see also *giri*

thundu kunaa – finely woven reed mats, particularly those from Gaafu Dhaalu

undholi – wooden seat, typically suspended under a shady tree so the swinging motion provides a cooling breeze

Wataniya – Kuwaiti mobile phone provider operating one of the Maldives' two networks

Behind the Scenes

SEND US YOUR FEEDBACK

We love to hear from travellers – your comments keep us on our toes and help make our books better. Our well-travelled team reads every word on what you loved or loathed about this book. Although we cannot reply individually to your submissions, we always guarantee that your feedback goes straight to the appropriate authors, in time for the next edition. Each person who sends us information is thanked in the next edition – the most useful submissions are rewarded with a selection of digital PDF chapters.

Visit **lonelyplanet.com/contact** to submit your updates and suggestions or to ask for help. Our award-winning website also features inspirational travel stories, news and discussions.

Note: We may edit, reproduce and incorporate your comments in Lonely Planet products such as guidebooks, websites and digital products, so let us know if you don't want your comments reproduced or your name acknowledged. For a copy of our privacy policy visit lonelyplanet.com/privacy.

OUR READERS

Many thanks to the travellers who used the last edition and wrote to us with helpful hints, useful advice and interesting anecdotes:

Janet Wishnetsky, Janice Douthwaite, Joe Sinclair, John May, Josh Lockington, Nitzan Winograd, and Rinse Balk, Bastiaan Balk & Ilse Harms

WRITER THANKS

Tom Masters

Huge thanks first of all to Moritz Estermann, who accompanied me on the first leg of this trip. Big thanks also to the scores of resort employees who helped me with my trip and went to great lengths to help me reach distant islands: you are way too many to thank, but know who you are. Big thanks also to Misbah, Shauna, Shamoon, Aziz, Paul, Basith, Clara, Richard and the whole team at MWSRP.

ACKNOWLEDGEMENTS

Climate map data adapted from Peel MC, Finlayson BL & McMahon TA (2007) 'Updated World Map of the Köppen-Geiger Climate Classification', Hydrology and Earth System Sciences, 11, 163344.

Cover photograph: Aerial view of an island in the North Male Atoll, Sakis Papadopoulos/Getty Images ©

THIS BOOK

This 10th edition of Lonely Planet's *Maldives* guidebook was researched and written by Tom Masters, who also wrote the previous three editions, and curated by Joe Bindloss. This guidebook was produced by the following:

Destination Editor Joe Bindloss
Senior Product Editor Kate Chapman
Product Editor Sam Wheeler
Senior Cartographer Valentina Kremenchutskaya
Book Designer Gwen Cotter
Assisting Editors Trent Holden, Tamara Sheward, Fionnuala Twomey, Maja Vatrić
Cover Researcher Naomi Parker
Thanks to Ronan Abayawickrema, Jennifer Carey, Bruce Evans, Sandie Kestell, Claire Naylor, Karyn Noble, Genna Patterson, Jessica Ryan, Angela Tinson

Index

Map Pages **000**
Photo Pages **000**

O

P

R

S

T

Map Pages **000**
Photo Pages **000**

Map Legend

Sights

- Beach
- Bird Sanctuary
- Buddhist
- Castle/Palace
- Christian
- Confucian
- Hindu
- Islamic
- Jain
- Jewish
- Monument
- Museum/Gallery/Historic Building
- Ruin
- Shinto
- Sikh
- Taoist
- Winery/Vineyard
- Zoo/Wildlife Sanctuary
- Other Sight

Activities, Courses & Tours

- Bodysurfing
- Diving
- Canoeing/Kayaking
- Course/Tour
- Sento Hot Baths/Onsen
- Skiing
- Snorkelling
- Surfing
- Swimming/Pool
- Walking
- Windsurfing
- Other Activity

Sleeping

- Sleeping
- Camping
- Hut/Shelter

Eating

- Eating

Drinking & Nightlife

- Drinking & Nightlife
- Cafe

Entertainment

- Entertainment

Shopping

- Shopping

Information

- Bank
- Embassy/Consulate
- Hospital/Medical
- Internet
- Police
- Post Office
- Telephone
- Toilet
- Tourist Information
- Other Information

Geographic

- Beach
- Gate
- Hut/Shelter
- Lighthouse
- Lookout
- Mountain/Volcano
- Oasis
- Park
- Pass
- Picnic Area
- Waterfall

Population

- Capital (National)
- Capital (State/Province)
- City/Large Town
- Town/Village

Transport

- Airport
- Border crossing
- Bus
- Cable car/Funicular
- Cycling
- Ferry
- Metro station
- Monorail
- Parking
- Petrol station
- Subway station
- Taxi
- Train station/Railway
- Tram
- Underground station
- Other Transport

Routes

- Tollway
- Freeway
- Primary
- Secondary
- Tertiary
- Lane
- Unsealed road
- Road under construction
- Plaza/Mall
- Steps
- Tunnel
- Pedestrian overpass
- Walking Tour
- Walking Tour detour
- Path/Walking Trail

Boundaries

- International
- State/Province
- Disputed
- Regional/Suburb
- Marine Park
- Cliff
- Wall

Hydrography

- River, Creek
- Intermittent River
- Canal
- Water
- Dry/Salt/Intermittent Lake
- Reef

Areas

- Airport/Runway
- Beach/Desert
- Cemetery (Christian)
- Cemetery (Other)
- Glacier
- Mudflat
- Park/Forest
- Sight (Building)
- Sportsground
- Swamp/Mangrove

Note: Not all symbols displayed above appear on the maps in this book

OUR STORY

A beat-up old car, a few dollars in the pocket and a sense of adventure. In 1972 that's all Tony and Maureen Wheeler needed for the trip of a lifetime – across Europe and Asia overland to Australia. It took several months, and at the end – broke but inspired – they sat at their kitchen table writing and stapling together their first travel guide, *Across Asia on the Cheap*. Within a week they'd sold 1500 copies. Lonely Planet was born.

Today, Lonely Planet has offices in Franklin, London, Melbourne, Oakland, Dublin, Beijing and Delhi, with more than 600 staff and writers. We share Tony's belief that 'a great guidebook should do three things: inform, educate and amuse'.

OUR WRITER

Tom Masters

Dreaming since he could walk of going to the most obscure places on earth, English-born Tom's writing career has taken him all over the world, including North Korea, the Arctic, Congo and Siberia. After graduating with a degree in Russian literature from the University of London, his first writing job was with the *St Petersburg Times*. He went on to work at the BBC World Service in London, then as a freelance contributor to newspapers and magazines around the world. He also spent several years working in television documentary production. Based in Berlin, his most recent projects include guides to the Russian Far East, Central Africa and Colombia. You can find him online at www.tommasters.net.

Published by Lonely Planet Global Limited
CRN 554153
10th edition – October 2018
ISBN 978 1 78657 168 7

10 9 8 7 6 5 4 3 2 1
Printed in Singapore